WITH RECIPES SELECTED FROM

Apples by Elaine Elliot and Virginia Lee

The Atlantic Cookbook by the readers of *Atlantic Insight*, edited by Patricia A. Holland

Blueberries by Elaine Elliot and Virginia Lee

Chowders, Bisques and Soups by Elaine Elliot and Virginia Lee

Cranberries by Elaine Elliot

Delicious DASH Flavours by Sandra Nowlan

Delicious Small Dishes by James MacDougall

Fall Flavours by Elaine Elliot and Virginia Lee

Fresh & Frugal by Craig Flinn

Fresh & Local by Craig Flinn

Fresh Canadian Bistro by Craig Flinn

Heritage Recipes from the Maritimes and Newfoundland by the readers and contributors of *Atlantic Insight*

Lobster by Elaine Elliot and Virginia Lee

Low-Salt DASH Dinners by Sandra Nowlan

Maple Syrup by Elaine Elliot

Maritime Flavours by Elaine Elliot and Virginia Lee

Molasses Inspirations by Joy Crosby

Pasta by Elaine Elliot

Patisseries by James MacDougall

Peaches, Pears & Plums by Elaine Elliot

Pumpkin & Squash by Elaine Elliot and Virginia Lee

Salads by Elaine Elliot

Salmon by Elaine Elliot and Virginia Lee

Scrumptious and Sustainable Fishcakes edited by the Formac cookbook team

Strawberries by Elaine Elliot

Summer Berries by Elizabeth Baird

Summer Drinks by Elizabeth Feltham

Summer Flavours by Elaine Elliot and Virginia Lee

Summer Vegetables by Elaine Elliot

Tomatoes by Elaine Elliot and Virginia Lee

BEST RECIPES
of the MARITIME
PROVINCES

THE BEST TASTING RECIPES FROM HOME COOKS AND LEADING CHEFS

RECIPES SELECTED AND WITH
AN INTRODUCTION BY
ELIZABETH BAIRD

FORMAC PUBLISHING COMPANY LIMITED
HALIFAX

Formac Publishing Company Limited recognizes the support of the Province of Nova Scotia through the Department of Communities, Culture and Heritage. We are pleased to work in partnership with the Culture Division to develop and promote our culture resources for all Nova Scotians. We acknowledge the financial support of the Government of Canada through the Canada Book Fund for our publishing activities. We acknowledge the support of the Canada Council for the Arts which last year invested $24.3 million in writing and publishing throughout Canada.

Design by Meghan Collins

Library and Archives Canada Cataloguing in Publication

Best recipes of the Maritime provinces : 400+ dishes : the best-tasting recipes from home cooks and leading chefs / selected and with an introduction by Elizabeth Baird.

Includes index.
Issued also in an electronic format.
ISBN 978-1-4595-0130-0

    1. Cooking—Maritime Provinces. 2. Cooking, Canadian— Maritime style. 3. Cookbooks— I. Baird, Elizabeth, 1939-

TX715.6.B4695 2012   641.59715   C2012-903134-8

Formac Publishing Company Limited
5502 Atlantic Street
Halifax, Nova Scotia, Canada
B3H 1G4
www.formac.ca

Printed and bound in Canada

CONTENTS

INTRODUCTION

EARLY LAST YEAR I WAS INVITED by James Lorimer, publisher of Formac Publishing and longtime friend, to do a little job for him; the very same James Lorimer who encouraged/cajoled me into writing my first cookbook, *Classic Canadian Cooking,* in 1974. That book became the entrée into almost 40 years of food writing and cookbooks.

It was hard to refuse the "little job," especially when it seemed so easy. The task? Read through all the cookbooks published by Formac Publishing in the past 25 years and pick out the recipes which would make up a one-volume collection of the best recipes from the Maritime provinces. Easy enough. But then the carton of books arrived, all 30 of them, starting with the 1985 *Nova Scotia Inns and Restaurants Cookbook* and a collection of recipes submitted by the readers of *Atlantic Insight* magazine in 1987 and finishing with *Scrumptious and Sustainable Fishcakes,* still warmish off the presses. Easy became intimidating as soon as I opened the carton.

Reading through this number of cookbooks turned out to be sheer pleasure. Once again the recipes and their stories transported me to Maritime memory land: a perch on the rocks on the Fundy shores, cracking lobsters boiled in sea water; spooning up a bowl of chanterelle soup prepared by Michael Smith in his kitchen, the chanterelles freshly gathered near his Bay Fortune home; tonging for oysters in Rocky Bay; trolling for extra slices of Donna Laceby's blueberry flan at the Amherst Shores Inn; biting into a real oatcake at Timmie's.

Over my two decades as food editor at *Canadian Living* magazine I had the privilege of visiting the Maritimes many times, though never enough, mind you. I have been welcomed into chefs' kitchens and gardens to see the link from the land and sea to the table, into home kitchens to whiff the tingling vapours rising from simmering bread and butter pickles, and into Canada's first whisky distillery to practise nosing a wee glass of Scotch. I have especially fond memories of kneading loaves of oats-topped brown bread; buying potatoes at a roadside stand, unmanned save for a cup left for money (and not a soul in sight to test your honesty); hauling up lobster traps; digging clams; judging culinary contests, chowder contests, iron-chef contests and even a baby contest; and casting approving looks at the long socks full of mussels suspended in sparkling clean water and rows of potatoes that seemed to run straight over the horizon.

I have long admired how a region could be at the forefront of farming, fishing and cooking technologies, and yet hang onto its roots, its dishes unique to the region's traditions and products. And with all these experiences, the people who make it happen — the chefs, the fishers, the teachers, the cheesemakers, the farmers — throwing everything they've got to make a go of raising sturgeon or oysters or sheep, or making a living running a bed and breakfast, filleting fish, smoking salmon and mackerel, making wine, waiting tables ... I could go on. But back to the task of reading through the cookbooks.

There were more than 1,000 recipes, written over a period of almost 30 years by a range of people from home economists, dieticians, home cooks, food writers and full-fledged chefs, the recipes as varied as the contributors. And the recipes reflected this range of contributors. It is a passion of mine to read recipes, following the steps as a dish comes together, and to imagine the person writing up the recipe. I was anxious to do justice to all the streams of cookery that makes up Atlantic Canada, ensuring that one province, one culture, one tradition or heritage, or one ingredient wasn't over-represented, knowing that there was a limit to how many I could include — 400 max, I was told. Which of the moist, spicy apple cakes would get the nod? How many taffy recipes could I include without sacrificing the soups and salads? It took a long time and a lot of thought.

Weaving together all these strands of culinary tradition and innovation was a challenge, but what makes this collection of recipes so amazing is the sense that they came from not from one cook or chef working in isolation, but a collective of cooks working within a framework of cooking every day with local products and drawing on their experience, specialties and creativity. These cooks speak to us through their recipes and invite the reader to share their traditions, especially in the introductions to their recipes that often speak of culinary traditions and introduce the people behind the recipes. For the most part, the introductions are from the original books so they offer an authenticity not often found in cookbooks. The result, I hope, is not only a collection of stories that you can read and enjoy but also recipes and ingredients that inspire you to try something new or to cook an old favourite.

There are some things I do need to bring to your attention. The 30-year span of cookbooks means that there are some delicious dishes, say from an inn in Saint John or a B&B on Cape Breton, which are fondly remembered, and deserve to be cooked by today's cooks — but, alas, the inn, or restaurant or festival no longer exists. This book offers you the chance to experience these flavours and favourite dishes all over again. You will also note that some of the recipes have been modified to include more details or to acknowledge that some ingredients are more or less available than many years ago.

Was it intimidating to choose 400 of the finest recipes from Atlantic Canada? Yes, but rewarding to witness a cuisine that honours its traditions, yet allows for creative new ways of interpreting them for today's families and guests. I invite you to draw a chair up to the table ... and enjoy.

— *Elizabeth Baird*

APPETIZERS

Seafood Cocktail, 10
Lobster-Stuffed Mushroom Caps, 10
Mushroom Spread, 11
Smoked Salmon Quiches, 11
Atlantic Smoked Salmon with Creamed Horseradish Sauce, 12
Salmon Terrine, 13
Smoked Salmon Crostini, 14
Salmon Roll, 14
Cream Cheese Crab Cakes, 15
Corn and Crab Fritters, 16
Brie Baked en Croute with Cranberry Sauce, 17
Rumrunner's Salmon, 17
Vegetable Crudités with Dip, 18
Heirloom Tomato Salsa, 19
Scotch Eggs, 19
Hot Atlantic Crab Dip, 20

SEAFOOD COCKTAIL

. . . .

ROSSMOUNT INN,
ST. ANDREWS BY-THE-SEA, N.B.

Rossmount Inn steps away from the traditional seafood cocktail to offer an interesting variation with scallops, shrimp and mussels served in a Dijon-style vinaigrette.

1 cup water
¼ cup dry white wine
1 bay leaf
5 black peppercorns
¼ small onion
1 celery stalk, quartered
24 mussels
12 scallops, halved if large
12 shrimp, peeled and deveined
6 cups shredded lettuce
6 each tomato slices, cucumber slices
  and lemon wedges
2 tablespoons minced fresh parsley

VINAIGRETTE

¼ cup extra-virgin olive oil
¼ cup vegetable oil
¼ cup red wine vinegar
1½ teaspoons Dijon mustard
Salt and pepper to taste

In a large pot, combine first 6 ingredients and bring to a boil. Poach mussels for 2 minutes and then add scallops and shrimp. Poach for 4 minutes, or until the mussels open and the scallops are just cooked.

Remove seafood from poaching liquid and cool. Remove 12 of the mussels from their shells.

VINAIGRETTE

Whisk together all ingredients. Combine all the seafood in the vinaigrette. Refrigerate for at least 3 hours. To serve, divide lettuce, tomato and cucumber among 6 serving dishes. Remove seafood from vinaigrette with a slotted spoon and place on top. Garnish with lemon and parsley.

Serves 6.

LOBSTER-STUFFED MUSHROOM CAPS

. . . .

Chef David Bradshaw combines garlic butter and fresh lobster to create these delightful hot mushroom treats.

¼ cup butter
2 cloves garlic, crushed
20 small mushroom caps, stems removed
3 tablespoons diced onion
1 cup chopped cooked lobster
⅓ cup mozzarella cheese, shredded

Combine butter and crushed garlic cloves to make garlic butter. In a skillet, sauté mushroom caps and onion in garlic butter until mushrooms are softened. Remove mushroom caps to escargot dishes. Add lobster to skillet and heat through. Place a piece of lobster in each mushroom. Cover mushrooms with any juices from skillet and top with shredded mozzarella cheese. Broil until the cheese is golden and bubbly.

Serves 4.

MUSHROOM SPREAD

Former innkeeper Joan Semple offered guests a variety of refreshing appetizers. This spread is easy to prepare and may be served warm or chilled, on small crackers or in tiny prebaked tart shells.

½ pound mushrooms
2 tablespoons butter
1 medium onion, finely chopped
2 teaspoons all-purpose flour
½ teaspoon salt
Pinch of pepper
Pinch of nutmeg
1 teaspoon lemon juice
½ cup sour cream
½ to 1 teaspoon dried dill weed

Clean and trim mushrooms before chopping finely. Melt butter and sauté mushrooms and onions, stirring often for 4 minutes. Sprinkle with flour, salt, pepper, nutmeg and lemon juice. Continue to cook for 1 to 2 minutes. Remove from heat and stir in sour cream and dill. Serve warm or chilled.

Serves 4 to 6.

SMOKED SALMON QUICHES

These tasty little quiches are designed to be served as an opener before the main meal or as part of an hors d'oeuvre offering at a larger gathering. They are easy to make and can be prepared in advance. To reheat, simply pop in a 350°F oven until heated through.

12 small, unbaked pastry shells
2 tablespoons unsalted butter
½ cup finely chopped button mushrooms
1 green onion, thinly sliced
1 large egg, beaten
⅓ cup sour cream
4 ounces smoked salmon, diced

Place pastry shells on a baking sheet; set aside.

Heat butter in a skillet over medium-high heat. Add mushrooms and onion and sauté until tender, about 3 minutes. Remove from heat and cool slightly.

In a small bowl, combine egg, sour cream and mushroom mixture. Divide salmon between pastry shells. Top with egg mixture. Bake at 375°F until golden, about 25 minutes. Serve warm.

Makes 12 tarts.

ATLANTIC SMOKED SALMON WITH CREAMED HORSERADISH SAUCE

. . . .

CATHERINE MCKINNON'S SPOT O'TEA RESTAURANT, STANLEY BRIDGE, P.E.I.

The Maritime shorelines are dotted with smokehouses, many of which invite passersby in to visit and shop. This recipe from Catherine McKinnon's fondly remembered restaurant calls for thinly sliced "cold-style" smoked salmon. Boston or Bibb lettuces are of the butterhead variety and are known for their soft, ruffled leaves.

Boston or Bibb lettuce leaves to line 6 salad plates
1 pound cold-smoked salmon, thinly sliced
2 tablespoons capers, drained
1 lemon, cut in 6 wedges
Cherry tomatoes or tomato wedges
½ English cucumber, thinly sliced
6 slices toast, crusts removed and sliced into triangles

SAUCE
½ cup heavy cream (35% mf)
1 ½ teaspoons grated onion
½ teaspoon salt
1 to 2 teaspoons prepared horseradish

SAUCE

In a chilled bowl, whip cream until it is stiff and has doubled in volume. Using a rubber spatula, fold in onion, salt and horseradish to taste. Refrigerate 2 hours to allow flavours to blend.

Makes 1 cup.

Line salad plates with lettuce leaves. Roll salmon slices and divide among plates. Sprinkle salmon with capers and garnish plates with lemon wedges, tomatoes, cucumber and a dollop of Creamed Horseradish Sauce. Serve with toast.

Serves 6.

SALMON TERRINE

· · · · · · · · · · · · ·

Speckled with salmon, onion and parsley, this rich terrine is simply delicious. The inn's signature recipe calls for both fresh and cold smoked salmon. Any unused terrine may be refrigerated for up to 5 days or frozen for up to 1 month.

1 pound skinless fresh Atlantic salmon

½ pound smoked Atlantic salmon, minced

2 tablespoons chopped fresh parsley

1 small red onion, finely diced

2 teaspoons fresh dill, more for garnish

½ cup butter, softened

¾ cup mayonnaise

2 tablespoons grainy Dijon mustard

2 tablespoons lemon juice

½ teaspoon pepper

½ teaspoon salt

Crackers or bread

Roast fresh salmon in 400°F oven, allowing 10 minutes per inch of thickness. Cool and flake with a fork. Combine smoked salmon, parsley, onion and dill with fresh salmon.

In a separate bowl, combine butter, mayonnaise, mustard, lemon juice, pepper and salt; mix well. Combine both mixtures and turn into a 1-quart loaf pan or mould that has been lined with plastic wrap. Gently press the salmon mixture with a spatula to remove any air bubbles.

Cover and refrigerate until firm, about 4 hours. Remove from the mould and serve with crackers or bread.

Serves 8 to 10.

SMOKED SALMON CROSTINI

. . . .

Chef Elizabeth Lee serves these delicious crostini with fresh greens as a first course dish or as individual hors d'oeuvres to accompany apéritifs and cocktails. Freeze extra crostini in freezer bags for instant appetizers when unexpected guests arrive.

1 baguette cut into 24 diagonal slices, ¼-inch thick
Extra-virgin olive oil
8 ounces cream cheese
2 green onions, thinly sliced
1½ tablespoons capers, drained
1½ teaspoons lemon juice
Salt and pepper to taste
4 ounces cold-smoked salmon, thinly sliced
Red onion, thinly sliced and separated into rings
Capers, extra-virgin olive oil and mixed greens tossed
  with vinaigrette of choice

Brush baguette slices with oil and season with salt and a generous amount of pepper. Arrange bread on a baking sheet and bake at 325°F, turning once, until crisp and lightly golden brown, about 12 minutes. Cool on rack.

In a bowl, blend together cream cheese, green onions, capers, lemon juice and salt and pepper to taste. Spread crostini with cream cheese mixture; cover with salmon, top each with an onion ring and 2 to 3 capers.

To serve, arrange 4 smoked salmon crostini spoke-like on each of 6 large plates. Place the mixed greens in the centre, where the crostini meet. In the areas between the crostini, sprinkle a few capers and drizzle a small amount of oil.

Serves 6.

SALMON ROLL

. . . .

Serve yourself — what could be easier for the busy host or hostess? The surprising addition of horseradish gives bite to this appetizer, and we suggest preparing it a day in advance, allowing the flavours to blend and the log to become firm.

7 ½-ounce can red sockeye salmon
8 ounces cream cheese, softened
1 tablespoon lemon juice
2 tablespoons minced onion
1 tablespoon prepared horseradish
¼ teaspoon salt
½ cup chopped walnuts or pecans
3 tablespoons chopped parsley

Drain salmon, remove skin and bones and flake with a fork. In a food processor, combine cream cheese, lemon juice, onion, horseradish and salt. Pulse until blended. Add salmon and pulse until just combined. Refrigerate 30 minutes.

Form cheese mixture into a log and roll in chopped nuts and parsley until coated. Wrap in plastic wrap and refrigerate at least 24 hours.

Serve with assorted crackers.

Makes 1 roll.

CREAM CHEESE CRAB CAKES

. . . .

BOFFINS CLUB, SASKATOON, SASK.

The sweet crab flavour and creamy cheese centre of these cakes make a delicious first course and won them a spot in a fishcakes cookbook collection. For a luncheon dish or main-course entrée, just add a salad and warm, crusty bread.

CRAB CAKES

¼ cup finely chopped sweet red pepper
¼ cup finely sliced green onion
¼ cup finely diced celery
1 tablespoon lemon juice
1 tablespoon jalapeño hot sauce, or to taste
8 ounces whipped cream cheese, at room temperature
1 cup fine breadcrumbs
½ teaspoon dried thyme
½ teaspoon dried basil
Pinch each of salt and pepper
1 pound Atlantic lump crabmeat
2 or 3 tablespoons butter
Fresh herbs, chopped
Lemon, cut in wedges

CREOLE MUSTARD SAUCE

3 tablespoons pepper jelly
¼ cup fresh orange juice
¼ cup Creole mustard

CRAB CAKES

In a skillet over medium heat, sauté pepper, onion, celery, lemon juice and jalapeño sauce until the vegetables wilt, about 5 minutes. Remove from heat and stir in whipped cream cheese until combined. Set aside. In a bowl, combine breadcrumbs, thyme, basil, salt and pepper. Set aside.

Clean and check crab for shell and cartilage; squeeze gently to remove excess liquid. Cup your hand and place about 2 tablespoons of the crabmeat into it. With a blunt knife, spread about 2 tablespoons of the cream cheese mixture over the crabmeat. Add another 2 tablespoons of the crabmeat, press down and form into a ball. Roll the ball in the crumb mixture until well coated. Place ball on a cutting board and press lightly to form a cake about ¾ inch thick. Repeat process to form 12 crab cakes.

Heat butter in a skillet over medium heat. Add crab cakes, being careful not to crowd, and sauté until golden on both sides.

To serve, arrange 2 or 3 cakes on each serving plate, spoon Creole Mustard Sauce around and garnish with herbs and lemon.

Serves 4 to 6.

CREOLE MUSTARD SAUCE

In a small saucepan over low heat, combine pepper jelly, orange juice and mustard. Stir until smooth. Serve warm.

Makes ½ cup.

CORN AND CRAB FRITTERS

· · · · · · · · · · ·

TEMPEST RESTAURANT, WOLFVILLE, N.S.

The flavours of corn and crab go so well together as they are both sweet in taste. A sprinkle of sea salt seems to intensify the sweetness.

1 cup all-purpose flour
1 cup cornmeal
1 teaspoon baking powder
Salt and pepper
1 large egg
1 large egg yolk
1 tablespoon butter, melted
½ sweet red pepper, chopped
½ sweet yellow pepper, chopped
1 cup corn kernels
1 shallot, chopped
2 cloves garlic, minced
2 tablespoons chopped cilantro
1 cup cooked Atlantic crabmeat
Paprika and cayenne to taste
⅔ cup beer
Vegetable oil, for deep frying
Coarse sea salt, to taste

Combine flour, cornmeal, baking powder, salt and pepper in a bowl and set aside. In a separate bowl, mix egg, egg yolk and melted butter. Melt butter in a pan over medium heat, sauté red and yellow peppers, corn kernels and shallot for 3 minutes. Add garlic, cook 1 minute, remove from heat and cool. Combine cilantro, crabmeat, paprika, cayenne and beer with the flour mixture. Refrigerate ½ hour.

Half fill a deep fryer with oil and heat to 320°F. Fry small scoops of batter until golden brown. Remove from oil, drop onto a platter lined with paper towel to absorb excess oil and sprinkle with coarse salt. Serve immediately.

Serves 12.

BRIE BAKED EN CROUTE WITH CRANBERRY SAUCE

LITTLE SHEMOGUE COUNTRY INN,
PORT ELGIN, N.B.

Baked Brie is an appetizer classic, especially enticing when paired with tangy cranberry sauce.

2 cups cranberries
1 cup granulated sugar
½ cup water
½ package frozen puff pastry, thawed
1 pound wheel Brie, chilled
1 large egg, whisked with 1 tablespoon water

In a saucepan over medium-high heat, combine cranberries, sugar and water. Bring to a boil, then reduce heat and simmer until berries are cooked and sauce has thickened, about 20 minutes. Let cool.

On a lightly floured surface, roll out pastry. Using Brie as a guide, cut a circle approximately 3 inches wider than the cheese. Brush edges with egg and water wash to ensure seal. Place Brie top down on pastry and wrap, pinching edges to seal. Pastry scraps may be used to make decorative pastry rounds for the top. Refrigerate Brie top side up, uncovered, for 30 minutes.

Bake at 425°F on a cookie sheet in the middle of the oven until pastry is puffed and lightly browned and cheese is melted, about 20 to 25 minutes. Remove from oven and let stand on cookie sheet for 20 minutes. Serve with cranberry sauce.

Serves 12 to 16.

RUMRUNNER'S SALMON

THE OLD FISH FACTORY RESTAURANT,
LUNENBURG, N.S.

For this dish, Chef Chris Profit was inspired by Lunenburg's reputation as a home to rumrunners and the town's abundant supply of fresh salmon.

1 boneless, skinless salmon fillet, about 8 ounces
⅓ cup pure maple syrup
¼ cup dark rum
2 tablespoons lemon juice
Salt and pepper to taste
Melba-toast rounds to serve 6

Rinse salmon fillet and pat dry. In a small bowl, whisk together maple syrup, rum, juice, salt and pepper. Place salmon in a shallow pan, drizzle with maple-syrup mixture and refrigerate for 12 hours, turning several times.

Drain salmon and bake in 350°F oven until fish flakes when tested, allowing 10 minutes per inch of thickness. Chill, slice and serve with Melba-toast rounds.

Serves 6.

VEGETABLE CRUDITÉS WITH DIP

. . . .

Everyone loves nibbling on crisp garden vegetables, so pick the freshest ones available. The sauce is also delicious on baked potatoes or for dipping corn chips and nachos.

Celery sticks
Baby carrots
Cauliflower florets
Broccoli florets
Cucumber slices
Sweet green or red pepper sticks
Cherry tomatoes

PARMESAN CHEESE DIP
½ cup light mayonnaise
½ cup light sour cream
½ cup grated Parmesan cheese
1 teaspoon Worcestershire sauce

Prepare vegetables in advance by washing, peeling if necessary and cutting into dip-size pieces. Place vegetables in separate bags and refrigerate.

To serve, arrange vegetables decoratively on a large serving dish. Accompany with Parmesan Cheese Dip.

PARMESAN CHEESE DIP
In a bowl, whisk together all ingredients until well blended. Remove to a serving bowl, cover and refrigerate for several hours to allow flavours to develop.

Serves 10.

HEIRLOOM TOMATO SALSA

• • • • • • • • • • • •

CHIVES CANADIAN BISTRO, HALIFAX, N.S.

Chef Craig Flinn notes that the beauty of this accompaniment is in its colour, texture and pure tomato flavour — if the tomatoes are perfectly ripe, of course! Serve as bruschetta topping, as a dip with tortilla chips or over grilled halibut.

1 large red field tomato, diced
1 large yellow tomato, diced
2 green zebra tomatoes, quartered
3 cups mixed cherry and grape tomatoes, halved
2 tablespoons minced red onion
2 tablespoons chopped fresh basil
3 tablespoons chopped chives
2 tablespoons balsamic vinegar
¼ cup extra-virgin olive oil
3 dashes Tabasco sauce
Sea salt

In a large bowl, combine tomatoes, onion, basil and chives. In a separate bowl, whisk together vinegar, olive oil and Tabasco sauce. Pour over tomato mixture and toss to coat. Adjust seasoning with sea salt. Set aside at room temperature 1 hour.

Makes 6 cups.

SCOTCH EGGS

• • • • • • • • • • •

LINDY GUILD, MAHONE BAY, N.S.

Says Lindy Guild, "Only my French grandmother could tamper with a traditional Scottish recipe like this and get away with it. She would not use prepared sausage meat, claiming it was too fatty and, of course, she added garlic. However, the English half of the family loved these eggs and they were always featured at her many family picnics when we were young children. She never had leftovers."

1 pound ground pork
2 teaspoons Worcestershire sauce
1 clove garlic, crushed
1 teaspoon prepared mustard
1 teaspoon salt
½ teaspoon pepper
½ teaspoon dried basil
½ teaspoon dried sage
4 large eggs, hardcooked and peeled
¼ cup all-purpose flour
1 large egg beaten with 1 tablespoon water
1 cup fine dry breadcrumbs
Salt and pepper to taste
Mustard

Mix together pork, sauce, garlic, mustard, salt, pepper and herbs. Divide into 4 portions. One at a time, roll cooked eggs in flour and press pork mixture evenly around each. Dip into the beaten egg and water mixture and then roll in breadcrumbs. Refrigerate 45 minutes. Fry in either shallow oil or deep fry, or bake in the oven on a nonstick cookie sheet. If frying, use moderate temperature and if baking, use 350°F and cook until nicely browned and pork is no longer pink. Serve with mustard.

Makes 4 whole eggs or 8 halves.

HOT ATLANTIC CRAB DIP

· · · · · · · · · · · ·

Easily prepared in advance, this dish has become a favourite at social gatherings. It will disappear quickly from your buffet table when your friends dig in!

12 ounces Atlantic crabmeat
8 ounces cream cheese, softened
¼ cup mayonnaise
Salt and pepper, to taste
Assorted crackers

Pick over crab to remove any shell or cartilage. Blend crab, cream cheese and mayonnaise; season with salt and pepper. Turn into a shallow baking dish; cover and refrigerate. At serving time, uncover and and bake in 325°F oven for 30 minutes or until browned on top and bubbly. Serve with assorted crackers.

Makes 2 cups.

SOUPS, CHOWDERS AND BISQUES

LOBSTER CHOWDER

· · · · · · · · · · · · · ·

A lobster chowder is luxurious — truly a special treat. In classic French cooking a lobster soup is a bisque, its base made from the lobster shells with vegetables and a small amount of tomato plus the lobster, of course. The result is a rich and creamy soup that tastes more like lobster than the meat itself. For this lobster chowder, start with a simple bisque-type broth then add potatoes and cooked lobster meat. Lobster is available year-round in the Maritimes and across Canada, but many consider that it is at its best in the spring -- say, on Mother's Day. Serve this as a lunch with freshly baked Buttermilk Biscuits (page 172) and butter.

2 cooked lobsters, about 1 pound each
1 large onion, coarsely chopped
1 stalk celery, coarsely chopped
1 carrot, coarsely chopped
2 cloves garlic, sliced
1 bay leaf
2 sprigs fresh thyme
2 tablespoons butter
2 tablespoons tomato paste
2 tablespoons all-purpose flour
½ cup dry vermouth or white wine
4 cups chicken stock
2 cups water
2 large yellow-fleshed potatoes, peeled and diced
1 leek, white part only, cleaned and chopped
1 cup heavy cream (35% mf)
Salt and pepper
Fresh tarragon or chopped chives

Crack lobster shells and remove meat from the claws and tails. Chop into bite-size pieces. Refrigerate in an airtight container.

Clean lobster shells under cool running water and remove head and liver. Place shells in a stockpot with onion, celery, carrot, garlic, bay leaf, thyme and butter and sauté for 10 minutes. Add tomato paste and flour and simmer for 5 minutes. Deglaze with vermouth and add chicken stock. Bring to a boil, reduce heat and simmer for 1 hour. Top up with the water when necessary to maintain the level.

In a food processor, purée shells, vegetables and stock and strain through a fine sieve. Discard contents of the sieve. Return liquid to clean stock pot. Add potatoes and leek and simmer, covered, until potatoes are tender, about 20 minutes. Add cream and chopped lobster meat and adjust seasonings with salt and pepper. Garnish with tarragon.

Serves 6.

CULLIN SKINK

SANDRA NOWLAN, HALIFAX, N.S.

Cullin Skink is a traditional Scottish soup from the shores of Moray Firth and it has long been a favourite with Sandra Nowlan's family in Canada. Skink means stew or soup. This simple but delicious dish made from finnan haddie (smoked haddock), potatoes and milk can be served thick as a stew or thin as a soup.

1 cup boiling water
1 cup milk, or ½ cup milk and ½ cup blend cream (10% mf) (approximate)
1½ pounds smoked haddock or cod fillets
1 medium onion, thinly sliced
6 medium potatoes, peeled and halved
1 tablespoon butter (approximate)
Pepper
Chopped parsley for garnish

In a pan over medium heat, combine boiling water and milk. Add fish and sliced onion. When liquid begins to simmer, reduce heat and cook for about 15 minutes or until fish flakes when tested. If the liquid boils, the fish will become tough. Transfer the fish to a plate and reserve the cooking liquid. Remove and discard bits of skin and bone and separate the fish into flakes.

Meanwhile, in a separate covered saucepan, boil the potatoes until tender. Drain and mash thoroughly in the saucepan. Strain the fish cooking liquid into the mashed potatoes and blend. Add flaked fish, butter and pepper. Add milk if a thinner consistency is desired. Serve piping hot with a small pat of butter on top and a generous sprinkle of parsley.

Serves 4 to 6.

ISLAND SEAFOOD CHOWDER

MOLLIE LEWIS ROBINSON, MISSISSAUGA, ONT.

When Mollie Lewis Robinson was growing up on Prince Edward Island, her mother often served clam chowder and oyster stew. She decided to combine these recipes and added some extra ingredients to come up with Island Seafood Chowder.

¼ pound salt pork, cut fine
2 tablespoons butter, approximate
1 cup diced onion
1 cup diced celery
1 cup diced potato
1 cup water
1 15-ounce can evaporated milk
2 cups cream
Salt and pepper to taste
1 cup scallops, cut into quarters
1 cup chopped cooked lobster
1 cup oysters with liquor
1 cup canned clams, drained

In a heavy saucepan, cook the salt pork in the butter over medium heat until the fat is rendered and the cracklings are crisp. Remove the salt pork with a slotted spoon. Add onions and celery and cook until softened. Remove onions and celery. Add potatoes and water. Cover and simmer until potatoes are tender. Drain.

In a large saucepan combine milk, cream, seafood, vegetables and cracklings. Simmer until hot, but do not boil. Pour into heated bowls. If desired, float a dab of butter on the top of each bowl of chowder.

Serves 6.

BAY OF FUNDY CLAM CHOWDER

. . . .

HAROLD A. BROWN, ST. GEORGE, N.B.

When New Brunswick native Harold Brown retired from The Montreal Star *in 1976, he came back to St. George, N.B. His recipe for Bay of Fundy clam chowder was handed down from his grandparents. Most people in the county eat fish quite frequently since they live near the fishing industry and the packing plants. He says he never gets the chowder the same twice, as the ingredients vary in strength. It can be adjusted as to the richness or the amount of salt that people prefer and he recommends tasting as you go along.*

1 pint shucked clams
Fistful of dried dulse
3 medium potatoes, peeled and diced
1 clove garlic, crushed, or onion, finely chopped
  (optional)
Milk or cream, to taste
Salt and pepper, to taste

Steam enough clams to make a pint after shucking. Save and filter the broth, keeping the clams aside. Add the dulse to the broth and boil for a few minutes until the dulse flavour is released. Remove what is left of the dulse leaves. Add potatoes to the liquid. At this point, some people like to add mashed garlic, sparingly; if not, add a quantity of finely cut onion. Simmer covered until potatoes are tender.

In a separate saucepan, heat the milk until bubbles form around the edge of the pan. Add the milk and clams to the broth mixture. Flavour with salt and pepper to taste. You may wish to alter the seasonings after trying it once or twice. Friends say the addition of the dulse improves the flavour.

Serves 4.

DEER ISLAND FISH CHOWDER

. . . .

SANDRA NOWLAN, HALIFAX, N.S.

Grandfather Simpson fished the waters around Deer Island, N.B., in his sailing vessel, the Oriola. *The fresh haddock and pollock that he brought home made a simple chowder. His son insists that the best chowders include a little salt fat pork and they must be slightly thickened with finely crushed soda crackers. Sandra (Simpson) Nowlan modifies the family recipe by adding clam broth and a pinch of thyme for extra flavour. The family digs clams in the summer and freezes the broth for winter chowders. The recipe becomes company fare by adding oysters, clams or lobster meat that has been sautéed in butter.*

1 or 2 ounces salt fat pork, finely diced
1 small onion, chopped
2 medium potatoes, diced
Pinch of dried thyme
1 to 2 cups clam broth or water
1 pound white fish fillets, cubed
1 cup evaporated milk, heated
2 cups whole milk, part can be light cream (20% mf),
  heated
5 ounces oysters (optional)
6 to 8 soda crackers, rolled fine
1 tablespoon butter
Paprika or parsley for garnish

Fry the salt pork until crispy. Remove and reserve for garnish. Cook the onion in the pork fat until soft. Add the potatoes, thyme and clam broth. Cover and simmer until the potatoes are tender. Add cubed fish and simmer gently, just until the fish flakes. Add evaporated and whole milk and oysters, if using. Stir in the cracker crumbs and butter. Keep the heat low so the chowder doesn't boil. Adjust the seasonings. Garnish each bowl of chowder with pork scraps and a bit of paprika or parsley.

Serves 4 to 6.

MARITIME CHEDDAR VEGETABLE CHOWDER

DEBRAH WESTERBURG, HALIFAX, N.S.

The chowder tradition has always been strong in the Maritimes. One of the first soups Debrah Westerburg learned to make from scratch was corn chowder. This recipe developed in the search for an updated version that reflected an interest in eating more vegetables without sacrificing the comfort of a milk-rich chowder.

1 tablespoon butter
1 large onion, minced
1 very small cabbage, cored and chopped
1 teaspoon caraway seeds
1 medium carrot, diced
1 medium parsnip, diced
1 small turnip, diced
2 large potatoes, diced
4 cups vegetable stock
1 cup cubed Cheddar cheese
2 cups light cream (20% mf)

In a large saucepan, melt the butter, sauté the onion, cabbage and caraway seeds until the onion is translucent and the scent of caraway is released. Add the rest of the vegetables. Pour in the stock and cover. Cook over medium heat until the stock boils and then turn it down to simmer until the vegetables are tender. Pour cream into a bowl. Take out 1 cup of stock and put it in a blender. Add the cheese and blend.

Gradually stir the hot cheese mixture into the cream. Pour the cheese-and-cream mixture into the soup pot. Mix well, stirring up from the bottom and keep on low heat until steaming and hot.

Serves 6 to 8.

ATLANTIC BLUE MUSSEL CHOWDER

What a wonderful way to utilize the Maritimes' famous mussels! The subtle flavour of this golden chowder is enhanced by the addition of curry.

2 pounds fresh mussels
½ cup dry white wine
¼ cup finely chopped shallots
⅓ cup finely chopped onion
A few sprigs each of parsley and dill
1 small bay leaf
2 tablespoons butter
½ cup julienned celery
½ cup julienned carrot
2 cups Fish Stock (page 39)
¾ cup heavy cream (35% mf)
1 large egg yolk, beaten
1 tablespoon curry powder (or to taste)
Salt and pepper to taste

Scrub and debeard the mussels, discarding any that remain open or have broken shells. In a large pot, bring to a boil wine, shallots, onion, parsley, dill and bay leaf. Add mussels and steam, covered, for 5 minutes or until they open. Strain cooking liquid through a fine sieve and reserve. Discard any mussels that do not fully open. Remove mussels from shells and reserve.

In a separate heavy-bottomed saucepan, melt butter and sauté celery and carrots until softened. Remove with a slotted spoon and reserve. Add fish stock and mussel liquid to saucepan. Bring to a boil and reduce by half. Add cream, mussels and julienned vegetables and remove from heat. Stir a small amount of hot liquid into beaten egg yolk, and stir back into saucepan. Add curry powder, season with salt and pepper and return to serving temperature, being careful not to boil.

Serves 4.

FIDDLEHEAD SOUP WITH SMOKED GOUDA SOUFFLÉS

. . . .

Fiddlehead ferns are the quintessential Maritime ingredient, but the season is short, especially when you are looking for perfect fiddleheads with tight spirals. You can garnish this puréed soup with a few sautéed fiddleheads, but for special occasions, try these twice-baked soufflés. There is no need to worry about them collapsing before they reach the table. You can make the day before and heat in the oven just before finishing the soup.

SOUP

1 cup chopped onion
½ cup chopped celery
3 cloves garlic
3 stalks fresh thyme
1 teaspoon salt
1 teaspoon pepper
2 tablespoons extra-virgin olive oil
2 tablespoons butter
½ cup white wine
5 cups fiddleheads, washed and trimmed
6 cups chicken or vegetable stock
1 cup heavy cream (35% mf) (optional)
2 teaspoons lemon juice

GARNISH

1 tablespoon butter
18 fiddleheads, washed and trimmed

SOUFFLÉS

⅔ cup unsalted butter
¾ cup all-purpose flour
2 cups milk
¼ cup minced shallots
1 clove garlic, minced
1 teaspoon salt
1 teaspoon white pepper
⅛ teaspoon nutmeg
5 large eggs, separated
1 cup shredded smoked Gouda cheese
3 tablespoons breadcrumbs

SOUP

Sauté onion, celery, garlic, thyme, salt and pepper in oil and butter over medium heat for 5 minutes. Deglaze the pan with white wine and bring to a boil. Add fiddleheads and stock and simmer for 20 minutes. Purée with an immersion blender or in batches in a regular blender. Strain into a clean saucepan and add cream, if using, and lemon juice.

SOUFFLÉS

Melt ½ cup of the butter in a small saucepan over medium heat and add flour. Mix well until a crumbly paste forms. Set aside to cool.

In a second saucepan, combine milk, shallots, garlic, salt, pepper and nutmeg and bring to a boil. Add to the cool roux (butter-flour mixture) in the first saucepan, stirring constantly. Set over medium heat and cook. As the sauce thickens, whisk to remove any lumps. Simmer over very low heat for 15 minutes. Scrape mixture into a bowl and refrigerate until cool.

Add cheese and egg yolks to the cool sauce. In a separate bowl, beat egg whites to stiff peaks. Fold in egg whites into cheese mixture. Grease 6 ramekins with remaining butter and dust with breadcrumbs. Fill ramekins with soufflé mixture and bake in a 375°F oven for 15 minutes or until soufflés are golden brown. Allow to cool for 30 minutes, then remove from ramekins. Prior to serving, reheat soufflés on a greased baking sheet in a 350°F oven for 7 minutes.

GARNISH

Meanwhile, melt butter in skillet. Add fiddleheads and sauté until hot and softened. Keep warm.

Ladle the soup into a heated shallow soup bowls and place a warmed soufflé in the centre of each bowl. Garnish with sautéed fiddleheads.

Serves 6 with some leftover soup for the next day.

SCALLOP CHOWDER

. . . .

MARY MOUZAR, HALIFAX, N.S.

A great way to release the exquisite flavour of scallops is to feature them alone in a chowder.

2 tablespoons butter
1 tablespoon minced shallots or onion
3 cups peeled and cubed potatoes
2 tablespoons water
2 cups scallops, well rinsed, cut into ½-inch pieces
2 cups coffee cream (18% mf) or light cream (12% mf)
Salt and pepper to taste
1 tablespoon chopped green onion tops (optional)
Dash of paprika (optional)

In a 1½-quart microwave-safe casserole, cover and microwave 1 tablespoon of butter and the shallots at 100% power for 45 seconds or until shallots are tender and translucent. Add potatoes and water. Cover and cook at 100% power for 6 minutes or until potatoes are tender, stirring once. Add scallops. Cover and cook at 100% power for 2 minutes 30 seconds or until mostly opaque, stirring once. Add cream, salt, pepper and remaining butter. Cover and heat at 50% power for 4 minutes or until hot. Sprinkle with green onion and paprika, if using. Let stand 3 minutes.

Serves 4.

ASPARAGUS SOUP WITH CREAM AND PARMESAN

. . . .

COOPER'S INN AND RESTAURANT, SHELBURNE, N.S.

This is a wonderful soup to prepare in late spring when the local asparagus season is at its height. We also tried this recipe using a combination of light cream and milk and though the result wasn't as creamy, it was just as yummy!

1 pound fresh asparagus
1 leek, white part only
2 tablespoons extra-virgin olive oil
¼ cup unsalted butter
2 cloves garlic, minced
2 medium potatoes, peeled and cubed
2½ cups chicken stock
1 cup heavy cream (35% mf)
Parmesan cheese, grated
Pepper

Remove and discard tough ends of the asparagus stalks. Rince the leeks to remove any grit then slice in 1-inch lengths.

In a large saucepan, heat oil and butter and sauté the leek and garlic. Add potatoes and stock, cover and gently boil until the potatoes are barely tender. Add the asparagus and cook until just crisp tender, being careful not to overcook.

Remove the asparagus with tongs, cut off and reserve the tips. Purée the asparagus stalks and contents of the saucepan in a food processor. Strain the purée through a fine sieve or food mill. Add reserved asparagus tips and cream to the soup and reheat, being careful not to boil. Serve in bowls garnished with a generous grating of Parmesan cheese and pepper.

Serves 4.

CREAM OF CHANTERELLE SOUP

CHANTERELLE COUNTRY INN,
BADDECK, N.S.

If chanterelles are unavailable, substitute other mushrooms such as shiitake, cremini or oyster to achieve an earthy flavour. For a lighter version, use blend cream (10% mf) instead of heavy cream.

1 medium onion, chopped
1 shallot, finely chopped
2 cloves garlic, finely diced
2 to 3 tablespoons extra-virgin olive oil
½ cup diced celery
¼ cup shredded carrot
½ pound chanterelles, coarsely chopped
2 cups chicken stock
1 cup heavy cream (35% mf)
Salt and pepper to taste
Snipped chervil or parsley

Sauté onion, shallot and garlic in oil until soft and lightly golden. Stir in celery and carrot and cook 1 minute. Add mushrooms and cook 2 minutes, stirring frequently. Add stock and simmer, covered, 10 minutes. In a food processor, pulse soup until slightly chunky. Return soup to saucepan, add cream and reheat, being careful not to boil. Adjust seasonings with salt and pepper and garnish with chervil or parsley.

Serves 4.

CREAM OF FIDDLEHEAD SOUP

AYLESFORD INN, CAMPBELLTON, N.B.

At the former Aylesford Inn, Shirley Ayles picked her fiddleheads and grew her own herbs to prepare this classic New Brunswick soup. While not quite as good as the fresh version, you can find fiddleheads in the frozen food section of most large supermarkets. Follow the cooking directions on the package.

1 pound fiddleheads, washed and trimmed
1 potato, peeled and cubed
2 cups water
3 tablespoons butter
3 tablespoons all-purpose flour
4 cups milk
½ cup heavy cream (35% mf)
Salt and pepper to taste
½ teaspoon dried tarragon
½ teaspoon dried rosemary
2 teaspoons dried chervil
1 teaspoon dried parsley

Cook fiddleheads and potatoes in the water until tender. Meanwhile, melt butter in a saucepan and whisk in flour. Slowly whisk in 2 cups of the milk and cook over medium heat until slightly thickened, whisking often.

Reserve 6 of the fiddleheads for garnish. Place potato and remaining fiddleheads in a blender with their cooking liquid and purée or use immersion blender right in the pot. Add thickened sauce mixture, remaining milk, cream, salt, pepper and herbs. Return to saucepan and reheat, being careful not to boil. Garnish each bowl with a reserved fiddlehead.

Serves 6.

GINGERED CARROT SOUP

. . . .

THE HATFIELD HERITAGE INN, HARTLAND, N.B.

This is an excellent vegetarian soup with a smooth, creamy texture and incredible flavour.

5 tablespoons butter
4 cups coarsely chopped carrot
3 cups coarsely chopped onion
3 tablespoons minced fresh ginger
6 cups vegetable stock
½ cup blend cream (10% mf)
Salt and white pepper to taste
Chopped parsley

In a large saucepan, melt butter over medium-low heat. Sauté carrot, onion and ginger, stirring occasionally until vegetables soften, about 10 to 15 minutes. Add stock and bring to a boil. Reduce heat to simmer. Cover loosely and cook until vegetables are tender, 30 to 40 minutes.

In a blender, purée soup in batches until smooth and creamy or purée with an immersion blender. Return soup to a clean saucepan and bring back to simmer. Add cream and bring back to serving temperature. Adjust seasoning with salt and pepper.

Serve in warmed soup bowls and garnish with parsley.

Serves 6 to 8.

HARVEST GOLD SOUP

. . . .

DUNCREIGAN COUNTRY INN, MABOU, N.S.

Eleanor Mullendore of Duncreigan Country Inn occasionally varied this recipe by adding ½ teaspoon curry or cumin to the soup.

1 medium onion, chopped
1 stalk celery, chopped
2 tablespoons butter
1 slice fresh ginger
1 large potato, peeled and diced
3 cups chicken stock
½ cup dry white wine
3 cups diced winter squash, such as Hubbard
½ cup heavy cream (35% mf)
Salt and pepper to taste
Sour cream

In a large saucepan, over medium heat, sauté onion and celery in butter until tender, being careful not to brown. Add ginger, potato, stock and wine. Cover and simmer for 10 minutes. Add squash and simmer, covered, until squash is tender, about 20 minutes. Remove ginger and purée soup in batches in a blender or food processor or in the pot with an immersion blender. Reheat and stir in cream, taking care not to bring soup to a boil. Season with salt and pepper and serve with a dollop of sour cream.

Serves 4 to 6.

CURRIED BUTTERNUT SQUASH AND CAULIFLOWER SOUP

. . . .

SCANWAY CATERING, HALIFAX, N.S.

"A heavenly taste as smooth as velvet" perfectly describes this creamy soup from well-known Halifax chef and restaurateur Unni Simensen.

2 tablespoons butter
2 cups chopped onion
1 tablespoon curry powder
½ teaspoon cinnamon
½ teaspoon salt
¼ teaspoon pepper
2 teaspoons liquid honey (approximate)
5 cups vegetable stock or chicken stock
2½ to 3 pounds butternut squash, peeled, seeded and
   cut in ½-inch dice
½ large or 1 medium cauliflower, cut into florets
⅔ cup heavy cream (35% mf)
Fresh thyme sprigs

Melt butter in a large saucepan over medium-low heat. Sauté onion until soft, stirring frequently, about 7 minutes. Add curry powder, cinnamon, salt, pepper and honey and stir to combine. Add stock, squash and cauliflower. Bring to a boil, reduce heat, cover and simmer until vegetables are soft, about 20 minutes.

In a blender, purée soup in batches until smooth and creamy. Or purée with an immersion blender. Return soup to a clean saucepan and stir in cream. Adjust seasoning and heat to serving temperature.

To serve, ladle into warmed soup bowls and garnish with a drizzle of honey and a sprig of fresh thyme.

Serves 6 to 8.

CREAM OF CAULIFLOWER SOUP

. . . .

KINGSBRAE GARDEN CAFÉ,
ST. ANDREWS BY-THE-SEA, N.B.

This smooth and creamy soup is an ideal starter for a special dinner. We prepared this soup twice, once using heavy cream and the second time using blend cream. While the heavy cream created a full-bodied soup, the flavour was not compromised in the lighter version.

¼ cup butter
1 medium onion, chopped
2 or 3 cloves garlic, minced
1 large cauliflower, trimmed
1 large potato, peeled and cubed
3 cups chicken stock
1 cup heavy cream (35% mf)
Salt and pepper to taste
Shredded aged Cheddar cheese
Parsley sprigs

In a large stockpot, melt butter over low heat. Stir in onion and garlic. Cover and cook on low, stirring often, until translucent but not browned, about 5 minutes. Divide cauliflower into florets. Add cauliflower and potato and stir to coat. Turn up heat slightly and sauté until softened but not browned, 10 minutes. Stir in stock and bring to a boil. Reduce to simmer and cook, covered, until vegetables are tender.

In a blender or with an immersion blender, purée in batches then return to a clean pot. Stir in cream. Return to serving temperature and adjust seasoning with salt and pepper. Garnish soup with cheese and parsley to serve.

Serves 4 to 6.

ONION SOUP

DAWN BREMNER, JEMSEG, N.B.

Dawn Bremner's grandmother made this dish, but never wrote down the recipe. After experimenting, Dawn arrived at a delicious facsimile that she and her family enjoy for lunch or supper on cold days.

4 large yellow onions, diced
1 medium potato, diced
1 or 2 stalks celery, diced (optional)
3 cups whole milk
1 teaspoon minced parsley
1 teaspoon pepper
¼ teaspoon salt
2 tablespoons butter
⅓ cup shredded Cheddar cheese

In a saucepan, cover and boil until tender onions, potatoes and celery in just enough water to cover. Drain, reserving stock for another use. Cool slightly. In a blender, combine vegetables with 2 cups of the milk. Blend until smooth. Put in a large clean saucepan. Add the remaining milk along with parsley, pepper and salt. Stir, then add butter. Heat gently until hot and the butter melts. Pour into warmed bowls, sprinkle with cheese and serve.

Serves 4.

MINESTRONE SOUP

SIRENELLA RISTORANTE, CHARLOTTETOWN, P.E.I.

Chef and owner Italo Marzari suggests adding a ham bone to the cooking broth to enrich the flavour of this soup. Should you wish to freeze the soup, add the pasta just at serving time.

2 tablespoons vegetable oil
1 cup diced onion
2 cloves garlic, crushed
5 cups chicken stock
2 carrots, peeled and diced
1½ cups diced red or green sweet pepper
2 small zucchini, seeded and diced
1½ cups small pasta
28-ounce can tomatoes, chopped, with liquid
2 cups diced cooked ham
14-ounce can chickpeas, drained and rinsed
14-ounce can red kidney beans, drained and rinsed
4 ounces fresh spinach
1 teaspoon dried thyme
¾ teaspoon dried summer savory
¾ teaspoon dried basil or oregano
Salt and pepper to taste

Heat oil in a large saucepan over medium heat. Sauté onion until tender, about 4 minutes. Add garlic, stock, carrots, sweet peppers and zucchini. Bring to a boil. Reduce heat and simmer vegetables until tender.

Add pasta, tomatoes, ham, chickpeas, kidney beans, spinach and herbs. Simmer 10 minutes or until pasta is al dente. Adjust seasoning with salt and pepper. Pour into warmed bowls.

Serves 6 to 8.

QUICK ROMANO BEAN AND PASTA SOUP

THE ITALIAN GOURMET, HALIFAX, N.S.

Chef and owner Kate Abato suggested cooking the pasta separately so that it does not absorb the liquid from the soup. At the Italian Gourmet, she served this hearty dish in many variations, at times using red or green peppers, squash or potato as the vegetable combination or substituting red kidney or white cannellini beans. You may use either vegetable or beef stock for a different flavoured soup.

1½ cups chopped mixed vegetables
  (onion, leek, carrot, celery)
2 cloves garlic, minced
¼ cup extra-virgin olive oil
28-ounce can tomatoes, coarsely chopped
4 cups chicken stock
1 tablespoon chopped fresh basil
1 tablespoon chopped fresh oregano
1 tablespoon chopped fresh parsley
Pinch of red pepper flakes
2 cups cooked Romano beans
Salt and pepper to taste
½ cup Italian soup pasta, such as stellete, farfaline,
  ditali or filini
½ cup freshly grated Parmesan cheese

Sauté vegetables and garlic in oil over medium heat until onions are translucent, about 10 minutes. Stir in tomatoes, stock, herbs and red pepper flakes and simmer 15 minutes, stirring occasionally. Add beans and simmer 10 minutes, stirring occasionally. Continue to cook until vegetables are tender. Adjust seasoning with salt and pepper.

In a separate pot, cook pasta al dente, according to package directions. Drain, but do not rinse.

To serve, place 3 tablespoons of cooked pasta in each soup bowl and top with soup. Serve garnished with grated Parmesan cheese and crusty bread.

Serves 6.

POTATO AND CHEESE SOUP

JOAN NEVERS, PLASTER ROCK, N.B.

Joan Nevers's grandparents came from England in the early 1900s, with her parents following in 1919 after World War I. The English are extremely fond of cheese. Joan recounts, "In the local country store, when I was small, cheese was cut from beautiful rounds and was called Rat Cheese or Chunk Cheese. At home the cheese was wrapped in cheesecloth and kept in the pantry. This very old soup recipe is nice and colourful."

2 tablespoons butter
1 onion, chopped
1 clove garlic or ¾ teaspoon pure garlic powder
3 medium potatoes, peeled and diced
1½ cups chicken stock
½ teaspoon poultry seasoning or ¼ teaspoon thyme
1½ to 2 cups milk
1½ cups shredded Cheddar cheese
Salt and pepper to taste
2 tablespoons minced parsley

Melt butter in heavy saucepan and add the onion and garlic. Cook until tender but not brown. Stir in potatoes, chicken stock and poultry seasoning. Cover saucepan and bring to boil. Cook gently for 15 to 20 minutes. Purée half of the soup in a blender and then return to the saucepan or buzz briefly with an immersion blender to purée some of the soup. Stir in milk and heat. Do not boil. Add cheese, cook and stir until the cheese is melted. Add salt and pepper. Sprinkle top of each serving with parsley.

Serves 4 to 6.

SPLIT PEA SOUP

· · · · · · · · · · · · · ·

EDNA WHITE, HALIFAX, N.S.

Edna White recalls her mother serving Split Pea Soup every Saturday. "She didn't believe in using a ham bone or ham, instead she used corned beef cut into small pieces. It really tasted good on a cold day. To complete the meal she served dumplings, which were cooked in the soup for 10 to 12 minutes just before serving." If you like, add diced carrot, turnip or potato to the soup with the onion and peas.

SOUP

2 cups split peas
1 pound corned beef, cut in small pieces
8 cups water (approximate)
1 medium onion, chopped
Salt and pepper to taste
Chopped carrots, turnip and potatoes (optional)

DUMPLINGS

2 cups sifted all-purpose flour
1 tablespoon baking powder
1 teaspoon salt
2 tablespoons butter
1 cup milk

SOUP

Separately soak peas and beef overnight then drain. Put beef in soup pot with 8 cups water and simmer for 1½ hours. Add peas, onion, salt and pepper and cook slowly for ½ hour, adding water as needed to maintain the level. Just before serving, add enough boiling water to double your soup.

DUMPLINGS

Sift together flour, baking powder and salt. Cut in butter until crumbly. Add milk and mix until smooth. Drop by spoonfuls into hot soup. Cover tightly and cook for 10 to 12 minutes without removing the cover.

Serves 6 to 8.

FRICOT SOUP

· · · · · · · · · · · · · ·

ANNE MARIE CURRIE, SYDNEY, N.S.

There were lots of Acadian dishes served in Anne Marie Currie's childhood home, and her favourite — especially during the cooler months — was Fricot. Served with hot biscuits or fresh rolls, it's delicious. Sometimes served as a first course, but substantial enough to be considered a meal.

1 pound beef or chicken, cubed
1 small onion, diced
1 teaspoon salted chives
⅛ teaspoon dried sage (optional)
Salt and pepper to taste
6¼ cups water
2 medium potatoes, diced and rinsed

In a large pot, combine beef with the onion, chives, sage (if using), salt and pepper and ¼ cup of the water. Cover and slowly stew meat until tender. Add 6 cups water and bring to a boil. Add potato. Cover and boil until tender. Lower heat to simmer.

Serves 6.

Tip: For a thicker soup, mix 2 tablespoons butter and 2 tablespoons flour together and add to pot until dissolved.

WILD RICE AND MUSHROOM SOUP

. . . .

PLANTERS' BARRACKS COUNTRY INN, STARRS POINT, N.S.

Sherry may replace the maple syrup in this recipe, producing an equally delicious soup.

3 cups chicken stock
⅓ cup raw wild rice, rinsed and drained
½ cup thinly sliced green onions
1 cup blend cream (10% mf)
2 tablespoons all-purpose flour
1 teaspoon chopped fresh thyme or ¼ teaspoon dried
Pepper to taste
½ cup thinly sliced mushrooms
1 tablespoon pure maple syrup

In a large saucepan, combine stock and rice. Bring to a boil, reduce heat and simmer, covered, for 40 minutes. Stir in onions and cook an additional 5 to 10 minutes until rice is tender. In a small bowl, whisk together cream, flour, thyme and pepper. Stir into soup mixture and add mushrooms. Cook, stirring frequently, until soup is thickened and bubbly. Stir in syrup and heat through. Serve in warmed bowls.

Serves 4.

ELEGANT SPLIT PEA SOUP WITH SMOKED TURKEY

· · · · · · · · · · · ·

PLANTERS' BARRACKS COUNTRY INN, STARRS POINT, N.S.

There are many ways to make split pea soup, but this one is a little different; smoked turkey legs in place of ham hocks and instead of a slightly chunky rustic soup this is a velvety smooth soup with a few leaves of puréed spinach in at the end for a vibrant green colour and the shredded turkey meat for texture. Serve for lunch with a roll or as a starter to a very elegant Saturday night meal.

2 large smoked turkey legs

12 cups cold water (approximate)

2 onions, 1 whole and 1 finely chopped

4 whole cloves

2 stalks celery, 1 whole and 1 finely chopped

1 whole carrot, peeled

3 sprigs fresh thyme

2 bay leaves

1 leek, white and pale green parts, cleaned and thinly sliced

1 pound green split peas, rinsed

1 cup lightly packed spinach leaves

½ cup heavy cream (35% mf)

Salt and pepper to taste

Crème fraîche

Sliced green onion tops

In a stockpot, bring turkey legs and water to a simmer. Stud whole onion with cloves and add to the pot along with whole celery stalk, whole carrot, thyme and bay leaves. Simmer for 2 hours or until meat is falling off the bone. Remove legs with a slotted spoon and set aside to cool. Remove celery stalk, carrot, whole onion and herbs and discard. If the pot has lost some of its liquid through evaporation, top it up with a little water.

Now add chopped onion and celery, leek and split peas to the pot. Simmer for 90 minutes covered and stirring often. Do not boil or the peas will stick. While the soup simmers, pick the meat off the turkey bones and shred into small pieces. Discard bones and skin. Reserve the meat.

When peas are soft, add spinach to the soup and immediately purée, in batches, in a blender or with an immersion blender. Pass through a sieve and add a little water if it seems a bit thick. Pour soup into a clean pot and add cream. Bring back to a simmer and adjust seasonings. Add turkey meat and return to simmer.

Ladle hot soup into soup bowls (a tea cup with saucer makes a nice presentation as well). Garnish with a dollop of crème fraîche and a couple of slices of green onion tops.

Serves 6, with leftovers.

CHILLED STRAWBERRY SOUP

. . . .

The pale pink colour of this soup presents beautifully. Prepare it early in the day to allow flavours to blend. Garnish with a swirl of sour cream and a modest sprinkle of diced strawberries.

2 cups hulled strawberries
⅓ cup granulated sugar
⅓ cup light sour cream
½ cup heavy cream (35% mf)
1½ cups water
½ cup mediumsweet red wine

Place strawberries in a blender and purée. Pour the purée into a bowl, whisk in remaining ingredients and refrigerate several hours before serving. Serve in chilled glasses or bowls.

Serves 4.

STRAWBERRY RHUBARB SOUP

. . . .

MURRAY MANOR BED AND BREAKFAST, YARMOUTH, N.S.

Sweet, yet tart, you may serve this soup warm or chilled. It is very flavourful, easy to prepare and lovely in its presentation.

2 cups strawberries
1½ cups chopped red rhubarb
1 cup granulated sugar
2 cups water
1 3-inch cinnamon stick
½ cup mediumsweet red wine
½ cup club soda
½ cup sour cream

Reserve 4 strawberries as garnish. Slice remaining strawberries and combine with rhubarb, sugar, water and cinnamon in a large saucepan. Bring to a boil, reduce heat and simmer until fruits are tender, about 8 minutes. Remove cinnamon stick and purée. Refrigerate.

At serving time, stir in wine and club soda. Serve chilled or reheated, garnished with remaining strawberries and a dollop of sour cream.

Serves 4.

CHILLED SWEET PEA, MINT AND YOGURT SOUP

ACTON'S GRILL AND CAFÉ, WOLFVILLE, N.S.

Fresh green peas and mint flavour this delightful soup — a perfect pick for a summer's day. Prepare this soup one day in advance to allow the flavours to blend.

2 cups chopped sweet onions
1 cup fresh mint leaves, chopped
2 tablespoon vegetable oil
2 cups fresh or frozen green peas
4 cups chicken stock
2 cups plain yogurt
6 drops Tabasco sauce

Sauté onions and mint in oil over medium heat until onions are caramelized, about 12 minutes. Stir in peas and chicken stock. Bring to a boil, reduce heat and simmer 10 minutes or until peas are tender. Cool slightly and purée in batches in a blender or with an immersion blender.

Let cool to room temperature, stir in yogurt and Tabasco sauce. Cover and refrigerate at least 8 hours.

Serves 4 to 6.

CHILLED BLUEBERRY SOUP

THE BLOMIDON INN, WOLFVILLE, N.S.

Blueberries have been designated the official berry of Nova Scotia. In honour of these berries, the chefs at Blomidon Inn used this fruit to star in this delightful chilled soup.

2 cups blueberries
¾ cup sour cream or plain yogurt
¾ cup Champagne or sparkling wine
1 cup blend cream (10% mf)
1½ teaspoon cassis liqueur
½ teaspoon lemon juice
Whipped cream
Fresh mint leaves

Combine blueberries, sour cream, Champagne, cream, cassis liqueur and lemon juice in a food processor or blender. Purée until smooth.

Serve in chilled bowls with an artful dollop of whipped cream and fresh mint leaves.

Serves 4.

FISH STOCK

. . . .

Use lean, white-fleshed fish such as cod, haddock, halibut, pollock or ocean perch to make fish stock. Fish with a high fat content, such as mackerel or salmon, will have a strong flavour that is not suited for fish stock.

2½ pounds fish trimmings with some
   flesh attached (bones, heads)
5 cups cold water, filtered if possible
1 cup dry white wine
1 carrot, chopped
1 small onion, chopped
10 sprigs fresh parsley
2 or 3 sprigs fresh thyme
Pinch of dried thyme
1 bay leaf

Discard tail, fat, gills, skin and all traces of blood from fish trimmings. Rinse with cold water and place the good trimmings in a stockpot. Add water to almost cover the trimmings, plus wine to completely cover. Add remaining ingredients and stir to combine.

Bring to a boil over medium heat. Adjust temperature to maintain a simmer and simmer uncovered 20 to 30 minutes, no longer. With a wooden spoon, occasionally stir and press the bones to release more flavour.

Remove from heat. Strain ingredients through a fine-mesh strainer lined with cheesecloth. With a spoon, skim the surface to remove any fat. Refrigerate for up to 3 days or freeze up to 2 months.

Makes 5 cups.

ROASTED VEGETABLE STOCK

. . . .

Prepare this stock when summer vegetables are at their freshest and store in containers in the freezer for future use.

2 medium carrots, chopped
3 small onions, chopped
2 stalks celery, chopped
3 leeks, white part only, chopped
1 medium fennel bulb, chopped
1 large tomato, chopped
2 tablespoons extra-virgin olive oil
12 cups water, filtered if possible
½ bunch green onions, chopped
5 sprigs Italian parsley

Place carrots, onions, celery, leeks, fennel and tomato in a large roasting pan. Drizzle with oil then toss vegetables to coat. Roast at 325°F for 45 minutes or until vegetables are tender and begin to colour.

Transfer to a large stockpot and cover with cold water. Add green onions and parsley sprigs. Bring to a boil. Skim any foam that appears on top. Reduce heat to simmer and cook uncovered for 2 hours.

Strain and refrigerate or freeze for future use.

Makes 8 to 10 cups.

CHICKEN STOCK

. . . .

Good restaurants rely on flavourful stock for everything from soups to risottos. Meat purveyors know this, and that is why frozen chicken bones, the basis of flavourful stock, are priced ridiculously high. What used to be scrap now costs almost as much as a whole bird by weight. Instead, consider using stewing hens instead of bones for stock. That way you can use the meat for pot pies, soups or salads, so nothing is wasted.

2 stewing hens (about 6 pounds each)
2 cups coarsely chopped onion
1 cup coarsely chopped white of leek
1½ cups coarsely chopped celery
1½ cups coarsely chopped carrot
4 bay leaves
3 sprigs fresh thyme
1 tablespoon whole black peppercorns
Cold water to cover (about 1½ gallons)

Cut hens into quarters and rinse well under cold water. Place all ingredients in a large stockpot with the chicken on top of the vegetables. This will make it easier to skim during the simmer. Cover with cold water (the water can rise about 1 inch above the level of the chicken, but no more). Bring to a boil on high and immediately reduce to a simmer. Cook for 3 hours, skimming any fat or scum from the top of the liquid. Strain stock through a fine sieve and refrigerate or freeze for future use. When the cooked chicken meat is cool to the touch remove from the bones and reserve for another use.

Makes 8 cups.

SKILLET CROUTONS

. . . .

These basic croutons adapt well to seasoning. Before removing from skillet, sprinkle with your favourite herb or spice and stir a couple of times.

3 tablespoon butter
3 slices good-quality white bread, crusts removed, cut into large cubes

In a skillet, heat butter over medium-high heat. Add croutons and stir until brown and crispy.

Makes 4 to 5 cups.

MAINS:
CHICKEN, TURKEY, DUCK
AND RABBIT

HERB-RUBBED TURKEY WITH SHERRY GRAVY

· · · · · · · · · · · ·

The size of your Thanksgiving or Christmas turkey will depend upon the number of people gracing your dining-room table. To calculate the size of turkey you'll need, allow 1 to 1½ pounds of uncooked turkey per person. And if you love leftover turkey, be sure to increase the weight by a few pounds. Prepare the Turkey Stock, Herb Rub and Seasoned Bread and Potato Stuffing (page 43) the day before roasting the turkey. On the big day you will be glad you did.

14-pound fresh turkey
¼ cup all-purpose flour
3 tablespoons dry sherry

HERB RUB

1 teaspoon dried oregano
1 teaspoon dried rosemary, crushed
1 teaspoon dried thyme
1 teaspoon dried sage
2 teaspoons sweet paprika
Pinch of ground ginger
¼ teaspoon salt
½ teaspoon pepper
1 tablespoon extra-virgin olive oil (approximate)

TURKEY STOCK

1 tablespoon extra-virgin olive oil
Neck and giblets (without the liver) from turkey
1 large carrot, chopped
1 medium red or sweet onion, chopped
1 stalk celery, chopped
Pinch of poultry seasoning
5 black peppercorns
1 cup dry white wine
5 cups chicken stock, water or combination of both

Prepare Turkey Stock, Herb Rub and Seasoned Bread and Potato Stuffing in advance.

Pat the turkey dry with paper towels. Loosely stuff turkey cavities with Seasoned Bread and Potato Stuffing. Close openings with skewers. Tie legs together and tuck wings back. Place the turkey, breast side up, on a rack set inside a large roasting pan and rub the exposed turkey skin with the Herb Rub.

Place the roasting pan on an oven rack set at the lowest position. Roast 1 hour and 15 minutes at 325°F, covering the turkey loosely with foil (shiny side down) if it's browning too quickly. Baste with pan drippings (if there are insufficient drippings, brush turkey with a little more oil) and re-cover with foil. Basting every 30 minutes, roast the turkey an additional 3 hours or until a thermometer inserted into the thickest part of the inner thigh registers 175°F. Remove foil during the last 30 minutes of roasting, allowing the turkey to brown. Transfer turkey to a platter, tent with foil and let stand 30 minutes before carving.

To make the gravy, skim fat off the drippings in the roasting pan. Place the roasting pan over 2 stove burners. Whisk the flour into the drippings until smooth. Cook and stir 3 minutes. Add sherry and Turkey Stock and whisk until smooth. Bring to a boil and add any additional turkey juices from the platter. Reduce heat and simmer until slightly thickened. Adjust seasoning and pour into gravy boat.

Serves 8.

HERB RUB

This rub works well with poultry, pork and beef.

In a small bowl, combine all ingredients and stir to blend.

Makes 3 tablespoons.

TURKEY STOCK

In a large heavy pot, heat oil over medium-high heat until fragrant. Add neck and giblets and brown, about 4 minutes. Add carrot, onion and celery and sauté, stirring frequently until golden, about 5 minutes. Add seasoning, peppercorns and wine. Bring to a boil and cook 1 minute. Add stock and cook at a brisk simmer until reduced to 3 cups of liquid, about 30 minutes.

Remove stock from heat. Strain and discard solids. Let cool to room temperature, skim off fat and reserve, covered, in the refrigerator.

Makes 3 cups.

Tip: Make the stock the day before you roast the turkey. On holidays such as Thanksgiving and Christmas, this eases kitchen clutter and stress.

SEASONED BREAD AND POTATO STUFFING

. . . .

This combination of good quality bread mixed with potato, celery, onion, nuts, dried fruit and herbs makes for a pleasing flavour that enhances but never overpowers the delicate taste of poultry. If you choose to bake the stuffing in the poultry cavities, pack it loosely and cook stuffing to 165°F.

2 tablespoons extra-virgin olive oil
2 tablespoons butter
1½ cups diced celery
1½ cups diced onion
4 cups roughly cubed day-old, rustic bread
3 cups mashed potato
1½ cups dried mixed fruit, chopped (apple, apricot, prune, cranberry)
1 cup pecan pieces
1 tablespoon dried summer savory or sage (or to taste)
¼ to ½ cup chicken stock
Salt and pepper

Heat oil and butter in a skillet over medium-low heat. Add celery and onion and sauté until softened, about 8 minutes. Remove onion and celery to a large bowl. Add the bread, potato, mixed fruit, pecans and savory and toss to combine. Add chicken stock, 2 tablespoons at a time, tossing the ingredients until stuffing is slightly moist. Add salt and pepper to taste. Cool until ready to use.

Lightly spoon dressing into a greased casserole and bake at 350°F for 45 minutes, until heated through and lightly crisped on top.

Makes 8 cups.

ROAST CHICKEN WITH ROOT VEGETABLES
(POULET ROTI)

· · · · · · · · · · · ·

Julia Child often commented that a cook's ability is determined by how perfectly he or she roasts a chicken. Start with a good chicken. Locally produced free-range chickens are generally available at good grocery stores or your local farmers' market. For simplicity, many cooks roast the root vegetables accompanying this dish in the same pan as the chicken, but the higher moisture content may prevent the chicken from developing a crispy skin. Cook them separately as shown below to achieve the ultimate roast.

ROAST CHICKEN

3½ to 4-pound free-range roasting chicken

¼ cup softened butter

2 teaspoons kosher or coarse sea salt

1 teaspoon pepper

2 sprigs fresh thyme

2 sprigs fresh rosemary

Several leaves fresh sage

Bunch of chervil or parsley

ROASTED ROOT VEGETABLES

3 medium potatoes, peeled

1 small celery root, peeled and diced into 1-inch cubes

1 pound baby carrots, with green tops on if available

½ medium turnip, diced

1 sweet potato, diced

3 tablespoons extra-virgin olive oil

1 teaspoon dried sage

3 tablespoons melted butter

1 teaspoon kosher or coarse sea salt

1 teaspoon pepper

ROAST CHICKEN

Pat chicken dry with paper towels. Rub entire bird, including internal cavity, with soft butter. Sprinkle with salt and pepper and fill cavity with fresh herbs.

It is essential to roast your chicken on a rack in a shallow roasting pan. This allows the pan drippings to fall away from the skin and also allows hot air to flow around the body. Roast in 425°F oven, breast side up, for 15 minutes. Lower the heat to 350°F and roast for 15 minutes. Carefully turn the chicken breast down. Roast for 15 minutes, basting regularly. When chicken has been in the oven for a total of 45 minutes, turn it breast side up. Roast for 30 to 45 minutes or until a thermometer inserted into the thigh reads 170 to 175°F. A 4-pound bird should take about 75 to 90 minutes total.

ROASTED ROOT VEGETABLES

Cover and cook potatoes in boiling water until tender. (Cooking the potatoes first allows them to be soft inside but crisp and golden outside.) Cut potatoes into wedges and place in a bowl with all other ingredients. Gently toss together and place on a nonstick roasting pan. Roast at 350°F for 45 minutes, or until golden brown.

Serves 4 to 6.

FREE-RANGE CHICKEN POT PIE

· · · · · · · · · · · ·

Perhaps the ultimate comfort food, chicken pot pie is a classic recipe for cold winter nights. But that doesn't mean it can't be enjoyed all year round. This pie is like British ones, the rich meat inside is bound in a small amount of sauce, and any vegetables are served on the side.

CHICKEN

1 whole free-range chicken
1 medium onion, coarsely chopped
1 stalk celery, coarsely chopped
1 carrot, coarsely chopped
2 bay leaves
4 sprigs fresh thyme or sage
2 cups unsalted chicken stock
Cold water

FILLING

1 small onion, minced
1 stalk celery, minced
1 clove garlic, minced
¼ cup butter
½ teaspoon dried summer savory
¼ cup all-purpose flour
¼ cup white wine or sherry
1 teaspoon salt
1 teaspoon pepper
2 tablespoons chopped fresh sage
2 tablespoons chopped fresh Italian parsley

PIE ASSEMBLY

Pastry for 10-inch Double-Crust Pie (page 205)
Chicken pie filling, chilled
1 large egg, beaten
1 teaspoon rock salt or sea salt such as fleur de sel

CHICKEN

Combine all ingredients in a stockpot, adding enough water to cover the bird. Bring to a boil, reduce the heat and simmer, covered, for 2 hours. Remove from the heat and chill the bird completely in the stock. (The meat hydrates completely as it cools.) Remove hard fat from the top. Remove chicken and discard all skin and visible fat. Pick meat completely off the carcass and shred by hand into small pieces. Strain stock and discard vegetables and herbs. In a clean pot, boil until reduced to 1½ cups. Cool reduced stock.

FILLING

Sauté onion, celery and garlic in butter until onions begin to turn slightly brown, about 15 minutes. Add summer savory and flour to form a roux. Stir in white wine, then add the reduced chicken stock. Season with salt and pepper. Whisk until very smooth. The mixture should be very thick. Stir in fresh herbs and combine sauce with the shredded chicken. Adjust seasoning, if desired. Refrigerate for 30 minutes.

PIE ASSEMBLY

Cut pastry in half and roll each piece into 2 rounds, approximately ¼-inch thick. Line a nonstick 9- to 10-inch tart pan or pie plate with the first layer of pastry. Smaller individual tart pans can also be used. Fill with chicken mixture until it heaps in the middle. Cover with the second piece of pastry and press the edges together and trim. Cut 3 small steam holes in the top of the pastry. Brush with beaten egg and sprinkle with salt. Bake for 35 minutes at 350°F or until crust is deep brown in colour.

Slice the pie in wedges, as you would a dessert pie, and serve immediately with your favourite vegetables.

Serves 6 to 8.

OLD-FASHIONED CHICKEN DUMPLINGS

. . . .

SANDRA NOWLAN, HALIFAX, N.S.

3- to 4-pound whole chicken

4 cups water

Salt and pepper to taste

4 onions, 1 sliced and 3 whole peeled

1 bay leaf

2 stalks celery, cut into 2-inch pieces, and celery
  leaves

½ teaspoon summer savory or thyme

1 clove garlic

4 medium potatoes, halved

6 carrots, halved

2 turnips, sliced ½-inch thick, cut in quarters

1 cup frozen peas

3 tablespoons all-purpose flour mixed with

6 tablespoons cold water

¼ cup finely chopped parsley

DUMPLINGS

1½ cups all-purpose flour

2 teaspoons baking powder

¾ teaspoon salt

½ teaspoon savory or thyme

3 tablespoons butter

¾ to 1 cup milk

Fancy molasses

Put chicken in Dutch oven and add the water. Season with salt and pepper, 1 sliced onion, a bay leaf, celery leaves, savory and garlic. Simmer for about 2 hours or until tender. Cool. Remove chicken from pot. Discard skin and bones. Set the meat aside. Skim fat from the stock. Add all remaining vegetables except peas to the stock. Cover and simmer until tender. Add peas and chicken and bring to a boil. Liquid should not quite cover the meat and vegetables. If it does, remove the excess. Stir in the flour mixture. Simmer until sauce thickens and boils.

DUMPLINGS

Meanwhile, blend dry ingredients. Cut in butter until crumbly. Mix in milk with a fork. Drop by spoonfuls onto the chicken and vegetables in the boiling sauce (not directly into the liquid). Reduce heat and cook slowly 10 minutes uncovered and another 10 minutes tightly covered.

Sprinkle generously with parsley. Serve with a small pitcher of molasses to eat with the dumplings.

Serves 4 to 6.

CHICKEN FRICOT WITH
SWEET POTATO DUMPLINGS

· · · · · · · · · · · ·

As anyone with Acadian heritage will know, fricot is basically chicken soup. It can most certainly be made with other birds or even hare, but chicken is the most traditional. Served simply with chunks of potatoes and onions, the meat is tender and moist. This recipe, more stew than soup, omits the potato and strays from tradition by adding small Italian dumplings or agnolotti, which work well with the fragrant summer savory that is so pronounced in any fricot. Wonton wrappers replace the traditional pasta for the agnolotti and stock the water Acadians would have used.

CHICKEN FRICOT

2 onions, finely chopped
1 stalk celery, finely chopped
1 tablespoon dried summer savory
1 teaspoon dried thyme
2 bay leaves
2 tablespoons butter
1 teaspoon salt
1 teaspoon pepper
5-pound free-range chicken
10 cups chicken stock, low sodium recommended

SWEET POTATO DUMPLINGS

1 pound sweet potatoes (3 medium)
2 large egg yolks
¼ whole nutmeg, grated
¼ cup grated Parmesan cheese
1 tablespoon chopped fresh sage
Salt and pepper to taste
1 package wonton wrappers, 3-inch square

CHICKEN FRICOT

In a stockpot that fits the whole chicken, sauté onions, celery, summer savory, thyme and bay leaves in butter for 3 or 4 minutes until onions are translucent. Add salt, pepper and chicken and cover with stock. Top up with water to cover chicken if necessary. Bring to a boil and reduce heat to a simmer. Cook for 90 minutes, until the meat is tender and falling from the bones.

FOR A RUSTIC SOUP

Remove chicken from the pot and pick meat from the bones. Discard bones and skin. Skim off the fat and discard. Return meat to pot and heat to serving temperature.

DUMPLINGS

Meanwhile, bake sweet potatoes, skin on, in a 350°F oven for 45 minutes to 1 hour, or until flesh is soft and creamy. Let cool to room temperature. Cut potatoes in half and scoop flesh into a mixing bowl. Mix in all remaining ingredients except the wrappers and refrigerate.

Spoon a heaping teaspoon of the filling in the centre of each wrapper, then run a finger dipped in cold water along 2 sides of the wrapper, folding over to form a triangle. Press edges to seal well.

Poach dumplings in boiling water until they float.

Place 2 dumplings in the bottom of a heated soup bowl (3 if you are really hungry). Ladle a healthy portion of soup overtop and serve.

Serves 8, with leftovers.

Tip: If making a large batch, lay them out on a baking sheet lined with parchment or wax paper. Freeze individually (making sure they do not touch on the sheet), and transfer to a freezer container once solid. They can be cooked from frozen.

HONEYED PAPRIKA CHICKEN

. . . .

SANDRA PHINNEY MACGREGOR,
EAST CANAAN, N.S.

Several years ago a group of ladies were served a supper dish featuring chicken. As they raved about it, the cook laughed and said it was just a bottle of salad dressing poured over some pieces of chicken and baked. Inspired by her friend, Sandra Phinney MacGregor combined her own marinade and her farm chickens, with rave results.

½ cup liquid honey
½ cup cider vinegar
1 small onion, finely chopped
2 to 3 cloves garlic, crushed
1 teaspoon salt
1 teaspoon paprika
1 teaspoon Worcestershire sauce
3-to 4-pound whole chicken
Water

Measure all the ingredients except chicken in a bowl and mix well. Cut chicken into serving pieces and arrange, skin side down, in a shallow baking pan. Cover with the honey marinade. Refrigerate for 2 to 4 hours, or as long as overnight. Bake, uncovered, at 400°F for 20 minutes. Turn the pieces, and bake until the juices run clear and skin is golden brown, about 20 minutes. Add a little water as necessary to retain a nice sauce. Serve hot with baked potatoes, which can cook at the same time, or pack pieces of the cold cooked chicken in lunch boxes or picnic baskets.

Serves 4 to 6.

DARREN'S COQ AU VIN

. . . .

Darren Lewis, Chef de Cuisine at Chives, has served this chicken classic many times over the years. Free-range chicken leg and thigh quarters and double-smoked German bacon are ideal for this recipe, and boiled baby potatoes and fresh green beans or haricots verts make an excellent accompaniment to a classic coq au vin.

2 teaspoons tomato paste

1 bottle (750 mL) good dry red wine

1 teaspoon sea salt

½ teaspoon pepper

2 bay leaves

4 sprigs fresh thyme

6 free-range chicken leg and thigh quarters, skin on

2 tablespoons extra-virgin olive oil

½ pound double-smoked bacon, chopped

2 teaspoons butter

20 pearl onions, blanched and peeled

1 head garlic, cloves separated and peeled

½ pound button mushrooms, halved

1 portobello mushroom, stem and gills removed, chopped

2 tablespoons all-purpose flour

¼ cup brandy

In a large bowl, combine tomato paste, wine, salt, pepper, bay leaves and thyme. Add chicken then cover and marinate for at least 12 hours in the refrigerator, turning chicken at least once. Remove chicken from marinade and pat dry with a paper towel. Reserve marinade for the sauce. In a large skillet or sauté pan, sear chicken in oil until both sides are browned. Remove from the pan and set aside on a plate.

Remove any fat from the pan and sauté bacon over medium heat until fat is rendered out and bacon is browned. The bacon fat can be discarded, if desired, but keeping it for the base sauce adds tremendous flavour. With a slotted spoon, remove bacon and add to chicken.

Add butter to the pan and cook onions, garlic and both mushrooms for about 10 minutes. When mushroom and onion mixture has some colour add flour and mix well to form a roux with the fat in the pan. Carefully deglaze the pan with brandy. As it ignites easily over an open flame, remove from the heat while deglazing. Return reserved marinade to the pan. Stir well, and over medium heat simmer to form a slightly thickened sauce. Return chicken and bacon to the pan and simmer, covered, until juices in the thighs run clear, about 30 minutes.

Serves 4 to 6.

CHICKEN SUPREME

. . . .

THE CAPTAIN'S HOUSE, CHESTER

You can serve this rich Sherry Cream Sauce over the chicken — or in a separate dish for diet-conscious diners.

4 boneless, skinless chicken breasts (6 ounces each)
2 tablespoons extra-virgin olive oil
½ pound mushrooms, chopped
1 clove garlic, minced
½ cup finely chopped onion
Salt and pepper to taste

SHERRY CREAM SAUCE

⅔ cup heavy cream (35% mf)
2 tablespoons butter
2 tablespoons sweet sherry
½ teaspoon cornstarch dissolved in 1 teaspoon cold water
Salt and pepper to taste

With a very sharp knife, cut into the underside of each chicken breast to form a pocket. Set aside. In a skillet, heat 1 tablespoon of the oil and sauté mushrooms, garlic and onion until soft. Season with salt and pepper to taste. Let cool.

Stuff the mushroom mixture into the pockets of the chicken breasts and turn over. Add remaining oil to the skillet and over moderate heat, quickly seal and brown the breasts all over. Transfer the breasts, pocket side down, to a shallow casserole and bake in a preheated 350°F oven for 20 minutes.

SHERRY CREAM SAUCE

Whisk cream, butter and sherry in a small saucepan over high heat. Gradually whisk in cornstarch and whisk until slightly thickened. Season with salt and pepper. Serve breasts with Sherry Cream Sauce.

Serves 4.

GRILLED BREAST OF CHICKEN WITH APPLE BRANDY SAUCE

. . . .

HALIBURTON HOUSE INN, HALIFAX, N.S.

This succulent chicken dish is sure to become a favourite in your recipe collection. The sauce recipe was created using Calvados brandy, but other brandies also give excellent results.

½ medium onion, chopped
1 clove garlic, chopped
1 cup apple juice
1½ cups heavy cream (35% mf)
1 tablespoon brandy
½ apple, peeled, cored and diced
Salt and pepper to taste
4 boneless, skinless chicken breasts (6 ounces each)

In saucepan over medium heat, combine onion, garlic and apple juice. Bring to a boil and reduce volume by three-quarters. Add cream and reduce volume by half. Press through a fine sieve, add brandy and apples. Adjust seasoning with salt and pepper.

Grill chicken breasts on a barbecue or electric grill until juices run clear, approximately 5 minutes per side, being careful not to overcook. Serve with sauce.

Serves 4.

SICILIAN CHICKEN

. . . .

BLUENOSE LODGE, LUNENBURG, N.S.

This is a healthy, low-fat recipe that is tasty with orange and vermouth — and elegant.

¼ cup all-purpose flour
1 tablespoon minced fresh parsley
½ teaspoon paprika
¼ teaspoon salt
¼ teaspoon pepper
¼ teaspoon dried oregano
4 boneless chicken breasts (6 ounces each)
1 tablespoon canola oil
8 slices fresh orange
¾ cup fresh orange juice
¼ cup sweet vermouth

Make a seasoned flour by combining flour, parsley, paprika, salt, pepper and oregano. Dredge chicken breasts in this seasoned flour. Heat oil in a large skillet and brown breasts on both sides until firm and almost cooked. Cover each breast with 2 slices of orange and add orange juice. Cover and cook another few minutes until juices in the breasts run clear. Remove breasts from skillet and keep warm.

Uncover skillet and reduce liquid to about ⅓ cup. Add vermouth and reduce slightly. Serve chicken with cooked orange slices topped with the orange-vermouth sauce.

Serves 4.

HEAVENLY CHICKEN

. . . .

THE INNLET CAFÉ, MAHONE BAY, N.S.

The chef of the Innlet Café serves this delightful dish in individual casseroles accompanied by rice pilaf and green salad.

8 to 10 medium mushrooms, sliced
¼ cup chopped shallots
⅓ cup butter
¾ cup water
¾ cup heavy cream (35% mf)
½ cup white wine
½ cup sour cream
1½ tablespoons soy sauce
¼ cup all-purpose flour
1 teaspoon paprika
2½ to 3 cups cooked chicken, in bite-size pieces

Sauté mushrooms and shallots in 1 tablespoon of the butter in a large skillet for a few minutes until wilted. Remove shallots and mushrooms to a bowl and wipe pan clean. Meanwhile, in a saucepan combine water, cream, wine, sour cream and soy sauce. Bring to a boil, reduce heat and simmer.

Melt remaining butter in skillet and whisk in flour and paprika. Cook 1 minute and remove from heat. Slowly add boiling wine-cream mixture, whisking constantly to prevent lumps. Fold in cooked chicken, shallots and mushrooms. Serve immediately or reheat at 350°F for 20 to 30 minutes.

Serves 4 to 6.

SEASON'S CRANBERRY-GLAZED CHICKEN

SEASONS IN THYME, SUMMERSIDE, P.E.I.

This is possibly one of the tastiest chicken recipes you will find. While you may choose any type of potato or vegetable, the chef suggests basil-sautéed carrots and pattypan squash or sautéed spinach.

4 chicken breasts, skin on and wishbone attached
12 leaves fresh sage or basil
Salt and pepper to taste
3 tablespoons extra-virgin olive oil

CRANBERRY GLAZE

½ tablespoon extra-virgin olive oil
1 tablespoon finely diced shallots
¼ cup whole cranberries
½ tablespoon finely chopped orange zest
¼ cup white wine
2 cups chicken stock
1 tablespoon unsalted butter
Salt and pepper to taste

Pat chicken breasts dry. Gently lift the skin and slide in 3 herb leaves so that they lie flat between the skin and the breast. Season breasts with salt and pepper.

Place a sauté pan or deep skillet over medium-high heat and add oil. Place the breasts in the pan, skin side down, and cook approximately 3 to 5 minutes until skin is golden. Turn and cook an additional 3 minutes. Remove breasts and finish off in a 350°F oven until juices run clear, 10 to 15 minutes. Allow to rest 4 to 6 minutes before carving. Drizzle with Seasons' Cranberry Glaze.

Serves 4.

CRANBERRY GLAZE

Heat oil in a small saucepan over medium-high heat. Add shallots and sauté approximately 1½ minutes, being careful not to brown. Add cranberries, zest and white wine then reduce by half. Add stock and boil to reduce by two-thirds. Swirl in butter with a small whisk and season with salt and pepper.

AMHERST SHORE CHICKEN WITH BLUEBERRY SAUCE

AMHERST SHORE COUNTRY INN, LORNEVILLE, N.S.

Nova Scotia's Cumberland County blueberries are at their peak during August, and Donna Laceby came up with innovative uses in several recipes.

4 boneless chicken breasts
2 tablespoons cornstarch
3 tablespoons water
2 cups fresh or frozen blueberries
3 tablespoons granulated sugar
½ cup dry red wine
Zest of 1 lemon

Pat dry chicken breasts. Over medium-high heat, grill breasts on a greased grill until grill-marked and browned, turning once. Remove to a 375°F oven and bake for 5 to 7 minutes, or until juices run clear and chicken is no longer pink in the centre.

Dissolve cornstarch in water and combine with blueberries and sugar in a saucepan. Cook over medium-high heat stirring often until berries break down and sauce thickens. Add wine and bring back to a boil. To serve, spread a small amount of blueberry sauce on each plate, top with chicken breast and drizzle with remaining sauce. Sprinkle with lemon zest to garnish.

Serves 4.

CHICKEN AND PEACHES

THE PALLISER, TRURO, N.S.

This dish is easily prepared. Pop it in the oven and it's ready to eat within the hour. Try it with rice, home-baked rolls and a crisp side salad.

2 tablespoons all-purpose flour
½ teaspoon salt
½ teaspoon paprika
4 to 6 chicken breasts, trimmed and skinned
½ cup peach jam
⅓ cup water
¼ cup barbecue sauce
¼ cup diced onions
¼ cup diced green pepper
1 tablespoon soy sauce
1 cup sliced peaches
⅓ cup sliced water chestnuts

Combine flour, salt and paprika. Dredge chicken in flour mixture and lay pieces in a large shallow casserole. In a bowl, combine jam, water and barbecue sauce. Stir in onions, green pepper and soy sauce and pour over chicken breasts. Bake, uncovered, in a preheated 350°F oven for 40 to 45 minutes, basting occasionally. Add peach slices and water chestnuts and bake for 10 minutes, basting once or twice to make sure that chicken and peaches are glazed.

Serves 4 to 6.

RABBIT IN GARLIC

MARY JANE LOSIER, BATHURST, N.B.

La Fine Grobe sur Mer is an art gallery, gourmet restaurant and auberge on New Brunswick's north shore at Nigadoo. Chef Georges Frachon is from France, but as he says, "I have no hat, no diploma. I just like cooking and I follow my intuition." He cautions that the rabbit has to cook slowly in its own juice. Serve with white rice or plain boiled potatoes.

1 fresh rabbit, cut in pieces
1½ tablespoons extra-virgin olive oil
1 teaspoon salt
1 teaspoon pepper
15 cloves garlic, peeled
Chopped fresh parsley

In a heavy frying pan, sauté the rabbit pieces in oil until they are well browned. Add salt, pepper and garlic cloves. Cover the pan and cook over low heat until the rabbit is tender, up to 2 hours. Check occasionally to make sure the liquid has not evaporated. Garnish with parsley.

Serves 4.

NOVA SCOTIA DUCK BREAST WITH FLAGEOLETS

CHIVES CANADIAN BISTRO, HALIFAX, N.S.

Flageolet beans have a delicate flavour that goes well with other ingredients. They come in different colours. Use white for the colour contrast in the sauce with the tomatoes.

4 boneless duck breasts
3 slices bacon, diced
½ leek, white part only
1 clove garlic
1 7-ounce can flageolet beans, drained
½ cup halved grape tomatoes
2 tablespoons chopped fresh sage
2 tablespoons red wine
Salt and pepper to taste
2 tablespoons extra-virgin olive oil

Using a sharp knife, score skin and fat of duck to help render the fat during cooking.

Roast duck breast, skin side down, until desired doneness. Let rest 5 minutes before slicing.

Meanwhile, in a large pot over medium heat, sauté bacon, leek and garlic until translucent. Turn heat to high and add beans, tomatoes and sage. Cook 2 minutes then add wine and season with salt and pepper to taste.

Divide bean mixture onto 4 plates and fan sliced duck over. Drizzle with olive oil.

Serves 4.

STUFFED CHICKEN BREASTS
WITH BLUEBERRY-MAPLE SAUCE

THE PINES RESORT HOTEL, DIGBY, N.S.

The goat's milk cheese in this recipe provides a distinctly sharp flavour that immediately distinguishes it from other cheeses. If you prefer a milder cheese flavour, substitute ¼ cup of the chèvre with cream cheese.

6 boneless, skinless chicken breasts (6 ounces each)
¾ cup chèvre cheese (soft goat's cheese)
2 tablespoons chopped pecans
2 tablespoons chopped fresh parsley, basil or thyme
Salt and pepper
1½ tablespoons extra-virgin olive oil
1 tablespoon butter
Cooked rice

BLUEBERRY-MAPLE SAUCE

1½ tablespoons butter
1 shallot, finely chopped
Salt and pepper
½ cup blueberries
2 cups red wine
1½ cups chicken stock
2 tablespoons pure maple syrup
4 drops hot pepper sauce, such as Tabasco
1 tablespoon all-purpose flour

Trim any fat from chicken breasts. Slice breasts halfway through thick side to form a pocket.

In a bowl, blend cheese, pecans and herbs. Spoon equal amounts of cheese mixture into breast pockets; press edges together to seal. Season with salt and pepper.

In a large ovenproof skillet, heat oil and butter over medium-high heat. Brown breasts, turning once. Remove skillet to 350°F oven and roast breasts until juices run clear, about 15 to 20 minutes. To serve, slice breasts diagonally. Drizzle serving plates with Blueberry-Maple Sauce, add rice and top with sliced chicken.

Serves 6.

BLUEBERRY-MAPLE SAUCE

In a saucepan over low heat, combine ½ tablespoon of the butter and shallot then sweat until shallot is softened, about 5 minutes. Season with salt and pepper. Add blueberries, red wine, chicken stock, maple syrup and hot pepper sauce. Increase heat to high. Bring sauce to a boil and simmer until reduced by three-quarters, about 20 minutes.

Mash together flour and remaining butter. Add a little at a time to simmering sauce. Stir constantly until sauce slightly thickens.

Makes 1 cup.

RAPPIE PIE

· · · · · · · · · · · · ·

Rappie pie is an Acadian dish derived from the French word for "grate," referring to the unique method of grating potatoes for the top layer of the pie. It can be made with nearly any meat, shellfish and, in the old days, sea birds. This is simple peasant cooking and variations are to be expected, so don't worry too much about how much potato or filling you have. Just pile it on and bake it until the crust is crisp and golden.

4 pounds peeled russet potatoes
1 teaspoon salt, approximate
7-pound chicken or stewing hen
2 medium onions, diced
2 stalks celery, 1 whole and 1 minced
1 carrot, split lengthwise
2 bay leaves
4 ounces salt pork, diced into 2-inch cubes
1 teaspoon dried thyme
½ teaspoon dried summer savory
¼ cup butter
Pepper

Using the fine side of a box grater, grate the potatoes into a large bowl. Add the salt and mix with your fingers, then place the grated potatoes in a pillowcase or several layers of cheesecloth; suspend above a bowl while the chicken cooks for the filling.

Meanwhile, in a large stockpot, place the chicken, half the diced onions, the whole stalk of celery, the carrot and the bay leaves. Add just enough cold water to cover everything. Bring to a boil and reduce the heat to a simmer. Cook for 1 hour until the chicken is tender. A stewing hen will take longer. Then let the chicken cool slightly in the poaching liquid.

When the chicken is cool enough to handle, remove from the broth and pick off all the meat, discarding the skin and bones. Reserve the broth for use with the potatoes. Chop the meat into bite-size chunks.

In a skillet over medium heat, cook the salt pork until the fat renders, then sauté the remaining onion, minced celery, thyme and summer savory in the pork fat until the onions are translucent. Combine this mixture with the chicken meat in the bottom of a large baking dish or casserole. Moisten the meat with several spoonfuls of the chicken broth.

Reheat the remaining chicken broth to a simmer. Firmly squeeze the potatoes in the bag, extracting as much water as possible. Empty the potatoes into a saucepan and cook for 3 minutes over medium-high heat, stirring. As the potatoes begin to heat, add about ½ cup of hot broth and stir continuously. Add another ½ cup and then another, and cook until the potatoes appear gluey and move as one mass in the pan. Season with salt and pepper, if desired.

Spread the potato mixture evenly over the chicken mixture in the dish, place several dollops of butter on top of the potato layer and bake in a 400°F oven until the potato crust is a deep golden brown, about 45 minutes to 1 hour. If the crust darkens too quickly, reduce the heat to 350°F to finish baking.

Allow pie to rest for at least 30 minutes before attempting to serve. Rappie pie is wonderful with a side salad, pickles of any sort or Christmas Cranberry Chutney (page 285).

Serves 6 to 8.

FRICOT AU LAPIN DES BOIS
(BRAISED WILD RABBIT HOT POT)

. . . .

CHIVES CANADIAN BISTRO, HALIFAX, N.S.

Chef Darren Lewis brought Acadian cultural dishes to the Chives menu from day one, including this warm and winter-perfect stew. "The Acadian people were good farmers and fishermen, as well as hunter-gatherers," says Darren, "skills they honed with the help of the First Nations peoples in the region. This recipe is a twist on an old Acadian favourite, traditionally made with wild hare, which they trapped themselves, and with the potatoes in the stew. But I prefer the flavour of the less gamey and more accessible farmed rabbit and to serve the potatoes on the side."

½ cup diced salt-cured pork belly

½ cup all-purpose flour

1 teaspoon fine sea salt (approximate)

1 teaspoon pepper (approximate)

1 farmed rabbit or wild, cut into 8 pieces

2 cups pearl onions

2 carrots, finely diced

2 stalks of celery, finely diced

1 shallot, minced

4 cloves garlic, minced

2 tablespoons dried summer savory

1 cup dry white wine

6 cups chicken stock

Place a ceramic-lined cast iron braising pot over medium-high heat and render salt pork until it is very crisp. Remove pork from the pan and set aside. Mix flour, salt and pepper together and dredge rabbit pieces in flour mixture. Brown rabbit pieces on all sides in the pork drippings. Remove rabbit and set aside. To the pot, add onions, carrots and celery and sauté for a few minutes until they begin to soften and take some colour, then add shallot, garlic and savory and sauté for another 5 minutes. Deglaze pot with wine and reduce it by half. Return rabbit pieces to the pot. Add chicken stock and bring to a boil.

Cover the pot and braise in 300°F oven for 1 hour. The meat should be fork-tender. Transfer rabbit pieces to a hot serving platter to keep warm. Using a slotted spoon, remove pearl onions from the broth and set aside. Place braising pot, uncovered, on high heat and boil to reduce until it coats the back of a wooden spoon. Strain sauce through a sieve and season to taste with salt and pepper. Return pearl onions to sauce.

PRESENTATION

Place 2 pieces of rabbit on each plate. Ladle some of the sauce over the meat and garnish with the reserved crispy pork belly. Serve with buttered baby red potatoes and haricots verts.

Serves 4.

MAINS:
BEEF, PORK, LAMB, VENISON AND MOOSE

PEPPERED BEEF TENDERLOIN

. . . .

INN ON THE LAKE, WAVERLEY, N.S.

The sauce for this impressive steak entrée may be made earlier in the day and reheated at serving time. Five Peppercorn Blend is a combination of colourful peppercorns and is found in most supermarkets.

4 beef tenderloin filets (6 ounces each)
Salt and pepper
1½ teaspoons vegetable oil
3 tablespoons Dijon mustard
¾ teaspoon Worcestershire sauce
¾ teaspoon dried rosemary, slightly crushed
2 to 3 teaspoons crushed Five Peppercorn Blend

PEPPERCORN SAUCE

2 tablespoons cold butter
1 tablespoon finely chopped shallots
1 teaspoon finely minced garlic
1½ teaspoons green peppercorns, drained
3 tablespoons brandy
¾ teaspoon dried thyme
⅓ cup white wine
1½ cups beef stock
⅓ cup heavy cream (35% mf)

Season beef filets with salt and pepper to taste. Heat a sauté pan or large skillet on high with oil. Sear the beef, making sure to move it around in the pan, browning it on all sides. Remove the filets from the pan and let rest for 10 minutes.

In a small bowl, combine mustard, Worcestershire sauce, rosemary and crushed peppercorns. Brush the mustard mixture over the beef and bake on a roasting rack in a 375°F oven, allowing 8 minutes for rare or 10 minutes for medium. Let the meat rest 5 minutes before serving on a pool of hot Peppercorn Sauce.

Serves 4.

PEPPERCORN SAUCE

Melt half of the butter over medium heat and sauté shallots, garlic and green peppercorns for 3 to 5 minutes. Increase heat, add brandy and ignite to flambé and burn off alcohol. Stir in the thyme and white wine and reduce by half. Add beef stock and bring to a boil, reduce by half. Stir in the cream and return to a boil. Reduce slowly until sauce thickens enough to coat the back of a wooden spoon. At serving time, return to a boil and whisk in remaining butter.

ZIPPY BEEF BURGERS

. . . .

The lineup will be long when the crowd hears you are barbecuing these burgers.

2 pounds lean ground beef
$\frac{1}{2}$ cup crumbled cooked bacon
$\frac{2}{3}$ cup dry breadcrumbs
$\frac{1}{2}$ cup finely diced onion
$\frac{1}{4}$ cup barbecue sauce
$\frac{1}{2}$ teaspoon salt
$\frac{1}{2}$ teaspoon pepper
8 to 10 large burger buns, toasted
Toppings: lettuce, tomato slices, red or green pepper
  slices, Swiss, Cheddar or Monterey Jack cheese slices,
  pickles or relish, ketchup, prepared or Dijon mustard

In a large bowl, combine beef, bacon, breadcrumbs, onion, barbecue sauce, salt and pepper. Shape into 8 to 10 patties $\frac{3}{4}$ inch thick. Cover and refrigerate until ready to cook.

Cook burgers on greased grill over medium-high heat, turning until no longer pink inside, for about 8 to 10 minutes. The internal temperature of the burgers must reach 160°F. Serve immediately on buns with toppings of choice.

Makes 8 to 10 burgers.

TOURTIÈRE PIE

. . . .

Every Christmas Eve thousands of Acadian families enjoy meat pie. Served with crunchy coleslaw, cranberry sauce or a traditional Québécois fruit relish, it is pure heaven.

1 small onion, minced
1 teaspoon cinnamon
1 teaspoon dried summer savory
1 teaspoon salt
1 teaspoon pepper
$\frac{1}{2}$ teaspoon cloves
$\frac{1}{2}$ teaspoon allspice
2 tablespoons rendered pork or bacon fat
1 pound ground beef
1 pound ground pork
$\frac{1}{2}$ cup beef stock
1 medium waxy potato, peeled and grated
Pastry for a deep 10-inch Double-Crust Pie (page 205)
1 large egg yolk, beaten
1 teaspoon rock salt

In a medium, steep-sided pot, sauté onion, spices and seasoning in pork fat until translucent. Add beef and pork, stock and grated potato. Stir well to combine. Cook for 15 minutes over medium heat, stirring often, until meat is no longer pink. Let cool. Roll out pie dough into 2 12-inch rounds. Fit one round into a deep 10-inch pie plate. Add cooled filling to pie shell, mounding it in the centre of the pie. Cover with a second piece of pie dough and trim the edges with a knife. Press edges and flute. Using a pastry tip or apple corer, make a $\frac{1}{2}$-inch vent hole in the centre of top crust. Brush with beaten egg yolk and sprinkle with salt. Bake in a 350°F oven for 45 minutes or until crust is deep brown in colour.

Serves 6.

MARINATED FLANK STEAK WITH FRIED POTATO GNOCCHI, FIDDLEHEADS, BALSAMIC AND PECORINO ROMANO

• • • • • • • • • • • •

This dish is incredibly simple to prepare, once you have the gnocchi made. Gnocchi are intimidating to many amateur cooks, but the little Italian dumplings are actually pretty foolproof if you have a solid recipe and a sense of adventure. Making them in advance and keeping them in the freezer is a great way to enjoy them anytime, either prepared as below or in a simple tomato sauce. Flank steak is cheap and requires only that you enjoy steak medium rare or rare; overcooking flank steak is a waste of money and time as it becomes tough and rubbery. Good balsamic vinegar is a sauce in itself; it's worth keeping a bottle in the pantry at all times.

FLANK STEAK

2 pounds flank steak
¼ cup balsamic vinegar
¼ cup red wine
2 tablespoons soy sauce
2 tablespoons brown sugar
1 teaspoon dried mustard or Dijon mustard
½ teaspoon dried oregano
½ teaspoon cracked black pepper
1 clove garlic, minced
1 shallot, minced

GNOCCHI

2 pounds russet potatoes
1 large egg
1 large egg yolk
½ teaspoon salt
1⅓ cups all-purpose flour
¼ cup butter
Salt and pepper to taste
½ cup shaved Pecorino Romano cheese
3 tablespoons excellent quality balsamic vinegar
2 tablespoons chopped chives

FIDDLEHEADS

1 pound fresh fiddleheads
1 teaspoon salt
1 tablespoon butter
Salt and pepper

FLANK STEAK

Cut the flank steak into easy-to-handle pieces, approximately 4 to 5 inches wide. Mix all the remaining ingredients together and pour this marinade into a large freezer bag. Add the steak. Press the air out of the bag and close the seal. Refrigerate for 4 to 6 hours.

Remove the meat from the marinade and pat dry with paper towels. Grill over high heat for about 3 minutes per side until it reaches an internal temperature of 125 to 135°F. Rest the steak for at least 15 minutes.

Meanwhile, pour the marinade into a pot. Bring to a boil and reduce until close to a syrup consistency. Remove from the heat and toss the flank steak in the syrupy marinade just before carving. Slice against the grain of the meat into ¼-inch strips.

Tip: Want to try the Marinated Flank Steak but don't have time to make the gnocchi? Enjoy the steak — and fiddleheads if you like — with some small new potatoes, boiled, drained and fried in butter like the gnocchi.

GNOCCHI

Bake potatoes in a 350°F oven until tender, about 1 hour. Scoop out the hot flesh, discarding the skins. Rice the potatoes in a potato ricer or food mill, or mash with a fork. While the potatoes are still hot, quickly mix in the egg and egg yolk along with the salt. Add the flour to the potatoes and stir with a wooden spoon until the flour is almost incorporated, then dump the contents onto a clean work surface and knead the dough just until it forms a smooth ball. Do not overknead.

Divide the dough into quarters and roll each into a long rope about ½ inch in diameter. Using a knife, cut into ¾-inch pieces. Cutting the rope will produce little pillow-shaped dumplings. (At this point you can place the gnocchi on a tray and freeze for later use.) Bring a pot of salted water to a boil. Drop the gnocchi, a quarter at a time, into the boiling water and cook until they float. In a nonstick frying pan, heat the butter until melted. Take the blanched gnocchi from the water using a slotted spoon and drain as well as possible before adding them to the buttered pan. Fry them until the gnocchi and the butter are slightly browned, about 3 to 5 minutes. Season with salt and pepper.

FIDDLEHEADS

Clean the fiddleheads of any brown ends and give them a good rinse under running water. Bring about 4 quarts of water to a boil and add the salt. When the water is at a full boil, blanch the fiddleheads for 3 minutes. Remove them with a slotted spoon and toss in butter. Season with salt and pepper to taste.

PRESENTATION

Place the gnocchi (about 10 per person) on a warm plate and lay several fiddleheads (about 6 or 8 per person) in and around them on the plate. Drizzle with aged balsamic vinegar and the browned butter that remains in the gnocchi pan. Place several slices of flank steak over top and garnish with Pecorino Romano cheese and chives.

Serves 4 to 6.

GLAZED BEEF SHORT RIBS WITH ROAST CORN POLENTA

· · · · · · · · · · ·

Succulent beef short ribs have been appearing more and more on restaurant menus across the continent for a couple of reasons: first, consumers appreciate full-flavoured food, and second, the price of premium cuts of beef continues to skyrocket. Like any braised dish, a little planning is required here, but really the dish is very simple to prepare.

BEEF SHORT RIBS

4 pounds bone-in beef short ribs (cut in 2-inch lengths)

½ cup all-purpose flour

1 teaspoon salt

1 teaspoon pepper

1 teaspoon onion powder (optional)

3 tablespoons vegetable oil

1 large onion, coarsely chopped

1 carrot, coarsely chopped

1 stalk celery, coarsely chopped

10 whole cloves garlic, peeled

1 bottle (750 mL) dry red wine

3 bay leaves

6 sprigs fresh thyme

1 star anise pod

1 sachet powdered demi-glace mixed with 1 cup cold water or 1 cup beef stock

1 tablespoon Worcestershire sauce

POLENTA

3 cobs corn, husked and desilked

1 shallot, minced

1 clove garlic, minced

¼ cup butter

2½ cups chicken stock, vegetable stock or water

½ teaspoon sea salt

½ cup cornmeal

½ cup grated Parmesan cheese

4 fresh sage leaves, shredded

Pepper to taste

Minced chives or parsley

BEEF SHORT RIBS

Pat ribs dry with paper towel. Mix the flour, salt, pepper and onion powder, if using, and dredge the ribs in it, shaking off the excess. Heat the oil in a large heavy-bottomed stainless steel braising pan with a tight-fitting lid or Dutch oven and sear the ribs on all sides until brown. Remove from the pan and add the onion, carrot, celery and garlic cloves to the oil remaining in the pan. Sauté for 5 minutes. Deglaze with red wine and add the bay leaves, thyme, star anise, demi-glace and Worcestershire sauce. Return the ribs to the pan, submerging them in the braising liquid as much as possible.

Meanwhile, increase the heat under the braising pan and bring the liquid to a boil. Cover the pot and place it on the middle rack of a 300°F oven. Braise for 2 hours or until the meat is tender and beginning to fall from the bone.

Let the ribs cool in the braising liquid. (The broth will permeate the meat as it cools, resulting in moister ribs.)

Transfer the ribs from the braising liquid into a casserole dish; cover and keep warm. Strain the braising liquid into a clean pan and boil until it measures about 1½ cups, or has thickened enough to coat the back of a spoon. Skim off any foam or impurities. Pour over the ribs.

POLENTA

Grill the husked cobs of corn over high heat until slightly caramelized all over, about 8 minutes. Cut the kernels off the cobs and set aside. (Note: For additional flavour, simmer the dekerneled cobs in the stock or water that will be used in the polenta for 30 minutes to an hour. This is not necessary, but it makes a big difference.)

In a heavy-bottomed pot, sauté the shallot and garlic in 1 tablespoon of the butter for a few minutes. Add the stock and salt and bring to a simmer. Pour the cornmeal into the simmering stock in a slow and steady stream, whisking continuously. When the mixture boils, reduce the heat to very low and add the grilled kernels. Cover and cook for 30 minutes. (You may need to add a bit more water if the polenta becomes too thick.)

Stir in the Parmesan cheese, sage and the remaining butter then finish with some freshly ground pepper.

PRESENTATION

Place a large spoonful of polenta in the centre of a warm plate or in a pasta bowl. Spread the polenta out slightly until it is about ½ inch thick. Place 2 or 3 ribs on top of the polenta and glaze with a little of the sauce. Garnish with chives.

Serves 4 to 6.

JIGGS' DINNER WITH PEASE PUDDING

· · · · · · · · · · · · · ·

Says chef Craig Flinn: "Jiggs' Dinner, also known as boiled dinner, is thought of as a dish from Newfoundland and Labrador, but I grew up eating it in Cape Breton and mainland Nova Scotia as well. On my last visit to England I was introduced to a kind of pease pudding made in cheesecloth that was a great accompaniment to beef stew. For me it's a logical combination due to the strong English influence in Newfoundland food culture. There is nothing fancy about this meal, just good food and plenty of it. Enjoy."

JIGGS' DINNER

3 pounds salted beef brisket (corned beef)

2 onions, peeled and quartered

1 teaspoon dried summer savory

2 bay leaves

½ teaspoon cracked black pepper

2 cups chicken stock (approximate)

Cold water to cover

1 small head of green cabbage, quartered

1 small turnip, peeled and cut into 2-inch dice

4 carrots, peeled and cut in 1-inch lengths

4 potatoes, peeled and halved

PEASE PUDDING

1½ cups yellow split peas

2 tablespoons minced onion or shallot

¼ teaspoon dried thyme

1 clove garlic, thinly sliced

Salt and pepper to taste

Butter

JIGGS' DINNER

Cover the salt beef with lots of cold water and soak for 12 hours or overnight, changing the water once halfway through.

PEASE PUDDING

Combine all the ingredients in a bowl and season with a little salt and pepper. Tie the mixture up into a ball, using at least 3 or 4 layers of cheesecloth tied at the top with string. Leave room in the bag for the peas to expand.

Place the beef, onions, savory, bay leaves and pepper in a large pot and cover with chicken stock and cold water. Place the pease pudding in the pot next to the beef, ensuring it too is covered completely by the liquid. Bring to a boil, reduce the heat and simmer, covered, for 90 minutes.

Add all the vegetables to the pot. Top off with more stock or water if needed and simmer, covered, until the vegetables are soft and tender and the beef is beginning to fall apart. (You may wish to add the cabbage and turnips a little sooner than the carrots and potatoes.)

Remove the vegetables and place them on the serving platter or bowl. Break the tender beef into chunks and lay them on the vegetables. Ladle on as much broth as required to warm the dish and give your guests something to dip their bread into. Remove the pease pudding from the cheesecloth bag and serve it with a pat of butter alongside the Jiggs' Dinner. Serve with mustard or Mustard Bean Pickles (page 291).

Serves 8.

PÂTÉ (ACADIAN MEAT PIE)

. . . .

ANNE MARIE CURRIE, SYDNEY, N.S.

Anne Marie Currie's parents came from the Cheticamp area of Nova Scotia where pâté was usually served as a celebration repast. In the early days, there was strict adherence to the meatless days prescribed by the Roman Catholic Church, so the serving of pâté was most welcome, especially after the seasons of fasting — Lent and Advent. Meat pie was always on the table for Christmas Eve, often with rabbit as the main ingredient. The filling makes 12 to 14 pies. The pastry recipe makes enough for 6 pies — make the pastry twice if you're making 12 pies or cut filling in half for 6 pies.

PASTRY

- 8 cups all-purpose flour
- 5 tablespoons baking powder
- 2 teaspoons salt
- 1 pound lard
- 2 cups milk (approximate)

MEAT MIXTURE

- 3 pounds beef, a good cut
- 3 pounds pork, include fat
- 3 pounds chicken (or deer, rabbit, partridge or pheasant)
- 2 onions, grated
- 1½ teaspoons pepper
- 1 to 2 teaspoons salt
- ¼ teaspoon dried sage
- ½ cup water

PASTRY

In a large bowl, combine all the dry ingredients. Cut in the lard with a pastry blender until of a fine mealy consistency. Then add milk and toss to combine. Add small amounts of milk if the dough is too dry for rolling. It should make 6 9-inch pies. If you are making more pies, repeat the pastry recipe as it's not advisable to double the ingredients.

MEAT MIXTURE

Cut the beef and pork into chunks and remove the chicken skin. Combine the meat, 1 of the onions, pepper, salt, sage and water in a large pot or Dutch oven. Stew covered very slowly over low heat for 3 to 4 hours until the meat falls from the bones. Remove from the heat and refrigerate in a bowl overnight. Very carefully remove all the bones and gristle (best done by hand). Do not discard any juice from the meat. Grate the remaining onion into the meat and mix. This mixture is enough for approximately 12 to 14 9-inch pies.

Roll out the pastry (not too thickly) for the top and bottom crusts for the 6 9-inch pie plates. Fill with 1 to 1½ inches of the meat mixture. Cover with a top pastry. Trim and flute edges to seal. Cut 3 steam holes in the centre of each pie. Bake at 350°F until golden brown, about 30 minutes. Serve hot. This dish is nice with cranberries.

Makes 12 to 14 pies.

WHOLE ROAST LOIN OF PORK WITH CARAMELIZED APPLES, SPAGHETTI SQUASH AND BRUSSELS SPROUT PETALS

. . . .

Applesauce and pork is a classic. This recipe adds some texture to the apple element by keeping them in slices. The spaghetti squash is simple to prepare and adds an interesting textural element as well. Finally, making the Brussels sprouts into petals lightens them up a bit. This way they are still slightly crisp and more like a salad side dish.

PORK ROAST

3-pound boneless pork loin (single loin, tied with string)

3 cloves garlic, quartered

2 sprigs fresh rosemary

1 tablespoon extra-virgin olive oil

1 teaspoon coarse sea salt

Pepper

2 tablespoons butter

4 Honeycrisp or Granny Smith apples, peeled, cored and cut into eighths

3 tablespoons apple cider

3 tablespoons granulated sugar

1 teaspoon cider vinegar or lemon juice

1 teaspoon chopped fresh tarragon (optional)

SPAGHETTI SQUASH

1 large spaghetti squash

1 tablespoon extra-virgin olive oil

2 tablespoons butter

Salt and pepper to taste

BRUSSELS SPROUT PETALS

2 cups Brussels sprouts

2 tablespoons butter

Salt and pepper to taste

PORK ROAST

Using a sharp paring knife, make many shallow slices in the fat cap, creating a crosshatched pattern. Then, pierce the fat and meat, making 12 very small pockets throughout the meat. These should go to the centre of the loin, not all the way through. Press a quarter sliver of garlic and a few rosemary needles into each of the pockets you made.

Heat a large skillet and add the oil. Place the loin, fat side down, in the oil and immediately reduce the heat to medium. Sear the loin on the fat side only and allow the fat to render. When the fat cap is deeply golden brown (about 7 or 8 minutes), remove the roast and place it on a roasting rack. Set the skillet and the rendered fat aside. Season the roast with salt and pepper. Roast in a 300°F oven for about 15 to 18 minutes per pound or until the internal temperature reaches 160°F. Rest the loin for at least 20 minutes before slicing.

Meanwhile, using the skillet in which you seared the loin, pour out all but a teaspoon of the pork fat. Add the butter and melt over high heat. Immediately add the apple wedges and lower the heat to medium. Fry the apples for 3 minutes, turn and fry for 2 minutes. Add the apple cider and sugar and bring to a boil. Cook for about 10 minutes to evaporate the cider and allow the sugar to caramelize. When the sauce in the pan is reduced, golden brown and sticky looking, add the vinegar and tarragon. Stir through and cook until the apple wedges are well glazed with the sweet sauce. Remove from the heat and allow to cool to room temperature. Serve the apples cool or warm with the pork roast.

SPAGHETTI SQUASH

Cut the squash in half from the stem end to the bottom. Scoop out the seeds and pulpy interior. Rub the oil over the cut sides and place the 2 halves cut side down on a greased nonstick baking tray. Roast the squash in a 350°F oven for 30 to 45 minutes until the skin blisters and the slices look slightly brown where they touch the baking tray.

Remove from the oven and hold one half of the squash in your hand using a clean, dry kitchen towel. Using a fork, scrape out the flesh into a bowl (using a fork helps keep the long strands of squash intact) and separate the strands as best you can with the fork. Repeat with the second half. Add the butter and season with salt and pepper.

BRUSSELS SPROUT PETALS

Bring a pot of heavily salted water to a boil. Cut off the root end of each Brussels sprout about ⅛" up from the bottom. Gently peel each layer of sprout away from the core. Blanch leaves in boiling water for 60 to 90 seconds and then remove. Heat butter in a large saute pan. Toss Brussels sprout petals in butter and salt and pepper.

PRESENTATION

Arrange apple slices with some of their sauce on warmed plates. Top with sliced pork loin and some of the Spaghetti Squash and Brussels Sprout Petals.

Serves 6.

MY MOTHER'S BAKED BEANS

. . . .

MARY I. ROBINSON, MISSISSAUGA, ONT.

Every Saturday night when two sisters were growing up on Prince Edward Island, their mother served baked beans, sausage and her homemade brown bread for supper. There was a woodstove in the kitchen and everything was cooked in it and there was always "extra beans in the pot" for frequent Saturday evening visitors. One of those sisters still makes baked beans, but instead of the cook stove, she uses a crockpot and the beans cook at a low simmer for 10 hours.

1 pound New Brunswick soldier beans or navy beans
Bouquet garni of 1 bay leaf, 2 sprigs celery leaves, 5
  sprigs fresh parsley
½ pound salt pork
½ cup fancy molasses
¼ cup packed brown sugar
2 teaspoons dry mustard
¼ teaspoon pepper
1 medium onion, chopped

Cover the beans with cold water and soak overnight. In the morning, drain and add enough fresh water to cover generously and the bouquet garni, wrapped in cheesecloth. Cook over low heat until the skins break if you blow on them, about 2 hours.

Drain the beans, reserving the liquid. Cut the salt pork into ¼-inch slices. Arrange the beans and half of the sliced pork in alternate layers in a crockpot, then the rest of the beans and pork. Mix the molasses, brown sugar, mustard, pepper and onion with 1 cup of the reserved bean liquid. Pour the mixture over the beans. Cover the crockpot and cook on low for 10 hours. Halfway through, uncover and stir, adding some of the reserved liquid if desired.

Serves 8.

ROLLED MOOSE STEAK

. . . .

MARION EVELIEGH, SEAL COVE, WHITE BAY, NFLD.

1 large moose steak
1 can mushrooms, drained or 8 ounces fresh
  mushrooms, sliced
½ cup chopped onions
2 tablespoons butter
1 cup dry breadcrumbs
1 teaspoon Worcestershire sauce
1 tablespoon vegetable oil
1 cup red wine
Salt and pepper to taste

Trim steak to 12-inch square. In a Dutch oven, sauté mushrooms and onions in butter. Mix with breadcrumbs and Worcestershire sauce. Sprinkle steak with salt and pepper and spread with mushrooms and onion mixture. Roll up loosely. Tie in 3 places with string. Heat the oil in a Dutch oven; sear the rolled steak on all sides. Pour in red wine. Bake at 325°F for 2 hours.

Serves 8.

PULLED PORK SANDWICH WITH MOLASSES BARBECUE SAUCE

JOY BISTRO, TORONTO, ONT.

This delicious, hearty sandwich is typical of the flavourful and extravagant tastes created by Chef Bryan Burke. The spices rubbed into the pork and the 36-hour marinating time enhance the tenderness and jolt your taste buds. Top it off with fresh barbeque sauce. Joy Bistro gave the recipe for this culinary treat to Craig Flinn for use in one of his cookbooks. It's good for any time of the day or night, and a delicious addition to Maritime cooking from Toronto!

PULLED PORK

2½ tablespoons kosher salt

2 teaspoons smoked sweet paprika

2 teaspoons garlic powder

2 teaspoons chili powder

2 teaspoons dry mustard

1 teaspoon cinnamon

1 teaspoon ginger

1 teaspoon pepper

½ teaspoon allspice

5 pounds boneless pork shoulder

1½ cups fancy molasses

¼ cup cooking oil

2 large white onions, chopped

2 cans dark beer

BARBECUE SAUCE

2 white onions, peeled

2 28-ounce cans tomatoes

3 cloves garlic

1 tablespoon grated fresh ginger

2 sprigs fresh thyme

1 tablespoon Dijon mustard

1 Granny Smith apple, cored, peeled and sliced

1 can dark beer

1 cup fancy molasses

¼ cup apple cider vinegar

1 bay leaf

Salt and pepper to taste

PULLED PORK

In a large bowl, mix the salt and all the dry spices together. Add the pork shoulder and vigorously rub the spice mixture over pork shoulder. Pour molasses over pork and turn to coat all over. Cover and marinate in the refrigerator for 36 hours. In a Dutch oven over medium-high heat, heat the oil until hot. Brown the pork shoulder on all sides. Add onions and beer. Cover and place in an oven at 275°F for about 4 hours, or until the meat is falling apart.

BARBECUE SAUCE

Meanwhile, slice onions in half and char on barbecue or grill pan over high heat until black. Combine with remaining ingredients except salt and pepper in a pot and simmer over low heat for 45 minutes, stirring regularly. Season to taste with salt and pepper and press through a sieve or food mill.

To serve, shred the cooked pork with 2 forks. Mix pork with enough barbecue sauce to make it sloppy and moist. Warm the pork mixture and serve in a crusty bun.

Serves 8 to 10.

PORK SCHNITZEL WITH FRIED FREE-RANGE EGG, SWISS CHARD AND BROWN BUTTER

· · · · · · · · · · · ·

Pork loin soaked in buttermilk replicates the traditional veal in both flavour and tenderness at about a third the cost. This dish is a lunch favourite in Austria and Switzerland and it can be garnished in many ways. Serve this with a salad or fried potatoes.

SCHNITZEL

1½ pounds boneless pork loin

½ cup buttermilk

½ cup all-purpose flour

2 large eggs, beaten and seasoned well with salt and pepper

1 cup panko or other dried breadcrumbs

¼ cup vegetable oil

2 tablespoons butter

½ teaspoon coarse sea salt such as fleur de sel

EGGS AND SWISS CHARD

4 large eggs

3 tablespoons butter (approximate)

Salt and pepper to taste

8 ounces cleaned Swiss chard leaves

1 tablespoon water

Juice of half a lemon

2 tablespoons sliced chives

SCHNITZEL

Clean the pork loin of any silverskin and fat. Cut it into 4 equal portions of about 6 ounces each. Slice each piece through the side about three-quarters of the way through. Butterfly the piece by opening it up in the cut and laying it flat, doubling its area. Place each between 2 pieces of plastic wrap and use a meat pounder to gently pound the meat until it doubles in size. You are looking for about a ¼ inch overall thickness.

Place the schnitzel pieces in a bowl or large freezer bag and pour in the buttermilk. Refrigerate for 1 hour. Remove and pat dry with a towel. Discard the buttermilk.

Bread the pieces using a standard breading procedure: dredge in flour, then dip in the seasoned egg mixture and finish in the breadcrumbs. Heat the largest frying pan you have over medium heat. You will likely have to fry the schnitzel in 2 batches, so heat your oven to 160°F or on the "warm" setting to hold over the pieces as you cook. Fry each piece in oil and butter until golden brown, about 3 minutes per side. Watch the temperature closely as they can brown quickly if too hot. Season each one with a little fleur de sel. The schnitzel will hold well for about 10 minutes while you prepare the eggs and Swiss chard.

EGGS AND SWISS CHARD

Place a large nonstick or well-seasoned cast-iron skillet over medium heat. Melt the butter in the pan and gently crack the eggs into the pan. Reduce the heat of the pan to low and cook the eggs until the whites are set but the yolks remain mostly runny (you will see the very bottom of the yolks start to turn opaque). Season with a little salt and pepper. Separate the eggs from each other with a knife or spatula and slide them onto a warm plate. Place them in the warming oven with the schnitzel while you cook the Swiss chard.

Set the skillet over medium heat again. There should be enough butter in the pan, but you can add another tablespoon of butter if needed. Gently heat the butter until it foams and begins to turn a nutty brown colour. Immediately add the chard and over medium-high heat sauté for a minute, then add a spoonful of water; steam the chard limp, about 2 minutes. Season with salt and pepper, squeeze the half lemon into the chard.

PRESENTATION

Place a schnitzel on each plate, make a pile of wilted Swiss chard on top and set a fried egg on each one. Garnish with some sliced chives and any of the brown butter remaining in the sauté pan.

Serves 4.

FRIED SWEET POTATOES WITH MAPLE SYRUP AND GRILLED SAUSAGES

. . . .

Craig Flinn tells the story of the origin of this recipe, "Many years ago, before I cooked for a living, I went to a friend's place for dinner. Neither my friend nor her boyfriend were very good cooks, so meals were simple and I usually pitched in a bit to help out. This time they made me wait as they were making their favourite late-night supper: sausages and potatoes with maple syrup. It was so delicious I have rarely eaten a sausage without maple syrup since then. In this recipe I bring back that evening with my own twist. Here I use sweet potatoes that have been breaded and fried in butter. It's luxurious, but cheap and pretty simple. Serve this with some green vegetables like steamed broccoli, chard or spinach."

3 large sweet potatoes

¼ cup all-purpose flour

2 large eggs, beaten and seasoned with salt and pepper

1 cup fresh or panko breadcrumbs

¼ cup butter or vegetable oil (approximate)

8 fresh, mild sausages (such as Oktoberfest, Cheddar Smokies or Knackwurst)

⅔ cup pure maple syrup (approximate)

Bake the sweet potatoes on the middle rack in a 350°F oven for 1 hour or until fork-tender. Let rest until completely cool. Peel and discard the skin and cut the potatoes lengthwise into ½-inch thick ovals. Dredge each slice in flour, then dip in the egg mixture and finally in the breadcrumbs.

Melt the butter in a large nonstick pan and fry the slices of sweet potato on both sides until golden brown. You may need a little more butter depending on the size of the potatoes. Since the potatoes are cooked you really only need to reheat and crisp them up a bit. This should take about 4 minutes per side over medium heat.

Grill the sausages on the barbecue or on a stovetop grill or griddle pan. Always use a moderate heat for sausages to prevent them charring too fast on the outside or bursting their casings. Cooking time will depend on the size of the sausages, but allow 15 minutes over medium heat, then reduce the heat to low for an additional 15 minutes to cook them through without drying them out. Let rest for 5 minutes before slicing so they retain all their juice.

PRESENTATION

Serve sausages with the crispy sweet potatoes. Drizzle 2 or 3 tablespoons of maple syrup over the sausages and the sweet potatoes. Place a container of maple syrup on the table as well so people can help themselves to a little more.

Serves 4.

NOVA SCOTIA MAPLE SYRUP BAKED BEANS

LISCOMBE LODGE, LISCOMB MILLS, N.S.

At Liscombe Lodge the chef served his maple-infused baked beans with his breakfast menu.

1 pound dry navy beans, rinsed and cleaned
6 cups water
6 slices bacon, cut in 2-inch pieces
1 small onion, chopped
1½ teaspoons salt
½ teaspoon dry mustard
½ cup pure dark maple syrup
2 tablespoons brown sugar
2 tablespoons butter

Bring the beans and water to a boil in a large saucepan and boil for 2 minutes. Remove from heat and let stand, covered, for an hour. Return to a boil, reduce heat and simmer, covered, adding more water as needed, for 40 minutes. Drain, reserving cooking liquid.

Place half of the bacon in a bean crocks and add beans. In a separate bowl combine the reserved cooking liquid, onion, salt, dry mustard and maple syrup. Pour over the beans and top with remaining bacon. Bake, covered, at 325°F for approximately 3 hours. From time to time check beans and add a small amount of water if they appear dry.

Blend together the brown sugar and butter. Sprinkle over the beans and bake, uncovered, an additional hour.

Serves 6 to 8.

COUNTRY HAM LOAF

LINDY GUILD, MAHONE BAY, N.S.

Lindy Guild was served this recipe by her mother-in-law when she had just arrived in Canada as a new bride. She says, "She served it cold at a picnic for the family and it reminded me of the veal and hampies I had eaten for years in England. I have added garlic, which grows so well in Nova Scotia, and my brand of mustard. But it is delicious without the garlic and served hot with sweet potatoes."

1½ pounds lean cooked ham
1½ pounds lean ground pork
2 large eggs
1 cup dry breadcrumbs
1 cup milk
1 clove garlic, crushed
¼ cup chopped parsley
Salt and pepper to taste
3 large eggs, hardcooked and shelled
¼ cup packed light brown sugar
2 teaspoons prepared mustard
1 teaspoon ginger

Grind the ham and pork alternately to get a good mix. In a large bowl, combine them with the eggs, breadcrumbs, milk, garlic, parsley, salt and pepper. Mix thoroughly — best done with your hands — and put half into a greased loaf pan. Place the hardcooked eggs lengthwise down the centre and cover with other half of meat mixture, pressing down lightly around eggs, leaving no space unfilled. Mix sugar, mustard and ginger together and spread on top of loaf. Bake for 1½ hours at 325°F and baste a couple of times. Cool on a rack and refrigerate.

Makes about 8 to 10 slices.

HAM AND POTATOES AU GRATIN

. . . .

ANNE MARIE CURRIE, SYDNEY, N.S.

What to do with leftovers must have taxed the ingenuity of our grandparents and great-grandparents, too. Not all of the remaining tender bits of a baked ham need be committed to the soup pot. Mayonnaise is a new addition to an old recipe.

¼ cup chopped onion
¼ cup chopped sweet green pepper (optional)
2 tablespoons butter
1 tablespoon all-purpose flour
Salt and pepper to taste
1 cup milk
1 cup shredded Cheddar cheese
¼ cup mayonnaise
3 cups mashed potatoes
2 cups diced cooked ham

Sauté onion and green pepper, if using, in butter until tender. Stir in flour, salt and pepper. Add milk all at once and bring to a boil, stirring or whisking constantly. Reduce heat and add cheese, mayonnaise, potatoes and cooked ham, stirring well after each addition. Spread in a large casserole and bake at 350°F for 30 minutes or until golden on top.

Serves 4.

SPRING LAMB CHOPS

. . . .

GLENORA INN AND DISTILLERY, GLENVILLE, N.S.

Take care not to overcook the lamb — the chops are small and will grill in a few minutes.

½ cup extra-virgin olive oil
1 tablespoon chokecherry or raspberry vinegar
Fresh rosemary to taste
8 loin lamb chops

Combine oil, vinegar and rosemary in a shallow dish. Place chops in marinade and turn to coat. Marinate in the refrigerator for 1 hour. Grill on a greased grill over medium-high heat or under the broiler, turning once, until meat is browned on the outside and pink on the inside, about 8 minutes.

Serves 4.

MARY RUSH'S PORK AND SAUERKRAUT

. . . .

NANCY E. REDDIN, MOUNT ALBION, P.E.I.

The Rush family came to Maine 154 years ago from Alsace-Lorraine where the name was spelled "Raesch." A descendant married into the Haines family of Moncton, N.B., whose granddaughter is Nancy Reddin of Mount Albion, P.E.I. The men of the Rush family make their own sauerkraut, but Nancy had never liked sauerkraut until she tried her mother-in-laws's dish, similar to choucroute garnie, one made in Alsace-Lorraine. The ingredients are not in precise measures; they are meant just as a guide.

Pork roast
28 to 32 ounces prepared sauerkraut, or
  4 cups of homemade sauerkraut
Water
Apple juice
Potatoes

Put a pork roast, any cut but preferably boneless, in a heavy pot that can hold it with a bit of room left over. Cover the pork with sauerkraut, including the juice, and add enough water just to cover the meat. You can use a cup or so of apple juice for part of the liquid. Cover, bring to a boil and simmer for at least 2 hours. The total amount of time depends on the size of the roast. When done, the meat will be tender and fall apart easily.

About 30 minutes before the meat is finished, add peeled whole potatoes, as many as you wish. Serve with carrots or turnip and lots of applesauce. The dish reheats well, but remove the potatoes before putting it in the fridge, otherwise the potatoes will be too salty.

Serves 6 to 8.

BARBECUED LAMB CHOPS

. . . .

JULIE V. WATSON, CHARLOTTETOWN, P.E.I.

The breeding of lamb and the raising of sheep in Prince Edward Island goes back to the late 18th century and the arrival of the Scottish settlers. Like families in those days, the Allmans of Ridgeview Farm in St. Ann's work as a team to care for and utilize the whole product — the meat and the wool. They have a flock of 70 sheep on their 86-acre farm and run a shop where they sell their woollen items. By cross-breeding, they are able to market their lamb in both spring and fall.

Jill Allman developed recipes for lamb when she was involved with the Prince Edward Island Lamb Co-op. She says, "The natural portion sizes of lamb fit what has become a trend towards eating smaller amounts of red meat. People like quality rather than quantity."

Zest from 1 lemon
2 tablespoons lemon juice
1 clove garlic, crushed
2 tablespoons vegetable oil
½ teaspoon dried rosemary
⅛ teaspoon pepper
3 pounds loin chops

Combine the zest and juice with the garlic, oil, rosemary and pepper and in a shallow dish. Add the chops and marinate for at least 15 minutes a side. Prepare the barbecue so that the coals are ready or heat barbecue to medium-high. Either spray or brush the rack with vegetable oil. Place the chops on the greased grill. Baste with any remaining marinade. Grill for 5 to 7 minutes, turn and complete cooking. The total time depends on the thickness of the meat.

Serves 6.

MAPLE-GLAZED HAM

. . . .

LOON BAY LODGE, ST. STEPHEN, N.B.

Loon Bay Lodge is located in a pristine setting beside the international St. Croix River. They served this delicious baked ham accompanied by scalloped potatoes and fresh garden vegetables.

1 ham, 4 to 6 pounds
½ cup water
¼ cup pure maple syrup
¼ cup table syrup
1 teaspoon soy sauce
1½ teaspoons cornstarch
1 to 2 tablespoons cold water
Granulated maple sugar to garnish

Place ham on a rack in a large roasting pan and add water. Cover with foil and bake in a 350°F oven, allowing 25 minutes per pound of meat.

A half hour before the end of baking time, combine maple syrup, table syrup and soy sauce in a small saucepan and bring to a boil. Combine cornstarch and cold water in a small bowl. Add enough cornstarch mixture to boiling sauce to thicken slightly.

Remove ham from oven and trim away any fatty layer on outside of roast. Score meat in a diamond pattern.

Reduce oven temperature to 325°F. Pour maple glaze over ham and bake, uncovered for 20 minutes. Insert a meat thermometer into the thickest part of the ham, being careful not to touch any bone. The ham is cooked when its internal temperature reaches 140°F, continue roasting if more time is needed. Remove from oven and allow to stand, tented with foil, for 15 minutes before carving.

Serves 6 to 8.

ALGONQUIN MAPLE AND MUSTARD BARBECUED LAMB CHOPS

. . . .

THE ALGONQUIN HOTEL, ST. ANDREWS BY-THE-SEA, N.B.

Executive Chef Willie White prepared his marinade a day in advance to allow the flavours to blend. He experiments by adding more garlic and ginger for a stronger flavour or chopped chili peppers for spice! While used for grilled lamb chops, the marinade is multi-purpose and will also complement chicken, pork or beef.

½ cup pure maple syrup
1 tablespoon grainy Dijon mustard
Grated zest and juice of 1 lemon
4 teaspoons balsamic vinegar
4 to 6 twists ground pepper
1 clove garlic, finely chopped
1 teaspoon finely grated fresh ginger
¼ cup canola oil
12 rib lamb chops (2 to 3 ounces each)

Blend together all ingredients except the lamb chops. Refrigerate, covered, for 24 hours.

Marinate the meat, refrigerated, for 45 minutes then barbecue over low to medium heat until meat is browned on the outside and pink on the inside.

Serves 4.

MEDITERRANEAN BRAISED LAMB SHANKS

RHUBARB GRILL & CAFÉ, INDIAN POINT, N.S.

Creamy garlic mashed potatoes and vegetable of choice are suggested to accompany the robust shanks.

4 lamb shanks
Sea salt and pepper
¼ cup all-purpose flour
3 tablespoons extra-virgin olive oil (approximate)
1 red onion, chopped
1 stalk celery, chopped
1 leek, white part, chopped
1 large carrot, peeled and chopped
4 cloves garlic, minced
1 cup dry red wine
1½ cups diced plum tomatoes
1 teaspoon dried thyme
1 teaspoon dried oregano 1 bay leaf
Sea salt and pepper
8 sprigs fresh thyme

Trim excess fat from lamb shanks and pat them dry. Season with salt and pepper and toss in flour to lightly coat. Heat 2 tablespoons of the oil in a large, heavy, ovenproof pot over high heat. Add lamb shanks, in batches if necessary, and brown on all sides. Remove shanks and reserve.

Lower heat to medium, add remaining oil if necessary and cook onion, celery, leek, carrot and garlic, adding them one type at a time and stirring each about 1 minute before adding the next. Cook, stirring frequently until caramelized, about 12 to 15 minutes.

Deglaze pot with wine, scraping the bottom to remove any brown bits, and cook about 2 to 3 minutes. Add tomatoes, thyme, oregano, bay leaf and reserved lamb shanks. Spoon sauce over shanks, cover and place in 250°F oven. Bake 3 to 4 hours or until lamb falls off the bone when pushed with the back of a fork.

Remove shanks with a slotted spoon, cover and keep warm. Strain liquid from pan through a sieve or food mill. Let liquid sit for a few minutes, skim fat from the surface and transfer to a new saucepan, discarding the residue that will have sunk to the bottom. Bring to a boil and reduce slightly. Adjust seasoning with salt and pepper.

To serve, place shanks on warmed plates and top with sauce. Garnish with thyme sprigs.

Serves 4.

CROWN ROAST OF SPRING LAMB WITH CRANBERRY WINE JUS

SHADOW LAWN INN, ROTHESAY, N.B.

The chef at Shadow Lawn Inn suggested serving these glamorous racks and the Cranberry Wine Jus with a medley of vegetables.

2 tablespoons canola oil
4 racks spring lamb
2 tablespoons butter
½ medium onion, minced
1 stalk celery, minced
2 cups bread cubes
¼ cup dried apricots, diced
¼ cup dried cranberries
½ teaspoon crumbled rosemary
Pinch of cloves
Small pinch of dried thyme
Salt and pepper to taste

CRANBERRY WINE JUS

1 cup full-bodied red wine (Cabernet Sauvignon or Merlot)
1 cup cranberry juice
¼ cup dried cranberries
1 sprig fresh rosemary
2 cups beef stock
1 tablespoon cornstarch dissolved in 1½ tablespoons water
Salt and pepper to taste

Heat oil in a skillet over medium-high heat and sear lamb racks one at a time, turning once. Remove to a platter.

In a deep skillet, melt butter over medium heat and sauté onion and celery until translucent. Add bread cubes, apricots, cranberries, rosemary, cloves and thyme, stirring to combine. Season with salt and pepper and set aside.

Place each lamb rack on a cutting board, bone side down. With a very sharp knife, slice partway through the loin of each rack. Using the photo as a guide, stand rack on end, curling the ribs into a crown with the meaty chops facing out. Tie each rack with string to help keep its shape. Place racks on a rimmed baking sheet. Fill the centre of each crown with the bread stuffing. Roast at 400°F, 15 minutes for medium-rare to 25 minutes for well done.

To serve, pour jus onto warmed plates. Remove string from crown roasts, cut into chops and arrange chops on the plate.

Serves 4.

CRANBERRY WINE JUS

Place wine, juice, dried cranberries and rosemary in a saucepan over medium heat. Boil until ½ cup liquid remains. Discard rosemary. Add stock and simmer 15 minutes. Dissolve cornstarch in water and add to sauce. Continue simmering until sauce is clear and shiny. Season with salt and pepper.

GRILLED LAMB KEBABS WITH TANGY COUSCOUS SALAD

· · · · · · · · · · · · · ·

For people who love lamb, eating it often can be a challenge because of the price. This is a great way to cook with ground lamb that doesn't break the bank, plus it is an easy recipe for entertaining as the salad can be done well in advance. The salad is inspired by tabouleh.

LAMB SKEWERS

1½ pounds finely ground lamb or ground lamb pulsed a few times in a food processor
4 cloves garlic, minced or grated
1 shallot, minced or grated
Zest and juice of 1 lemon
2 tablespoons extra-virgin olive oil
¼ cup chopped flat-leaf parsley
1 teaspoon dried oregano
½ teaspoon salt
½ teaspoon pepper
½ teaspoon ground cumin
½ teaspoon fennel seed
3 dashes of hot sauce, such as Tabasco
2 teaspoons Worcestershire sauce
1 large egg yolk

COUSCOUS

1 cup couscous
1½ cups boiling water
½ small red onion, finely chopped
½ sweet red pepper, diced small
½ sweet green pepper, diced small
2 plum tomatoes, seeded and diced
½ cup chopped flat-leaf parsley
2 tablespoons chopped fresh mint

DRESSING

3 cloves garlic, minced or grated
Zest and juice of 1 lemon
¼ cup red wine vinegar
¼ cup extra-virgin olive oil
1 teaspoon pepper
½ teaspoon salt
½ teaspoon hot sauce, such as Tabasco

LAMB SKEWERS

Combine all the ingredients in a bowl and mix very well with your hands. Press the meat mixture into 4 8-inch-sausages around 4 flat metal skewers. Refrigerate for 30 minutes to firm the meat before grilling.

Grill the skewers on a greased grill over high heat for 4 minutes on each side, then lower the heat and finish cooking for an additional 5 minutes.

COUSCOUS

Combine the couscous and water in a large bowl and stir. Cover the bowl and let stand for 12 to 15 minutes. Fluff with a fork. Let cool then add all of the vegetables and fresh herbs. Toss with the dressing and refrigerate. Serve cold, or warmed in the microwave, if desired.

DRESSING

Combine all the ingredients in a bowl. If possible, let stand for an hour to develop flavours.

Serves 4, with leftovers.

THE TASTIEST SHEPHERD'S PIE

· · · · · · · · · · · ·

Craig Flinn says, "I always enjoyed shepherd's pie as a child, but even more so when I was travelling throughout the U.K., where it is often featured on pub menus. Of course, "shepherd's pie" contains lamb and "cottage pie" uses beef, though on our continent ground beef is usually the favourite choice. I prefer to serve the vegetables on the side, but you can add some peas, carrots or corn if you wish. It can either be made in a single casserole dish or individual dishes. The idea here is to worry less about looks and more about taste. This is simple rustic bistro food, and I doubt if you have ever had a tastier version."

FILLING

2-pound boneless lamb shoulder
3 tablespoons extra-virgin olive oil
1 medium onion, diced
1 carrot, diced
1 stalk celery, diced
2 cups beef or lamb stock
2 cups red wine
2 bay leaves
4 sprigs fresh mint
Salt and pepper

CHEDDAR POTATO PURÉE

2 pounds unpeeled potatoes
1 cup milk
½ cup heavy cream (35% mf)
½ pound salted butter
1 teaspoon sea salt (approximate)
1 teaspoon pepper
1 teaspoon nutmeg
1 cup shredded old white Cheddar
½ cup corn or frozen sweet peas

FILLING

In a large, heavy pot brown lamb in oil. Add the onion, carrot and celery, stock, wine, bay leaves and mint. Bring pot just to a boil. Cover and braise in 300°F oven for 2 to 2½ hours, or until meat is very tender. Let meat cool in braising liquid for at least 1 hour.

Remove lamb from braising liquid and set aside. Strain contents of the pot through a sieve into a clean saucepan, discarding vegetables and herbs. Bring the liquid to a boil. Reduce by half, or until it coats the back of a spoon.

Pull meat apart, into shreds or bite-size pieces. Add reduced sauce to meat and mix well. Adjust seasonings with salt and pepper if needed and refrigerate.

CHEDDAR POTATO PURÉE

Meanwhile, cook potatoes, covered, in boiling salted water until fork-tender. Drain and, using a towel to protect your hands, peel potatoes while hot. Mill or rice potatoes into a large bowl. Heat milk, cream, butter, salt, pepper and nutmeg in a small saucepan. Pour into potatoes and beat with a whisk. Add cheese and adjust seasoning if necessary with a little salt.

TO ASSEMBLE

Fill the bottom half of individual ramekins or a large casserole dish with lamb. Pat meat down using the back of a spoon. Add corn then spread potato purée evenly over the corn or pipe potato overtop.

Bake in a 350°F oven until slightly browned on top and hot all the way through, about 20 to 30 minutes, depending on the size.

Serve with a simple salad, some steamed peas and carrots, or on their own.

Serves 6 to 8.

VENISON GOULASH

A traditional goulash can be made with three essential ingredients: stewing meat, onions and paprika. Many modern variations include pasta, potatoes and many more vegetables, but this version is a truly peasant dish that is more Hungarian in its roots. You can add a bit of tomato and red pepper to this recipe, but it isn't necessary if you don't have any. The slow cooking melts the onions into a sauce similar to the classic sauce "soubise." Of course, venison is lean and sometimes an acquired taste, so if you prefer to use beef, go right ahead. It's a great slow-cooker recipe as well.

2 pounds onions, sliced
2 tablespoons olive oil
2 pounds cubed venison stew meat
2 cloves garlic, minced
2 tablespoons paprika
$\frac{1}{2}$ teaspoon cayenne pepper or chili flakes
$\frac{1}{4}$ teaspoon cumin
1 teaspoon brown sugar
1 sweet red pepper, sliced
1 tomato, diced
$\frac{1}{2}$ cup beef stock, water or red wine

Place a large heavy pot over high heat and sauté the onions in the oil until slightly brown. Add all of the remaining ingredients and bring the liquid to a boil. Reduce heat and cover. Cook for 15 minutes until the vegetables look limp and have released their water. Uncover the pot and cook the goulash over low heat until the onions are melted and the venison is tender, about 3 hours, adding a little liquid from time to time, depending on the rate of reduction.

Serve the goulash with buttered noodles, steamed rice or potatoes.

Serves 6 to 8.

GLAZED LAMB SHANKS WITH
SIMPLY PERFECT RISOTTO

. . . .

This is a wonderful bistro dish. It is unbelievably flavourful, rich and rooted in culinary history. Nova Scotia lamb is among the best in the world, but as long as you choose locally raised, grass-fed lamb, your end result will be every bit as good. Making a simple lamb broth with a pound of bones from your butcher is well worth the effort for this recipe, but beef broth is a good substitute.

LAMB

2 heads garlic

6 lamb shanks

½ cup bacon or duck fat or vegetable oil (approximate)

2 onions, coarsely chopped

2 stalks celery, coarsely chopped

2 medium carrots, coarsely chopped

2 cups dry sherry

2 cups medium-bodied red wine (Merlot or Shiraz)

2 cups lamb stock

6 sprigs fresh thyme

4 sprigs fresh mint

4 bay leaves

Salt and pepper to taste

Chopped chives

RISOTTO

1 medium onion, minced

1 clove garlic, minced

½ teaspoon salt

½ teaspoon pepper

2 tablespoons extra-virgin olive oil

1 cup Caranoli rice

½ cup dry vermouth

3½ cups hot chicken stock

½ cup grated Parmigiano Reggiano cheese

2 tablespoons butter

LAMB

Wrap garlic in foil for and roast at 350°F until soft, about 30 to 40 minutes. Let cool and squeeze cloves out of the papery skins. Mash roughly with a fork and set aside.

In a large heavy pot, heat a quarter of the fat. Add the lamb shanks and brown on all sides, adding more of the fat if needed. Transfer to a braising pan or steep-sided roasting pan. Remove excess fat from pan, then sauté onions, celery and carrots for 10 minutes, until slightly caramelized. Deglaze the pan with sherry. Add the sherry, wine, stock, thyme, mint, bay leaves and roasted garlic to the braising pan. There should be enough liquid to completely cover the shanks.

Bring to a boil and transfer to a 300°F oven and braise, covered, for 2½ to 3 hours. Remove from oven and let shanks rest in braising liquor for 1 hour. Remove shanks to a second ovenproof pan and cover. Strain braising liquor into a saucepan and reduce over medium heat by two-thirds, or until liquid will coat the back of a wooden spoon. Season with a salt and pepper.

Ladle sauce over shanks and place in a 350°F oven to reheat, about 10 minutes. The sauce will glaze the shanks as they reheat.

In a heavy-bottomed sauté pan, or deep skillet over medium heat, sauté onion, garlic, salt and pepper in oil for 5 minutes or until soft. Add rice and cook for 3 minutes until grains look translucent. Deglaze pan with vermouth and cook until the bottom of the pan is dry. Begin adding hot broth one 8-ounce ladle at a time, stirring constantly. The risotto will take about 15 to 18 minutes to cook depending on the variety of rice. When risotto is fully cooked but still al dente (the grain still gives some resistance when bitten) remove from heat and stir in Parmesan cheese and butter. Cover and rest for 5 minutes off the heat, then serve immediately.

Spoon a helping of risotto in the centre of a large pasta bowl or soup bowl. Place a lamb shank on top of the risotto and sprinkle with freshly chopped chives. Serve with your favourite vegetables: green beans or steamed broccoli are good choices.

Serves 6.

PORK TENDERLOIN WITH PEPPERCORN-MUSTARD CRUST AND CIDER GRAVY

· · · · · · · · · · · · ·

AUBERGE LE VIEUX PRESBYTÈRE, BOUCTOUCHE, N.B.

Chef de cuisine Marcelle Albert shared this recipe from her menu at Le Tire-bouchon — "The Corkscrew" — dining room. This pork tenderloin with peppercorn-mustard crust and cider gravy has been a hallmark recipe.

2 pork tenderloins, about 1½ pounds total

2 tablespoons butter

1 tablespoon all-purpose flour

1 tablespoon Dijon mustard

½ tablespoon each cracked black, green and white peppercorns

½ tablespoon whole mustard seeds

1 teaspoon brown sugar

1 teaspoon crumbled dried thyme

CIDER GRAVY

1 cup sweet apple cider

2 tablespoons Cognac

1½ tablespoons all-purpose flour

⅓ cup chicken stock

2 teaspoons cider vinegar

⅔ teaspoon Dijon mustard

Salt and pepper

Remove all fat and tissue from tenderloins and tuck tail under so meat is of uniform thickness. In a bowl, combine butter, flour, mustard, peppercorns, mustard seeds, sugar and thyme. Spread all over the tenderloins. Place on a rack in a roasting pan and roast in a 350°F oven for 35 minutes until internal temperature reaches 160°F and meat is just barely pink inside. Transfer to a cutting board and tent with foil.

CIDER GRAVY

Place 1½ tablespoons of the pan drippings from the roasting pan in a heavy saucepan and set aside. Discard remaining drippings from roasting pan and place the roasting pan over medium-low heat. Deglaze pan with cider. Boil until liquid is reduced by half, about 6 minutes. Stir in Cognac and boil 1 minute longer.

Meanwhile, heat reserved drippings over medium-high heat, add flour and stir until golden brown, about 2 minutes. Whisk in cider mixture from the roasting pan and stock. Simmer until thickened, stirring occasionally, about 2 minutes. Remove from heat and mix in vinegar and mustard. Season with salt and pepper.

Slice the tenderloin and serve with the Cider Gravy.

Serves 4 to 6.

MAINS:
FISH AND SEAFOOD

FRESHLY STEAMED LOBSTER

. . . .

This foolproof recipe for freshly steamed lobster comes from innkeepers in Lunenburg, N.S. Remove the rubber bands from the lobster claws before cooking, as they give the lobster a rubber taste.

2 lobsters
½ cup melted butter
1 lemon, cut in wedges
Romaine leaves
Parsley sprigs

Use a steamer pot or place a vegetable steamer in an appropriate size pot with enough water to cover the bottom of the steamer by 1 inch. Bring the water to a hard boil, place lobsters in the steamer and cover. Cooking time will vary depending on the size of the lobsters, but a 1-pound lobster is cooked in 15 minutes.

When cooked, remove the lobster from the pot and briefly cool under cold water. For ease of eating, crack the lobster in the kitchen: place the lobster upside down; take a cleaver and place the point at the beginning of the tail; slice down the middle, breaking right through the outer shell. With the lobster still on its back, bring the cleaver sharply down on each claw and twist sideways, forcing the claw shell apart.

For presentation, put 2 romaine leaves on a plate and place the lobster on top, with the front covering the stems of the romaine. Between the claws place a small bowl of melted butter. Position 2 lemon wedges where the claws join the body and parsley sprigs between the lemons and along the cut made in the tail. Take a paper towel dipped in a small amount of the melted butter and rub over the lobster shell. Bon appétit!

Serves 2.

LOBSTER SUPREME

. . . .

GWEN MACKAY, VICTORIA, B.C.

For a transplanted Maritimer, there's no better place to live than Victoria, B.C. Gwen MacKay enjoys the ocean air of the Pacific as much as she did the Atlantic breezes. And what better occupation than to open a seafood market where there is access to the fresh fish she loved at home. She created a recipe for entertaining both East and West Coast friends with her all-time favourite — the Atlantic lobster. Serve with a salad.

2 tablespoons butter
1 small onion, chopped
Juice of ½ lemon
2 teaspoons all-purpose flour
¼ teaspoon pepper
½ cup milk
½ cup light cream (20% mf)
2 tablespoons dry sherry
½ cup mayonnaise
1 pound cooked lobster meat, chopped
Grated Parmesan cheese
Pinch of pepper and paprika

Melt butter in a saucepan over medium heat. Add onion and lemon juice and sauté until lightly browned. Add flour. Stir until well blended and then gradually add milk, cream and sherry. Cook until thick and smooth, stirring constantly. Remove from the heat. Stir in mayonnaise and salt. In a bowl combine lobster meat and sauce. Spoon into individual gratin dishes. Sprinkle tops with Parmesan cheese, pepper and paprika. Bake in 400°F oven until lightly browned, about 10 minutes.

Serves 4.

LOBSTER CLUB SANDWICH

. . . .

The ultimate lobster sandwich — served Maritime-style with a side of coleslaw and fries!

3 slices white bread, toasted
Mayonnaise
Lettuce, shredded
Tomato, thinly sliced
3 strips bacon, cooked crisp and drained
4 ounces lobster meat

Spread first slice of toast with mayonnaise and cover with lettuce, tomato and bacon. Cover with second slice of toast, spread with mayonnaise and lobster meat. Spread mayonnaise on one side of the third slice of toast and place on top of the sandwich. To serve, cut in quarters and secure with toothpicks.

Serves 1.

LOBSTER SHANNON

. . . .

UPPER DECK WATERFRONT FISHERY AND GRILL, HALIFAX, N.S.

Lobster is the most frequently requested seafood in Maritime restaurants. This lobster linguini recipe from Halifax's Upper Deck is one to remember.

1 can frozen lobster meat (about 11 ounces)
2 tablespoons butter
2 tablespoons all-purpose flour
1 cup Fish Stock (page 39) or reserved lobster juice
12 ounces linguini or fettucini
½ cup white wine
2 tablespoons lemon juice
¼ teaspoon freshly crushed peppercorn
½ cup heavy cream (35% mf)
Salt and pepper

Drain lobster, reserving juice. Chop lobster into bite-size pieces. Melt butter in a saucepan over low heat. Add flour, blending well. Whisk in stock. Bring to a boil, stirring until the first bubbles appear. Reduce the heat and cook over very low heat for 30 minutes, stirring frequently until smooth and thickened.

Meanwhile, boil pasta in a pot of boiling, salted water until al dente, drain.

Mix together the wine, lemon juice, crushed pepper and lobster in a large skillet. Quickly heat until warmed, add sauce, cream and pasta. Simmer gently until hot, 3 to 4 minutes. Add salt and pepper to taste.

Serves 4.

"LOBSTER" ROLLS

· · · · · · · · · · · ·

MOUNTAIN GAP INN, SMITHS COVE, N.S.

This traditional Maritime lobster roll is also served with fries and coleslaw. This recipe includes a roll recipe from the Compass Rose B&B, Grand Manan Island when it was operated by Cecelia Bowden and Linda L'Aventure.

3 cups chopped cooked lobster meat, in bite-size
  pieces
¼ cup finely chopped celery
Mayonnaise
Salt and pepper to taste
2 cups shredded lettuce
4 "lobster" rolls or other short hot-dog-style bun

"LOBSTER" ROLLS

1 tablespoon dry yeast
⅓ cup granulated sugar
½ cup lukewarm water
1 teaspoon salt
⅓ cup vegetable oil
1⅓ cups warm water
5 to 6 cups all-purpose flour
1 tablespoon butter

Combine lobster and celery with just enough mayonnaise to bind them. Season with salt and pepper. Split 4 rolls almost through and toast lightly. Place lettuce on rolls and fill with lobster mixture.

Serves 4.

"LOBSTER" ROLLS

Dissolve yeast and 1 teaspoon of the sugar in lukewarm water and let froth to at least 1 cup in volume. In a large bowl, combine remaining sugar, salt, oil and warm water and whisk briskly. Add yeast mixture and beat until smooth. Gradually add flour, a cupful at a time, beating after each addition, until you need to use a wooden spoon and your hands to add in the remainder.

Turn out on a flour-covered surface and knead until smooth and slightly sticky, about 5 minutes. Place in a greased bowl and turn to grease all over. Cover and let rise until doubled in bulk, about 45 minutes in a warm, draft-free place.

Punch down. Divide into 12 pieces and shape into 12 oblong rolls. Place on a greased baking sheet, cover loosely and let rise again for 45 minutes.

Bake rolls in 375°F oven for 12 to 15 minutes, until slightly golden. Remove from oven, brush tops with butter and cool on wire racks.

Makes 12 rolls. Freeze extras.

LOBSTER THERMIDOR

. . . .

CANDLERIGGS, INDIAN HARBOUR, N.S.

This recipe makes an excellent choice for guests. It not only tastes delicious but is both make-ahead and impressive in its presentation.

Water sufficient to boil lobsters
1 onion, chopped
1 celery stalk, chopped
1 bay leaf
1 lemon, sliced
4 uncooked lobsters (1¼ to 1½ pounds each)
2 tablespoons melted butter
¼ cup butter
2 tablespoons chopped chives
¼ cup all-purpose flour
⅔ cup blend cream (10% mf)
¼ cup dry sherry
½ teaspoon dry mustard
Salt and pepper to taste
½ cup fine soft breadcrumbs
⅓ cup shredded Swiss or grated Parmesan cheese
Fresh parsley or dill for garnish

Pour water into a large pot and add onion, celery, bay leaf and lemon slices. Bring to a boil, cover and reduce heat to simmer for 10 minutes. Add lobsters and bring back to a boil. Skim off foam and simmer for 10 to 12 minutes. Transfer lobsters to cutting board. Strain broth and reserve 1 cup.

Split lobster tails and bodies, cutting lengthwise. Remove meat from tails, knuckles and claws and cut into bite-size pieces. Discard all shells except lobster bodies and tails. Clean shells under running water and brush inside and out with the melted butter. Set aside on a greased broiler pan.

In a saucepan melt the ¼ cup of butter over low heat and cook chives for 1 minute. Stir in flour. Gradually whisk in cream and reserved broth, stirring over medium heat until smooth and thickened. Add sherry and mustard, cooking for 1 minute. Season with salt and pepper and stir in breadcrumbs and lobster chunks.

Spoon the lobster mixture into the shells. Top with cheese and broil until golden and heated through, about 7 minutes. Lower rack if necessary to heat the lobster mixture through without burning the top. Garnish with fresh parsley or dill.

Serves 8.

SEAFOOD LASAGNA

. . . .

This house speciality was shared by a New Brunswick chef many years ago. The inn was perched on the Bay of Fundy shore, and the chef made use of the fresh seafood that was readily available.

1½ pounds raw seafood

1 pound spinach, rinsed and trimmed

4 large eggs

1 pound cottage cheese

⅛ teaspoon nutmeg

Salt and pepper to taste

6 tablespoons butter

1 medium onion, chopped

1 garlic clove, crushed

1 tablespoon chopped fresh dill

6 tablespoons all-purpose flour

3 cups light cream (20% mf)

2 tablespoons sherry

1 cup shredded Swiss cheese

10 lasagna noodles, cooked al dente

½ cup grated Parmesan cheese

In simmering salted water, poach raw seafood until barely cooked. Drain and reserve.

In a large covered pot, briefly cook spinach until wilted. Drain, press out liquid and chop.

In a large bowl whisk eggs, mix in spinach, cottage cheese, nutmeg and season with salt and pepper. Set aside.

Melt butter over medium heat and sauté onion and garlic until softened, but not brown. Add dill, sprinkle with flour and cook, stirring constantly for 1 minute. Whisk cream and sherry, a little at a time, into flour mixture and cook until well blended and slightly thickened. Stir in Swiss cheese and reserved seafood. Season with salt and pepper.

To assemble, place half the prepared noodles in a greased 9- by 13-inch lasagna pan. Spread half the spinach mixture over the noodles and cover with half the seafood mixture. Repeat these 3 layers. Sprinkle top with Parmesan cheese and bake at 350°F for 45 minutes to 1 hour or until bubbly and browned. Remove from oven and let stand 10 minutes before serving.

Serves 6 to 8.

SCALLOP BUBBLY BAKE

. . . .

THE WEST POINT LIGHTHOUSE, WEST POINT, P.E.I.

Cooks will find that this easily prepared seafood casserole, served with pasta or rice pilaf and accompanying side salad, is a delicious meal.

1 pound scallops
½ cup finely chopped onion
1 cup sliced mushrooms
1 cup chopped sweet green pepper
1 cup chopped celery
6 tablespoons butter
¼ cup all-purpose flour
½ teaspoon salt
2 cups milk
½ cup breadcrumbs
Cheddar or Parmesan cheese, grated

Cut large scallops in half. Poach scallops in simmering, salted water for 1 minute. Drain and set aside. Meanwhile, sauté onion, mushrooms, green pepper and celery in 2 tablespoons of the butter until onion is softened; set aside.

In a separate saucepan, melt remaining butter and whisk in flour and salt. Add milk, whisking constantly and cook until sauce is thickened and bubbly. Fold scallops and vegetables into the sauce and pour into a buttered 8-cup casserole. Top with breadcrumbs and a sprinkling of grated cheese. Bake in 350°F oven for 25 to 30 minutes, until browned and bubbly.

Serves 4.

GABRIEAU'S FETTUCCINI WITH SCALLOPS AND SHRIMP

. . . .

GABRIEAU'S BISTRO, ANTIGONISH, N.S.

Created by owner-chef Mark Gabrieau, this entrée is seafood at its finest!

1½ tablespoons extra-virgin olive oil
1½ tablespoons butter
¾ pound bay scallops
¾ pound cooked medium shrimp, peeled and deveined
1 sweet red pepper, roasted and sliced*
1 cup fresh peas
1 large clove garlic, minced
1 tablespoon chopped fresh tarragon
Salt and pepper to taste
½ cup white wine
1 cup heavy cream (35% mf)
12 ounces fettuccini, cooked al dente
Fresh parsley, chopped
Freshly grated Parmesan cheese

Heat oil and butter over medium-high heat in a large skillet. Add scallops, shrimp, red pepper, peas, garlic and tarragon and sauté 2 to 3 minutes. Season with salt and pepper. Remove to a plate and keep warm.

Deglaze pan with white wine, stir in cream and bring to a boil. Reduce heat and simmer until slightly thickened. Add fettuccini and toss to coat. Stir in reserved scallop mixture and serve garnished with fresh parsley and grated Parmesan cheese.

Serves 4.

* To roast a red pepper: Grill pepper until it is black on all sides. Immediately place in a brown paper bag until cooled. Peel skin from pepper. Remove stalk and inner seeds and slice.

ITALIAN SEAFOOD STEW

• • • • • • • • • • • •

THE ITALIAN GOURMET, HALIFAX, N.S.

An abundant supply of fresh seafood and a love of Italian cuisine marry beautifully in this seafood stew prepared by Chef Kate Abato. The seafood is cooked separately from the stew stock, then combined during the last five minutes of preparation to avoid overcooking the fish. At The Italian Gourmet the stew was served with crusty bread, a side salad and a glass of red wine.

STEW STOCK

1 tablespoon extra-virgin olive oil
1 small sweet green pepper, finely chopped
1 small onion, finely chopped
1 clove garlic, crushed
1 cup Fish Stock (page 39)
1 cup fruity red wine
1 cup seeded and diced Roma plum tomatoes
½ teaspoon dried Italian seasoning

SEAFOOD

2½ pound mixed seafood, such as scallops, salmon and
   white fish
2 tablespoons extra-virgin olive oil
1 medium onion, finely chopped
1 clove garlic, crushed
Salt and pepper
Fresh basil or parsley for garnish

STEW STOCK

For the stew stock, heat oil in a large skillet over medium heat. Sauté green pepper, onion and garlic, stirring frequently, until onion is translucent, about 5 minutes. Add fish stock and wine, reduce heat and simmer 20 minutes, stirring occasionally. Add tomatoes and Italian seasoning. Simmer until tomatoes soften and stock is slightly reduced, about 20 minutes. Keep warm.

SEAFOOD

Rinse and pat dry seafood, cutting into a uniform 1½-inch pieces. Heat oil in a large skillet over medium heat. Sauté onion and garlic, stirring frequently until translucent, about 5 minutes. Add all the seafood, being careful to distribute it evenly in the skillet. Cook 3 to 4 minutes on one side, turn over gently and cook 2 minutes. Transfer contents of skillet to stew base and simmer 5 minutes. Adjust seasoning with salt and pepper.

To serve, ladle into shallow bowls. Garnish with fresh basil.

Serves 6.

OYSTER AND SNOW CRAB GRATIN

. . . .

This is a fun way to cook with oysters and the presentation is beautiful. This dish can be served as a main or appetizer. In Nova Scotia, particularly in Cape Breton, snow crab is available year round, as are oysters.

1 large snow crab

18 large choice oysters

¼ cup minced red onions or shallots

2 tablespoons butter

½ cup sour cream

½ cup cream cheese, softened

Zest and juice of 1 lemon

1 teaspoon grated or prepared horseradish

1 teaspoon Worcestershire sauce

1 teaspoon hot sauce such as Tabasco

¼ teaspoon salt

¼ teaspoon pepper

2 tablespoons chopped chives

½ cup panko or fresh breadcrumbs

2 tablespoons melted butter

Cook snow crab legs in 1 inch of water for 10 minutes, or steam them for the same period. Cool and remove meat from shells. Make sure meat contains no bits of shell or cartilage, and pick into ½-inch chunks. One large crab should yield about 1 cup of cooked meat.

Shuck oysters using a proper oyster knife, and detach meat from adductor muscle underneath. Pour off oyster liquor into a small, fine sieve to remove any sand or bits of shell, and reserve. Take bottom half of each oyster shell and rinse very well under running water. It is a good idea to scrub shells with a brush as well to remove any sand. Dry shells and place a single oyster in each. Set on a rimmed baking sheet, cover and refrigerate.

Sauté onions in butter until translucent. Add to a food processor along with sour cream, cream cheese, lemon zest and juice, horseradish, Worcestershire, Tabasco, salt, pepper and reserved oyster liquor. Purée until smooth. Remove the processor bowl from its base and gently stir in picked crabmeat and chopped chives so crab does not break apart too much.

Combine breadcrumbs and melted butter in a small bowl.

To assemble gratins, divide crab mixture among the oysters in their shells. Spread evenly and sprinkle with breadcrumbs. Broil in a 500°F oven until breadcrumbs are golden and cheese is bubbling. Allow to stand for 3 minutes before serving.

Serves 6.

CRAB CAKES DE BOUCTOUCHE

AUBERGE LE VIEUX PRESBYTÈRE RESTAURANT, BOUCTOUCHE, N.B.

Baking powder gives a lightness to these moist cakes.

1 pound crabmeat, drained and pressed
1 cup fresh breadcrumbs
⅓ cup milk
¼ cup mayonnaise
1 large egg
2 tablespoons finely chopped green onions
1 tablespoon chopped fresh parsley
½ teaspoon baking powder
½ teaspoon salt
¼ teaspoon white pepper
2 tablespoons butter
2 tablespoons vegetable oil
All-purpose flour

Place crabmeat in large bowl. Check for bits of shell. Add breadcrumbs and milk. In a separate bowl, combine mayonnaise, egg, green onions, parsley, baking powder, salt and pepper. Pour over crab mixture and gently toss until mixed.

Form into patties. Cover and refrigerate on a baking sheet for at least 1 hour.

Heat butter with oil in large skillet over medium heat.

Dust cakes lightly with flour and fry until golden brown, about 4 minutes each side.

Makes 8 cakes.

SIMPLY STEAMED CLAMS

C RESTAURANT, VANCOUVER, B.C.

Executive chef Robert Clark of Vancouver's famed C Restaurant shared this recipe with Elaine Elliot and Virginia Lee for their lobster (and other shellfish) cookbook. Clams are a favourite on the West Coast as well as the East Coast, and this recipe from an outstanding seafood restaurant may seem simple. It is indeed simple to prepare — but the flavour is anything but ordinary. Be sure to have plenty of warm crusty bread on hand for dipping in the buttery herb sauce.

4 pounds clams in the shell
⅓ cup butter
⅓ cup chopped shallots
⅔ cup white wine
1 cup cherry or grape tomatoes, cut in quarters
2 tablespoons chopped fresh herbs of choice

Wash clams. In a heavy sauté pan over medium-high heat, heat 2 tablespoons of the butter. Add clams; cover and steam for 2 minutes. Lower heat to medium, add shallots and sweat for about 2 minutes. Raise heat slightly, add wine and cook until clams open, about 2 to 4 minutes. Add remaining butter, tomatoes and herbs. Toss together until butter is melted and tomatoes are slightly wilted.

To serve, discard any clams that did not open. Divide clams with sauce into 4 large bowls.

Serves 4.

MEDUSA MUSSELS

· · · · · · · · · · · ·

FLEX MUSSELS, CHARLOTTETOWN, P.E.I.

Flex Mussels rightly boasted that all its mussel dishes had a unique flavour. This recipe, featuring fresh tomato with a hint of oregano and permeated with lemon zest, was a winner. Chef Garner Quain explained that the key to making great mussels is speed. Using high heat and a short cooking time, you prevent overcooking. Have all your ingredients ready and don't overload the pot with mussels. If you are cooking a large quantity it's smart to make several smaller batches.

2 to 3 pounds fresh mussels
1 teaspoon extra-virgin olive oil
1 teaspoon minced garlic
1 large tomato, chopped
Zest of 1 lemon
2 sprigs fresh oregano
½ cup white wine
½ cup crumbled feta cheese
Crusty baguette, sliced

Scrub and debeard mussels, discarding any that do not close when lightly tapped or have broken shells. Reserve.

Heat oil in a large, heavy saucepan over medium-high heat. Add garlic, tomato, lemon zest and oregano and sauté, stirring frequently until tomatoes begin to break down, about 2 minutes.

Deglaze the pan with wine, stirring with a wooden spoon and gently scraping the bottom of the sauccpan to combine all the ingredients. Cook 1 minute. Add mussels, cover and bring to a boil. Cook 4 to 6 minutes, stirring midway, until all mussels are open. Remove lid and boil to reduce the sauce by one-third or to desired consistency.

To serve, using a slotted spoon, remove mussels to a warm serving dish, discarding any not fully opened. Sprinkle feta cheese over mussels and top with sauce. Serve with lots of fresh, sliced baguette.

Serves 4.

THE DUNES' CURRIED MUSSELS

. . . .

THE DUNES CAFÉ AND GARDENS,
BRACKLEY BEACH, P.E.I.

Thankfully, due to the successful mussel-farming industry in Atlantic Canada, succulent fresh mussels are available almost everywhere in North America. The chef at the Dunes Café and Gardens enhances this dish with a touch of curry.

3 to 4 pounds fresh mussels
2 to 3 cloves garlic, minced
1 tablespoon curry powder, or to taste
¾ cup white wine
1½ cups heavy cream (35% mf)
1½ cups chopped leeks, white part only

Scrub and debeard mussels, discarding any that do not close when lightly tapped or with broken shells, and set aside. In a large heavy saucepan, combine garlic, curry, wine, cream and leeks. Mix well and bring to a simmer over medium heat. Add mussels, stirring to cover with sauce, and cover pan. Steam mussels until fully opened, approximately 6 to 7 minutes. Before serving, discard any unopened mussels. Serve sauce separately in 4 individual bowls with the mussels on the side.

Serves 4.

STEAMED MUSSELS ACADIAN STYLE

. . . .

Mussels make excellent appetizers or mains for casual dining. Live mussels should have a closed shell, although those exposed to air may gape slightly but should close when lightly tapped.

5 pounds fresh mussels
⅓ cup butter
1 small onion, chopped
3 cloves garlic, minced
1 small carrot, peeled and grated
2 plum tomatoes, finely chopped
1 cup white wine
2 tablespoons chopped parsley
Freshly ground pepper
Crusty baguette, sliced

Scrub and debeard mussels in cold running water, discarding any that do not close when lightly tapped or with broken shells. Combine all ingredients except mussels in a large heavy saucepan and bring to a boil, stirring constantly. Add mussels and stir to coat them evenly with sauce. Cover, reduce heat to medium and steam for 5 to 7 minutes, being careful not to overcook. Remove mussels to serving bowls, discarding any that have not opened. Pour sauce overtop. Serve with baguette.

Serves 4 to 6 as appetizers, 2 to 3 as a main course.

HONEY-MUSTARD GLAZED SALMON

. . . .

This salmon entrée is sweet, yet it has a definite bite. The glaze is equally tasty as a dipping sauce for shrimp and scallops.

2 tablespoons finely chopped onion
⅔ cup whole grain Dijon mustard
½ cup liquid honey
6 salmon steaks or fillets (6 ounces each)
¼ cup all-purpose flour
Salt and pepper
1 to 2 tablespoons vegetable oil

In a small saucepan combine onion, mustard and honey and cook over low heat, stirring frequently until onion is tender. Reserve and keep warm.

Lightly dust the salmon with flour and season with salt and pepper. Heat oil in a heavy ovenproof skillet over high heat. Add salmon and sear 2 minutes per side. Remove to 350°F oven and bake for 5 minutes. Remove skillet from oven.

Turn oven to broil. Pour glaze over salmon and broil until brown and bubbly, about 1 minute.

Serves 6.

CEDAR-PLANKED SALMON

. . . .

A SNUG HARBOUR INN, UCLUELET, B.C.

Sue Brown, owner-chef of A Snug Harbour Inn in Ucluelet, on Vancouver Island, naturally uses West Coast salmon for this dish. She shared it with Elaine Elliot and Virginia Lee for their salmon cookbook. Elaine and Virginia found that it works just as well with Atlantic salmon, even though this variety is no longer available wild. The recipe was handed down through generations of West Coast fishermen and may be prepared either in the oven or on the barbecue grill. If using a grill, adjust the heat so the board does not ignite or cook over indirect heat.

1 untreated cedar plank, slightly larger than the size of the fish you wish to cook
¼ cup extra-virgin olive oil
Juice of 1 lemon
1 tablespoon chopped fresh basil
½ teaspoon salt
1 teaspoon pepper
1 salmon fillet (1 to 2 pounds)

Soak cedar plank for several hours in room-temperature water. It is a good idea to place something heavy on the plank to be sure that all the wood is submerged and soaked.

In a shallow baking dish, combine all ingredients except the salmon. Add salmon, turn to coat and marinate, covered and refrigerated for several hours.

Place soaked plank in 450°F oven and heat 5 minutes. Remove fish from marinade and place on plank. Bake until fish flakes when tested, about 10 to 12 minutes, depending upon thickness.

Serves 4 to 6.

POACHED SALMON

. . . .

SHAW'S HOTEL, BRACKLEY BEACH, P.E.I.

This whole poached Atlantic salmon is a specialty at Shaw's Hotel. It is easy to prepare and delicious when napped with their White Wine Sauce.

2½ to 3 pounds fresh Atlantic salmon
1 cup dry white wine
½ cup lemon juice
6 to 8 peppercorns
1 teaspoon salt
1 large carrot, peeled and diced
1 medium onion, peeled and sliced
1 large stalk celery with top, sliced
¼ cup chopped fresh tarragon

WHITE WINE SAUCE

2 tablespoons butter
2 tablespoons all-purpose flour
⅔ cup milk
⅓ cup heavy cream (35% mf)
2 tablespoons dry white wine
Salt and white pepper
1 tablespoon chopped parsley

Rinse and pat dry salmon. Place on a rack in a poaching pan and add enough cold water to cover fish. Add remaining ingredients to pan and bring to a boil. Reduce heat and simmer, covered, 2 minutes per pound of fish. Turn off heat and let stand in water, 1 hour. Carefully remove salmon from pan, remove skin and place fish on a serving platter. Serve with White Wine Sauce and vegetables of choice.

Serves 6.

WHITE WINE SAUCE

In a small saucepan, melt butter and stir in flour to form a roux. Cook until bubbly, 1 to 2 minutes, stirring constantly. Whisk in milk, cream and wine. Cook over medium heat until thickened. Adjust seasoning with salt, pepper and parsley. Serve immediately.

Makes 1 cup.

HIGHLAND SALMON

• • • • • • • • • •

INN ON THE COVE AND SPA, SAINT JOHN, N.B.

Innkeeper Ross Mavis says that this marinade enhances but does not mask the wonderful flavour of Atlantic salmon. The recipe was featured on Tide's Table, *a Maritime television cooking show filmed at the inn prior to the fire that damaged it seriously in 2012.*

4 Atlantic salmon fillets (6 ounces each)
Zest of 1 orange
½ cup orange juice
⅓ cup whisky or rye
1½ tablespoons pure maple syrup
1 tablespoon grainy Dijon mustard
2 teaspoons Worcestershire sauce
1 teaspoon pepper
¾ teaspoon salt
2 teaspoons butter
4 green onions, chopped
Orange slices, for garnish

Place salmon fillets in a shallow glass baking dish. In a bowl, whisk together zest and juice, whisky, maple syrup, mustard, Worcestershire sauce, pepper and salt. Pour over salmon. Refrigerate 2 to 4 hours, turning fish at least once.

Remove salmon from marinade, place on greased grill and grill over high heat about 4 minutes on each side, until opaque and flesh flakes easily with a fork.

Meanwhile, heat butter in a small skillet over medium heat, add green onion and sauté until just heated through. Reserve and keep warm.

To serve, portion fillets on plates. Garnish with sautéed green onions and orange slices.

Serves 4.

GRILLED SALMON WITH SAGE BUTTER

• • • • • • • • • • • • •

THE NORMAWAY INN, MARGAREE VALLEY, N.S.

Atlantic salmon grills better and has a more fragrant flavour than Pacific salmon due to its higher fat content.

½ cup diced onion
1 cup, cold unsalted butter, cubed
2½ cups fresh sage leaves
Pinch each of salt and pepper
Dash of lemon juice
4 to 6 salmon fillets, unskinned

In a skillet, slowly sauté onion in ½ teaspoon of the butter until golden brown. Remove to a fine mesh strainer and drain. In a food processor, combine onion and sage leaves and whirl until leaves are chopped. Add salt, pepper, lemon juice and butter, 1 cube at a time, and whirl until smooth.

Reserve ⅓ cup of the sage butter for salmon, and place remaining sage butter on plastic wrap and roll up into a log. Wrap and seal ends. Freeze for up to 2 weeks and slice off portions to use with fish, meats or vegetables.

Grill salmon fillets on flesh side for about 6 to 7 minutes, turn over to skin side and grill 2 to 3 minutes or until fish flakes easily and is opaque. To serve, remove skin from fillets and add a pat of sage butter to melt over the top.

Serves 4 to 6.

FILLET OF SALMON WITH CREAM LEEK SAUCE

. . . .

THE QUACO INN, ST. MARTINS, N.B.

The Quaco Inn (now renamed the Tidal Watch Inn), with its close proximity to the Bay of Fundy, always featured Atlantic salmon on the menu. This special entrée was a signature dish.

3 tablespoons butter
2 green onions, cut into thin 3-inch julienne strips
1 leek, white part only, cut into thin 3-inch julienne strips
⅔ cup Fish Stock (page 39)
1 cup heavy cream (35% mf)
1½ tablespoons dry vermouth
Salt and pepper to taste
Pinch of cayenne pepper
4 salmon fillets (5 ounces each)
Fresh dill sprigs

Heat butter in a skillet over medium heat. Add green onions and leeks and sauté, stirring frequently, until softened, about 2 minutes. Add fish stock and cook until vegetables are tender. Add cream and simmer until mixture begins to thicken, about 8 minutes. Add vermouth and simmer gently, 5 minutes. Adjust seasoning with salt, pepper and cayenne.

Rinse and pat dry salmon fillets. Place salmon on greased grill 3 inches from high heat and cook, turning once, 5 minutes per side or until salmon flakes easily and is opaque.

To serve, place fillets on plates and nap with sauce. Garnish with dill.

Serves 4.

SALMON CAKES

. . . .

BLOMIDON INN, WOLFVILLE, N.S.

Chef Sean Laceby noted that it is important to put the breadcrumb coating on at the last minute, just before frying: "This really helps to give a crisp exterior and to keep the flavour at its best." This has been one of the inn's most popular dishes. We suggest serving with fresh garden vegetables.

12 ounces boneless salmon fillets
1 cup mashed potatoes
1 large egg, lightly beaten
¼ cup sour cream
1 cup fresh breadcrumbs
1 tablespoon chopped fresh dill
2 teaspoons salt
1 teaspoon pepper
Vegetable oil

Bring saucepan or deep skillet of water to boil. Turn heat to medium and place salmon in pan, ensuring water covers fish. Cook until salmon flakes apart easily then drain. Let cool and flake, discarding skin if any.

In large bowl, combine salmon, potatoes, egg, sour cream, half the breadcrumbs, dill, salt and pepper.

Mix well and form into 4 patties. Coat with remaining breadcrumbs.

Heat vegetable oil in large skillet over medium heat, add cakes and brown and crisp on both sides, turning once.

Serves 2.

SALMON LOAF WITH PARSLEY EGG SAUCE

. . . .

Both fresh and canned salmon work equally well in this flavourful "comfort-food" dish. If using canned salmon, be sure to drain and remove all skin and bones.

2 cups flaked cooked fresh or canned salmon
2 tablespoons lemon juice
¾ teaspoon salt
2 green onions, chopped
2 cups soft breadcrumbs
2 large eggs, beaten
½ cup mayonnaise
¼ cup whole milk

PARSLEY EGG SAUCE
1½ tablespoons butter
1½ tablespoons all-purpose flour
1 cup whole milk, heated
1 large egg, hard cooked and finely diced
2 tablespoons chopped fresh parsley
Salt and white pepper

In a bowl, gently combine all ingredients. Pour into a buttered 6-cup loaf pan. Bake at 350°F for 35 minutes until golden on top. Let cool slightly, remove from pan and slice.

PARSLEY EGG SAUCE
Meanwhile, in a saucepan melt butter over medium heat. Whisk in flour, stirring constantly, cook 2 minutes. Whisk in milk and bring to a boil. Reduce heat and simmer until sauce has thickened. Fold egg and parsley into sauce. Adjust seasoning with salt and pepper.

  Serve slices topped with Parsley Egg Sauce.

Serves 4 to 6.

GRILLED HALIBUT

. . . .

The North Atlantic species of halibut is the largest member of the flatfish family, at times reaching 300 pounds. Its mild-flavoured, firm white flesh tends to be rather lean and must never be overcooked.

2 to 2½ pounds halibut steaks or fillets
¼ cup extra-virgin olive oil
Freshly ground mixed peppercorns*
Fresh lemon juice
Lemon twists

Preheat one side of grill to high. If using halibut steaks, cut in half through centre bone. Brush fish with oil and grill on greased grill for 2 to 3 minutes per side. If fish appears to be drying out, brush again with oil. Transfer fish to unheated side of grill. Close lid and cook for 2 to 3 minutes longer or until fish is opaque and flakes easily. Grilling time will depend upon thickness of fish.

  Transfer fillets to serving plates. Sprinkle with freshly ground mixed peppercorns, drizzle with fresh lemon juice and garnish with lemon twists.

Serves 6.

* Mixed peppercorns are a combination of black, white, green and pink peppercorns. A word of warning: once you use this blend, it will be difficult to return to regular black pepper.

SALMON À LA KING WITH SWEET PEAS, LEEKS AND CHOPPED EGG

. . . .

This dish makes a lovely entrée or appetizer and takes a twist on the more common Chicken à la King, served in puff pastry vol-au-vents. These are available in the freezer section of your grocery store and can be baked ahead of time.

1 package frozen puff pastry shells or vol-au-vents

3 large eggs

3 tablespoons butter

1 cup sliced white of leek

¼ cup all-purpose flour

½ teaspoon salt

¼ teaspoon white pepper

¼ cup white wine

1 cup cold milk

¼ cup heavy cream (35% mf)

Pinch of nutmeg

1 teaspoon chopped fresh dill or tarragon

1½ pound fresh salmon fillet, skinned and cut into bite-size cubes

½ cup frozen peas

Fresh dill sprigs for garnish

Prepare the puff pastry shells as directed on the package. (They can be made ahead of time and warmed in the oven just prior to serving.)

Boil the eggs in water for 10 minutes and cool under running water. Peel the eggs and then cut them in half, removing the yolks. Chop the whites coarsely and set aside. Grate the egg yolks through the finer holes of a grater and set aside.

Heat the butter in a sauté pan and cook the leeks for a few minutes until they wilt and soften. Add the flour, salt and pepper and mix well. Cook over medium heat for about 3 minutes. Add the wine, stirring very well. This will form a sticky-looking paste as the wine heats. Cook this for 3 minutes and then add the milk, whisking as the milk heats. Whisk in the cream, nutmeg and dill. Cook the sauce for a few minutes and then add the peas and cubed salmon. Cook on medium heat for about 10 minutes, gently stirring a few times. Fold in the reserved chopped egg white.

PRESENTATION

Ladle the salmon mixture into the warm pastry shells. Pile it high and don't worry if extra sauce spills over onto the plate. Use a teaspoon to sprinkle some grated egg yolk over top and garnish with a sprig of fresh dill.

Serves 6.

SALMON AND SPINACH LASAGNA

. . . .

This appetizing salmon lasagna was a creation of chef-owner Axel Begner of the Dufferin Inn in Saint John. It is based on a creamy béchamel sauce and can be prepared in advance. Simply pop in the oven when guests arrive and serve it with a Caesar salad and warm garlic bread.

1 pound fresh spinach, stems removed and rinsed
8 ounces lasagna pasta sheets
1¼ pound skinless salmon fillet, cut in ½-inch slices
Salt and pepper
¼ cup freshly grated Parmesan cheese
4 ounces mozzarella cheese, shredded
Chopped fresh dill

BÉCHAMEL SAUCE

2 tablespoons butter
2 tablespoons all-purpose flour
2 cups milk
½ teaspoon salt
¼ teaspoon white pepper
Pinch of nutmeg
2 large egg yolks

BÉCHAMEL SAUCE

In a large saucepan, melt butter over medium heat, whisk in flour, and cook, without browning, about 3 minutes. Gradually whisk in milk and bring to a boil, stirring constantly. Stir in salt, pepper and nutmeg. In a small bowl, beat egg yolks lightly and stir in a little of the hot mixture. Blend thoroughly and then stir back into the saucepan. Continue to cook sauce, stirring constantly until thickened. Set aside and keep warm.

Meanwhile, blanch spinach in boiling salted water, 1 minute, drain and press firmly to remove water. Prepare lasagna sheets following package directions, drain.

In a greased 8- by 10-inch baking pan, spread a layer of béchamel sauce. Add a layer of pasta sheets, top with a layer of salmon and a layer of spinach. Repeat with sauce, pasta, salmon and spinach ending with a layer of sauce. Top with Parmesan and mozzarella cheese. Bake in 350°F oven for 40 to 50 minutes, until top is browned and lasagna is bubbly. Sprinkle with dill.

Serves 4.

PENNE WITH SMOKED SALMON AND CREAM CHEESE SAUCE

. . . .

MICHAEL SMITH, FOOD NETWORK CANADA, FORTUNE, P.E.I.

Michael loves cooking for his family and says, "This is my family's all-time favourite dinner party pasta dish. Our friends request it all the time. It's easy to make too, because it makes its own sauce! You can toss steaming wet, just-cooked pasta with melting cream cheese to form an incredibly smooth, luxurious sauce. The smoked salmon adds extravagance balanced by other familiar flavours: dill, lemon, onion, mustard and capers." If you have the time, smoking your own salmon on the barbecue is fun and makes this dish extra special, but with so many great Canadian smokehouses, high-quality smoked fish is available almost everywhere.

1 pound penne pasta

2 cups cream cheese at room temperature, cubed

¼ cup chopped fresh dill

4 green onions, thinly sliced

Zest and juice and of 1 lemon

4 teaspoons Dijon mustard

¼ cup capers, rinsed

1 pound hot-smoked salmon, flaked

½ teaspoon salt

½ teaspoon pepper

Bring a large pot of water to a boil. Season it liberally with salt until it tastes like seawater. When it is boiling furiously, add the pasta. Cook to al dente, until the pasta is cooked through but still pleasantly chewy.

Scoop out some of the starchy cooking water and reserve. Drain pasta but not quite all the way — leave it a bit wet. Return pasta to the pot, along with 1 or 2 splashes of the reserved water, perhaps ¾ cup or so in total.

While pasta is still steaming hot, immediately add all remaining ingredients except salmon and seasonings. Stir with a wooden spoon as cheese melts and forms a creamy sauce. At the last second, briefly fold in smoked salmon so it won't break up too much. Season with salt and pepper.

Serves 4.

BUTTER-ROASTED HALIBUT WITH
ASPARAGUS "NOODLES" AND BEURRE BLANC

· · · · · · · · · · ·

In great bistros, fish dishes usually take a just-caught piece of seafood, cook it at the very last minute and accompany it with something fresh and light, often a vegetable. The beauty of this recipe is that it follows this path by taking a few simple ingredients, at the peak of freshness, and elevating them into an elegant dish. The key here is to find the right cut of halibut and to follow the method of butter-basting it in the pan. Ask your fishmonger for a thick-cut, boneless halibut loin from the centre of the fish, away from the tail. This makes the fish a bit sturdier in the pan and prevents it from overcooking and crumbling. The beurre blanc can be made just before you start the fish and held warm until you are ready to serve.

ASPARAGUS "NOODLES"

2 pounds fresh asparagus
1 tablespoon chopped flat-leaf parsley
1 teaspoon chopped fresh tarragon
1 teaspoon chopped thyme
Salt and pepper

BUTTER-ROASTED HALIBUT

3 tablespoons olive or vegetable oil
3 pounds boneless halibut loin (centre of the fish)
1 cup melted butter
Grated zest of ½ lemon
Coarse sea salt
Pepper

BEURRE BLANC

1 shallot, minced
1 bay leaf
1 sprig thyme
6 black peppercorns
Juice of ½ lemon
½ cup dry vermouth
¼ cup white wine vinegar
2 tablespoons heavy cream (35% mf)
1 cup cold salted butter, cubed
Sliced chives

ASPARAGUS "NOODLES"

Prepare asparagus by snapping off woody ends of stalks. Using a vegetable peeler or mandolin slicer, cut each asparagus stalk lengthwise into ribbons. Each ribbon will be approximately 5 or 6 inches in length. Set aside.

HALIBUT

Heat a skillet over medium-high heat. Add oil and sear presentation side of halibut for 2 minutes, until slightly browned. Reduce the heat to low and add butter and lemon zest. Using a large spoon, baste halibut fillets with butter. Baste for about 8 minutes, turning fish once or twice in the pan. When fish is firm to the touch, remove from the heat and let stand for 3 minutes, presentation side up. Sprinkle with salt and pepper.

Meanwhile, drop asparagus ribbons into boiling water and cook for 2 minutes until just tender. Remove from water using tongs, place in a bowl. Toss with parsley, tarragon, thyme and about 2 tablespoons of butter from the halibut pan. Season with a little salt and pepper, if desired.

BEURRE BLANC

In a saucepan, combine shallot, bay leaf, thyme, peppercorns, lemon juice, vermouth and vinegar and bring to a boil. Reduce liquid until only ¼ cup remains. Strain into a clean saucepan, discarding shallots and herbs. Add cream and just bring back to a simmer. Begin whisking in cold butter over very low heat, 1 or 2 cubes at a time, until sauce begins to thicken. When only one cube of butter remains, remove sauce from the heat and whisk the last one in to the side of the stove. If you are using unsalted butter you may need to adjust seasoning at this stage. Do not boil the beurre blanc after the emulsion has formed or the sauce will break.

PRESENTATION

Make a mound of asparagus in the centre of a pasta bowl, as you would with linguini or spaghetti noodles. Place a piece of fish on top and then pour a couple of spoonfuls of beurre blanc over the top. Garnish with sliced chives.

Serves 6.

PAN-FRIED HADDOCK WITH
SOFT-POACHED EGG AND GREEN BEANS

· · · · · · · · · · ·

Pan-fried haddock is such a simple dish but incredibly popular both in pubs and in home kitchens. As with most seafood, the dish really begins with the choosing of the freshest fish possible. It's best to use fresh instead of frozen haddock because this dish is about tasting the sea in each bite. The sauce is the egg yolk, buttery and silky smooth when you let it douse the crunchy outer layer of the fish. Serve this with a pickle such as Green Tomato Chow Chow (page 285). This is perfect, satisfying food.

FISH

4 slices white sandwich bread
4 haddock fillets
½ cup all-purpose flour
2 large eggs, beaten and seasoned well with salt
  and pepper
¼ cup vegetable oil
½ teaspoon coarse sea salt such as fleur de sel
Fresh chives, chervil or chopped parsley

POACHED EGGS

1 tablespoon white vinegar
4 large eggs

GREEN BEANS

1 pound green beans
1 tablespoon salt
2 tablespoons butter
Pepper

FISH

Using a food processor, pulse the bread until you have fine fresh breadcrumbs. Pour into a large, shallow bowl.

Feel the fillets for any small bones along the belly line and remove them with a paring knife. Dredge each fillet in flour, dip in the egg mixture, then coat in the breadcrumbs.

Heat the vegetable oil in a large frying pan over medium-high heat. Fry the fillets until golden brown on both sides, about 6 minutes in total. Each fillet can be seasoned with a little fleur de sel before serving.

POACHED EGGS

Meanwhile, heat a deep skillet of water to a gentle simmer and add the vinegar. A thermometer would read 180°F for the perfect poaching temperature. Crack the eggs on a saucer (this prevents shards of shell from getting into the whites). Gently slide the eggs into the water. With a wooden spoon, gently roll the white of each egg over its yolk for several seconds until the eggs begin to set. Poaching will take 4 to 5 minutes. Remove from the water using a slotted spoon and drain off excess water by tapping the spoon on a kitchen towel. (Make ahead: The eggs can be shocked and held in ice-cold water until ready to serve then reheated in simmering, salted water for a minute, or they can be served immediately.)

GREEN BEANS

Meanwhile, remove the stem ends of beans. Do not cut off the elegant little "tail" on the other end, it is lovely for presentation. Bring a large pot of water to a boil and add the salt. Cook the beans for 3 minutes at a full rolling boil. While they cook, heat a large skillet and melt the butter. Remove the beans from the water when they are cooked but still firm to the bite. Toss them in the hot butter until all the water has evaporated and the beans are glazed. Season with a few grindings of pepper.

PRESENTATION

Make a small pile of green beans in the centre of a warm plate. Place a fillet of haddock on top and lay the poached egg on the fish. Garnish with fresh chives.

Serves 4.

MI'KMAQ BAKED HADDOCK FILLETS

. . . .

SALMON RIVER HOUSE COUNTRY INN,
SALMON RIVER, N.S.

It is said that pioneers learned to bake fish from the local natives who wrapped their catch in wet leaves with a combination of herbs, fruits and roots, then baked it in a fire. Adrien Blanchette, owner of the Salmon River House Country Inn, substituted foil for wet leaves.

1½ pounds haddock fillet
8 slices of apple
8 thin slices of onion
8 slices of lemon
8 slices of tomato
2 teaspoons butter
Summer savory
Salt and pepper to taste

Removing any bones from fillet, cut into 4 portions and place each on a large square of foil. Alternate slices of apple, onion, lemon and tomato on each fillet and dot with butter. Season with a pinch of summer savory, salt and pepper.

Enclose fillets in the foil, being careful to seal all edges. Bake in a 325°F oven for approximately 20 to 25 minutes, depending on the thickness of the fish. Serve by folding back the foil to form a boat that retains the juices.

Serves 4.

BAKED STUFFED WHOLE HADDOCK

. . . .

M. HELEN DECOSTE, RIVERVIEW, N.B.

In Mulgrave, N.S., 50 years ago, fish was eaten more often than meat. It was more economical to buy and a mother found many different ways to serve it, hoping the family would forget they were having "fish again." It was creamed, baked, poached, fried and made into chowders. Baked whole and stuffed, haddock was a dish everyone liked.

Whole haddock, 2 to 4 pounds, cleaned
Salt
2 cups fresh white bread cubes
3 tablespoons finely chopped onion
1 teaspoon poultry seasoning
Salt and pepper to taste
½ cup hot water (approximate)
3 tablespoons melted butter
3 or 4 strips bacon
Celery salt

Dry haddock with a cloth and sprinkle salt in the cavity. Combine the remaining ingredients except for the bacon and celery salt, adding more or less water until the mixture has a doughy rather than a crumbly texture. Spoon into the cavity. Place fish in a small roasting pan. Cover the fish with the bacon. Season with salt, pepper and celery salt. Bake at 450°F for about 20 minutes for a medium-size haddock, or until the white meat loses its transparent look.

Serves 4 to 6.

FISH CAKES

At Seawind Landing, located in a beautiful seaside location in Guysborough Country, Nova Scotia, these authentic Maritime fish cakes are served for a hearty breakfast.

1 pound salt cod
1½ cup finely diced onions
2 tablespoons butter
4 cups mashed potatoes
¼ teaspoon dried summer savory
½ teaspoon dried thyme
½ teaspoon dried parsley
1 large egg, beaten
Pepper to taste
Butter, to fry

Soak fish 8 to 10 hours in cold water, changing water 4 to 5 times. Drain well.

Boil fish until tender and flaky, 15 to 20 minutes. Drain and flake.

Sauté onions in butter until soft, set aside.

In a large bowl, combine potatoes, fish, onions, savory, thyme, parsley and egg.

Season to taste, being careful not to over salt.

Let cool and form into patties.

Pan-fry in butter or oil until golden brown.

Serves 6 to 8.

TRADITIONAL BREADED FISH CAKES

Chef Chris Sheppard who served these at his restaurant Gaffer's Bistro says that you can prepare these fish cakes ahead and freeze them. Then when unexpected company arrive, you can impress them with an instant fish cake meal.

5 ounces fresh cod
3 tablespoons butter
½ cup finely diced onions
½ cup finely diced celery
2 cups mashed potatoes
2 teaspoons salt
1 teaspoon white pepper
2 large eggs, beaten
¼ cup milk
1 cup all-purpose flour
2 cups fine dry breadcrumbs

Place cod in pan, cover with water and simmer 8 to 10 minutes over medium heat, until fish flakes easily.

In 1 tablespoon of the butter, sauté onions and celery until soft.

In large bowl, combine cod, potatoes, onion mixture, salt and pepper.

Let cool, and form into patties.

Combine eggs and milk.

Set up breading station: 3 bowls left to right, first flour, then egg mixture, then breadcrumbs. Dip cakes in flour, shake off excess, dip in egg mixture, then coat in breadcrumbs.

Pan-fry in remaining butter until golden brown on each side.

Serves 6.

FISH 'N' CHIPS

. . . .

Fish 'n' chips is easily the most common restaurant menu item in the Maritimes, if not all of Canada. This is a fun version with fennel coleslaw that you can try at home.

FISH 'N' CHIPS

1 pound fresh cod cheeks (or fillets)

½ cup all-purpose flour

1 tablespoon salt

1 teaspoon pepper

2 large eggs

3 tablespoons milk

1 cup panko or breadcrumbs

10 fingerling potatoes, about 3 inches long

8 cups canola oil

COLESLAW

1 fennel bulb, cored and thinly sliced

¼ cup julienned sweet red pepper

Grated zest and juice and of 1 lemon

2 tablespoons chopped fennel fronds

¼ cup extra-virgin olive oil

¼ teaspoon salt

¼ teaspoon pepper

Each cod cheek has a small muscle and membrane on its side that is easy to remove with your fingers. Pat cheeks dry using paper towel. To bread the cod you will require 3 bowls. In the first bowl, mix flour, 1 teaspoon of the salt and the pepper. In the second bowl, mix eggs and milk, and in the third bowl place breadcrumbs. Dredge cod cheeks in flour, then in egg mixture and finally in breadcrumbs. Set aside on a clean plate.

Slice fingerling potatoes on a mandoline or with a knife as thinly as you can. Rinse in cold water then dry as much as possible on towels.

Use a steep-sided pot with a wide mouth for deep-frying. The oil should go no more than one-fifth of the way up the sides. Heat the canola oil to 300°F, using a deep-fry thermometer. Begin with the potatoes as you will serve these cold like potato chips. Carefully drop them in the fat, keeping slices separate and fry until lightly golden. Remove from heat and place in a bowl lined with paper towel. Season with the remaining salt.

Increase the heat of the oil until the thermometer reads 360°F. Fry cod cheeks until they float and are a deep golden brown.

COLESLAW

Mix all ingredients in a bowl and refrigerate overnight.

Serves 4 to 6.

SMOKED HADDOCK FISH CAKES WITH CELERY ROOT, APPLE AND GOLDEN BEET SALAD

· · · · · · · · · · · · ·

RENEE LAVALLÉE, FIVE FISHERMEN, HALIFAX, N.S.

Renee Lavallée contributed this recipe to Craig Flinn for his cookbook Fresh Canadian Bistro. *"For me fish cakes are comforting cold-weather food, sometimes served with baked beans for a weekend supper." They make a great morning brunch with eggs over-easy and Green Tomato Chow Chow (page 285), or as a lunch or appetizer with a unique coleslaw-inspired salad. You could use any fish for a fish cake, but smoked haddock is a great choice for flavour, aroma and affordability. The white truffle oil Renee uses is available at most supermarkets and will keep for a long time in the fridge.*

FISH CAKES

1 pound smoked haddock
1 pound baby red- or yellow-fleshed potatoes
1 teaspoon sea salt
Several grindings of black pepper
Grated zest and juice of 1 lemon
3 tablespoons extra-virgin olive oil
½ cup grated Parmesan cheese
¼ cup chopped fresh tarragon
1 teaspoon white truffle oil
1 cup panko breadcrumbs
½ cup canola oil

SALAD

1 small celery root, peeled and julienned
1 firm, tart apple, peeled, cored and julienned
1 golden beet, peeled and julienned
Zest and juice of ½ lemon
1 teaspoon liquid honey
½ cup chopped flat-leaf parsley
¼ cup extra-virgin olive oil
Salt and pepper to taste

FISH CAKES

Flake smoked haddock and set aside. Steam or boil potatoes until cooked. Place still-warm potatoes in a stand mixer with paddle or with a potato masher, crush slightly, making sure not to overmash. Add flaked haddock, salt, pepper, lemon zest and juice and mix to combine. Add olive oil while mixing on slow speed or beating until mixture starts to stick together. Add Parmesan, tarragon and truffle oil, if using. Taste for seasoning and add more if you feel that it is needed.

Using an ice cream scoop, form fish mixture into balls, then pat into cakes. Dip cakes into panko crumbs. Pour canola oil into pan and place over high heat. Cook cakes one side for 1½ minutes, or until golden brown, then turn over. Fry for 1 minute and remove from oil. Place onto a baking tray and into a preheated 400°F oven to finish cooking through, about 3 to 4 minutes.

SALAD

Mix celery root, apple and beet in a bowl. In a separate bowl, mix together lemon zest and juice, honey, parsley, olive oil and seasonings. Combine with apple mixture, mix and marinate for 1 hour before serving.

Serve fish cakes with or on a large spoonful of salad.

Serves 6.

SMOKED LINE-CAUGHT HADDOCK CAKES WITH SWEET CORN AND TARTAR SAUCE

· · · · · · · · · ·

This is no ordinary fish cake and no ordinary tartar sauce. The smoky haddock and sweet corn work perfectly together and the crunchy and slightly tart condiment finish it off beautifully. There are many very good smokehouses that make a great smoked haddock, so pick some up if you can. Smoked mackerel or hot-smoked salmon make very good substitutes here.

FISH CAKES

¼ cup each minced red onion, celery and sweet red pepper
1 clove garlic, minced
1 cup fresh corn kernels
3 tablespoons butter
1 teaspoon salt
1½ pounds smoked haddock
1 medium potato, peeled, cooked and grated
½ cup fresh breadcrumbs
1 cup mayonnaise
1 teaspoon hot sauce, such as Tabasco
1 teaspoon Worcestershire sauce
2 tablespoons chopped green onion tops or chives

BREADING

3 large eggs
¼ teaspoon salt
¼ teaspoon pepper
½ cup all-purpose flour
1½ cups panko or regular dried breadcrumbs
¼ cup vegetable oil

TARTAR SAUCE

3 tablespoons minced pickled red onion or fresh red onion
2 tablespoons finely chopped capers
¼ cup diced gherkins
1 tablespoon sweet green relish
1 cup mayonnaise
¼ cup sour cream
1 teaspoon hot sauce, such as Tabasco
1 teaspoon Worcestershire sauce
Zest and juice of 1 lemon

½ teaspoon salt
¼ teaspoon pepper
2 tablespoons chopped chives (optional)

FISH CAKES

In a skillet over low heat, sweat onion, celery, red pepper, garlic and corn in butter and salt until onions are translucent. In a large mixing bowl, flake haddock into small pieces using your fingers. Add potato, breadcrumbs, sweated vegetables, mayonnaise, hot sauce, Worcestershire sauce and green onions. Mix thoroughly using your hands. Form into 5-ounce cakes and refrigerate on a tray for a minimum of 1 hour before breading.

BREADING

In a small mixing bowl, beat eggs with salt and pepper. Dredge fish cakes first in flour, then egg mixture and finally breadcrumbs. Heat vegetable oil in a nonstick frying pan and fry fish cakes over medium heat until crisp and golden, about 6 minutes per side.

TARTAR SAUCE

Combine all ingredients in a small bowl.

Store in a sealed container, refrigerated, for up to 10 days.

Serve 2 cakes with a heaping spoonful of tartar sauce and garnish with herbs or microgreens.

Serves 8 as an appetizer or 4 as an entrée.

MAINS:
EGGS, CHEESE
AND VEGETARIAN

FRESH ASPARAGUS OMELET

. . . .

SANDRA PHINNEY MACGREGOR,
EAST CANAAN, N.S.

The asparagus season is early, short and furious, and for one of the Heritage Recipe Contest finalists that time is even more intense. Sandra Phinney MacGregor grows asparagus on her farm in East Canaan, N.S., not just for family consumption, but to sell to farm markets. While the growing requires years of patience before the first crop is ready, the caring for and marketing of asparagus and other garden produce leaves Sandra little time to enjoy the taste. This recipe takes only 10 to 15 minutes altogether. Serve it as a fast, nutritious lunch or with baked ham and a salad for a brunch or dinner dish.

2 cups fresh asparagus, cut in 1-inch lengths
2 small cloves garlic, finely chopped
2 tablespoons butter, melted
3 tablespoons grated Parmesan cheese
Salt and pepper to taste
6 large eggs, beaten
Butter

Cook asparagus in a small amount of boiling water until barely tender, about 2 minutes. Drain well. Combine with garlic, butter, cheese, salt and pepper then set aside. It's ready to fill the omelets.

   Into a large buttered skillet on medium to high heat, pour half of the eggs. When they look set enough to turn over, do so and cook for 8 to 10 seconds more. (The whole procedure takes less than 1 minute.) Take half the asparagus mixture and pour down the centre of the cooked eggs. Flip one side over, cut in half and serve immediately. Repeat procedure using the remaining eggs and asparagus mixture, or use 2 frying pans to make all the servings at once.

Serves 4.

FIVE-ONION RISOTTO WITH CHARRED PEPPER COULIS

. . . .

INN ON THE LAKE, WAVERLEY, N.S.

It might take a little extra time to prepare this dish but the results are so worthwhile!

¼ cup butter
1 leek, white and pale green part only, finely chopped
1 Spanish onion, finely chopped
8 pearl onions, peeled
3 shallots, chopped
1 red onion, finely chopped
2 cloves garlic, minced
1 cup arborio rice
4 cups hot chicken stock
½ cup Parmesan cheese
Snipped chives

CHARRED PEPPER COULIS
4 sweet red peppers
1 cup chicken stock
Salt and pepper to taste

Melt butter in a large saucepan over medium heat and sauté the leek, onions, shallots and garlic until translucent. Stir in rice and cook, stirring constantly for 3 to 4 minutes. Add ¼ cup hot stock and stir until absorbed. Continue to add stock in ¼ cup amounts until rice is cooked and creamy. Gently stir in cheese.

   To serve, divide rice between 4 3-inch ring moulds and centre each on a plate. Remove moulds and spoon Charred Pepper Coulis around rice. Garnish with a sprinkling of snipped chives.

Serves 4.

CHARRED PEPPER COULIS
Grill or broil peppers until black on all sides. Immediately place in a brown paper bag until cooled.

   Peel skin from peppers, remove stalks and inner seeds. Combine peppers and stock in a saucepan and cook until tender. Purée mixture and season with salt and pepper. Keep warm.

CORN COB AND AGED CHEDDAR SOUFFLÉ

. . . .

Soufflés have a reputation as being difficult, but they are actually a lot of fun to make. Fresh corn for this recipe really makes a difference, but use frozen in a pinch. White Canadian Cheddar is delicious in this recipe, but orange Cheddar, Gruyere, Gouda or Oka are also great choices.

4 ears fresh corn
½ cup unsalted butter
¾ cup all-purpose flour
2 cups 2% milk
¼ cup minced shallots
1 clove garlic, minced
½ teaspoon salt
½ teaspoon white pepper
Pinch of nutmeg
5 large eggs, separated
1 cup shredded aged Cheddar cheese
Butter
3 tablespoons grated Parmesan cheese

Cut kernels from corn cobs with a sharp knife. Reserve the cobs. Place kernels in a food processor and purée until relatively smooth.

In a small saucepan, melt butter over medium heat and add flour. Mix well until a crumbly paste forms. Set aside to cool.

In a second saucepan, combine milk, puréed kernels, corn cobs, shallots, garlic, salt, pepper and nutmeg and bring to a boil. Simmer gently for 30 minutes; remove the cobs.

Stirring constantly, add hot liquid to cooled flour mixture. Simmer on very low heat for 15 minutes, whisking often. Refrigerate until cool. Stir in yolks and Cheddar.

Beat egg whites to stiff peaks. Fold into Cheddar mixture. Grease 6 8-ounce ramekins with butter and dust with half of the Parmesan. Fill ramekins with Cheddar mixture. Dust with remaining Parmesan and bake in a 425°F oven for 10 minutes. Reduce the temperature to 350°F and bake for 6 minutes. Serve immediately.

Serves 6.

QUICHES AU CRABE

. . . .

HOTEL PAULIN, CARAQUET, N.B.

Chef Girard Paulin is from the third generation of the family that, for over 100 years, has managed Hotel Paulin in Caraquet, N.B. In the summer, he serves mainly fish dishes and his philosophy is, "Simple, nutritious food, prepared as fresh as possible." Paulin's favourite recipe book is an old scribbler that his mother used to jot down some of her recipes in pencil. The ingredients and instructions for crab quiche are from that scribbler.

3 single 9-inch pie crusts
1 pound fresh Atlantic crabmeat
3 cups shredded Swiss cheese
6 large eggs, beaten
¾ cup chopped green onions
1½ cups light cream (20% mf)
1½ cups milk
1½ teaspoons salt
1 teaspoon grated lemon zest
1 teaspoon dry mustard
1¼ teaspoons nutmeg
Sliced mushrooms and almonds

Cover the bottom of the pie shells with the crabmeat and sprinkle with the cheese. Mix all the other ingredients and pour over the cheese and crab. Sprinkle mushrooms and almonds overtop. Bake at 325°F for 45 minutes.

Makes 3 quiches.

BAKED BROCCOLI CASSEROLE

. . . .

THE LEDGES INN, DOAKTOWN, N.B.

Innkeeper Caroline Taylor liked having a dish or two prepared in advance of dinner. This Baked Broccoli Casserole lends itself well to early preparation and may accompany a main dish in the oven.

2 bunches fresh broccoli, trimmed
3 tablespoons butter
3 tablespoons all-purpose flour
½ cup chicken stock
1 cups milk
1 cup shredded aged white Cheddar cheese
15 Ritz crackers, crushed

Separate broccoli into florets and blanch in boiling, salted water for 4 minutes. Drain and chill in ice water to stop cooking process. Thoroughly drain and place in a lightly greased casserole.

Melt butter in a saucepan and whisk in flour, stirring constantly for 2 minutes. Whisk in stock and milk until thickened and smooth. Add cheese and stir until melted.

Pour sauce over broccoli and sprinkle cracker crumbs overtop. Bake in 350°F oven until bubbly and broccoli is tender, about 20 to 30 minutes.

Serves 6 to 8.

ROOT VEGETABLE TART

. . . .

Unlike a gratin, which is generally saucy and needs to be scooped out of a deep dish casserole, this tart is firm enough to cut and serve like a square or pie. It is particularly good with turkey, chicken or pork loin, as the sage and cranberries are an obvious match.

1 small turnip (about 1¼ pounds)

2 sweet potatoes

1 medium celery root

4 parsnips

4 carrots

½ pound butter

2 cups cranberries

1 cup minced onion

¼ cup chicken, beef or vegetable stock

¼ cup chopped fresh sage

2 tablespoons salt

Black pepper

Peel all the vegetables and slice into large rounds or ovals about ⅛-inch thick. (A mandoline works best, but a sharp knife is effective.) Line a casserole dish with a piece of parchment paper cut to fit the bottom exactly. Rub paper liberally with some of the butter. Layer vegetables, beginning with the largest pieces of sweet potato. This will be the top of the tart when it is flipped out of the pan and the orange colour will be visible. Alternate types of vegetables, but in 2 of the layers add cranberries and minced onions along with a drizzle of stock. Season each layer with a little fresh sage, salt and pepper. Place a few dollops of the butter in with the seasonings. The last layer of the tart, which will be the eventual bottom, should be turnip. These slices are larger and will give the tart stability when plated.

Set another piece of buttered parchment cut to fit and buttered side down on the top. Using another casserole dish, slightly smaller than the first, weight the vegetables and place in a 350°F oven for 1 hour. At this point remove the second casserole dish and parchment and return to the oven for another hour. When a knife goes through the centre with ease, remove from the oven and allow to cool. Unmould the tart carefully onto a cutting board and slice into pieces. (Reheat pieces in the oven or microwave before serving, if desired.)

Serves 6, with leftovers.

FRESH ATLANTIC LOBSTER SOUFFLÉ

• • • • • • • • • • •

ACTON'S GRILL AND CAFÉ, WOLFVILLE, N.S.

At Acton's, this soufflé is usually accompanied by assorted greens dressed with a fresh herb vinaigrette. Always serve a soufflé straight from the oven before it collapses.

16 cups water

1 tablespoon salt

1 medium onion, peeled and halved

1 medium carrot, peeled and diced

2 stalks celery

2 small bay leaves

6 whole allspice

4 whole cloves

2 or 3 tomatoes, cut in chunks

1 tablespoon sweet paprika

1½ pound lobster

2 tablespoons unsalted butter

2 tablespoons all-purpose flour

¼ cup heavy cream (35% mf), warmed

1 tablespoon brandy

¼ teaspoon lemon juice

6 large eggs, separated

Salt and white pepper to taste

Pour water into large stockpot. Add salt, onion, carrot, celery, bay leaves, allspice, cloves, tomatoes and paprika. Bring to a boil, then reduce heat and simmer 15 minutes. Return to full boil, add lobster, cover and cook 15 minutes. Remove lobster from pot and set aside to cool.

Twist the tail and claws from the lobster body. Remove meat from shells, cut into small chunks and reserve. Split body shell in half, place in stockpot and return to a boil. Reduce heat and simmer 1 hour. Strain, discarding solids and reserving stock.

In a heavy saucepan, melt butter and whisk in flour. Cook over low heat for 1 minute, then add 1 cup of the reserved lobster stock and cream. Bring to a boil, whisking constantly until sauce thickens. Remove from heat. Whisk in brandy, lemon juice and egg yolks. Add lobster meat, season with salt and pepper and set aside.

Butter and lightly flour a 2-quart soufflé dish. Beat egg whites until stiff, but not dry, then gently fold into the lobster mixture. Pour into soufflé dish and bake at 400°F for 15 to 20 minutes, until puffed and browned. Serve immediately.

Serves 4.

KING CRAB AND MASCARPONE RISOTTO

. . . .

In his cookbook Fresh & Local *Craig Flinn recounts the conception of this recipe: "Every now and then a group of friends and I gather for a full Sunday of cooking. Usually we have hobby chefs coming through my good friend John Corney's kitchen all day long, drinking wine and tasting a new dish. John is very particular about his food and is very hard to please. One day we made more than 13 dishes, and even John was impressed with this winner of a risotto. We used fresh crab just caught near Cheticamp, Cape Breton."*

2 shallots, minced
1 clove garlic, minced
¼ fennel bulb, cored and minced
¼ cup butter
½ teaspoon pepper
1 cup Italian arborio rice
3 cups low-sodium chicken stock (approximate)
1 cup clam juice
½ cup dry vermouth
2 cups cooked and chunked king crab meat
1 cup mascarpone cheese
Fresh chervil leaves, for garnish

Sauté shallots, garlic and fennel in butter over medium heat for 10 minutes until soft and translucent. Add pepper and rice and stir well to coat in fat. Cook for 3 minutes until rice looks translucent. In a separate pot, bring chicken stock, clam juice and vermouth to a boil. Keep hot. Add hot stock mixture one ladle at a time to the rice mixture, stirring until liquid is fully incorporated. Repeat adding liquid, cooking and stirring. The rice will take about 15 to 18 minutes to cook until tender but firm to the bite. Add crab and mascarpone cheese and just heat through. For a soupier risotto add another ½ cup of hot chicken stock at the end. Adjust salt to taste as many commercially available stocks and clam-juice products have a high sodium content.

Serve in soup bowls, garnished with a few leaves of fresh chervil.

Serves 6.

GARDENER'S PIE

· · · · · · · · · · · · ·

This is a vegetarian version of shepherd's pie. It has a sweet potato crust, along with corn and a hot pepper spice for a little south-of-the-border feel. One essential ingredient here is the mushrooms. They add a rich, earthy, almost meaty taste and consistency to the filling. Serve with a salad.

SWEET POTATO CRUST

3 large sweet potatoes
2 tablespoons butter (use extra-virgin olive oil for vegan version)
Salt and pepper to taste

FILLING

4 portobello mushroom caps
10 button mushrooms
2 tablespoons extra-virgin olive oil
1 medium onion, minced
2 cloves garlic, minced
1 stalk celery, minced
1 carrot, peeled and finely chopped
1 teaspoon smoked paprika
1 fresh hot red chili, seeds removed and finely chopped
1 cup cooked green or brown lentils
1 cup corn kernels
½ cup fresh peas
½ cup vegetable stock
Salt and pepper to taste
1 tomato, chopped
Assorted fresh herbs, to taste

CRUST

Bake the sweet potatoes in a 350°F oven for 1 hour, until the insides are easily pierced with a knife. Cut them in half and scoop the flesh into a bowl. Mash well with a potato masher, adding the butter and seasonings. Cover and keep warm until ready to assemble the pie.

FILLING

With a spoon, scrape the gills out of the portobello. Discard the gills and break the caps into smaller pieces with your fingers. Add to a food processor with the button mushrooms and pulse until the mushrooms are finely chopped. Place the mushrooms into a large sauté pan and cook in the oil until they release their water and turn dark brown in colour. This should take about 10 minutes. Add the onion, garlic, celery and carrot and cook until the vegetables are soft, about 10 minutes. Add the paprika, fresh chili, lentils, corn, peas and stock. Boil, stirring often, until the liquid evaporates. Season with salt and pepper and add the chopped tomato and any fresh herbs you have around (such as parsley, basil, thyme or chives).

Spoon the filling into a casserole or lasagna dish; smooth top. Cover with an even layer of the sweet potato mixture. (Choose a dish that will allow the filling and the sweet potato crust to fill the pan, so a nice crust will develop.) Bake at 350°F about 30 minutes or until hot through and crusty on top. Let the casserole to rest for 15 minutes before serving.

Serves 6.

HARVEST VEGETABLE POLENTA TORTE

. . . .

INN ON THE LAKE, WAVERLEY, N.S.

Polenta is a hearty staple of northern Italian cuisine. At Inn on the Lake, the chef enriched his polenta with autumn vegetables, layered it with tortillas and served it as a luncheon dish or a side dish at dinner.

1 cup diced sweet green peppers
2 tablespoons extra-virgin olive oil
1 cup diced cooked beets
½ cup cooked corn kernels
½ cup diced cooked carrots
1 cup whole milk
1 cup chicken stock
2 cloves garlic, minced
3 sprigs fresh thyme
½ cup cornmeal
½ teaspoon salt
¼ teaspoon white pepper
2 large eggs
½ cup freshly grated Parmesan cheese
4 9-inch round corn tortillas or flatbreads
½ cup shredded Monterey Jack cheese
Guacamole, salsa and sour cream, for garnish

Sauté green peppers in oil over medium heat until tender. Set aside in a medium bowl. In separate medium bowls, set aside beets, corn and carrots.

In a large saucepan, bring milk, stock, garlic and thyme to a simmer. Turn off heat, steep for 20 minutes and remove thyme. Return to a boil. Slowly add cornmeal in a steady thin stream, stirring constantly, until cornmeal is incorporated, about 5 minutes. Stir in salt and pepper. Reduce heat to very low, cover saucepan and cook very gently 10 minutes, stirring occasionally.

Remove polenta to a mixing bowl and beat in the eggs, one at a time. Stir in the Parmesan cheese. Divide the polenta evenly among the 3 bowls of vegetables and mix well. Keep each bowl covered.

To assemble the torte, lightly grease a 9-inch springform cake pan with butter or oil. Place a tortilla in the bottom of the pan and spread with the green pepper polenta. Top this layer with another tortilla and spread with the beet polenta. Top with another tortilla and spread with the corn and carrot polenta. Top with the last tortilla. Sprinkle with Monterey Jack cheese. Cover pan with foil and bake at 350°F for 45 to 55 minutes, removing the foil for the last 15 minutes to allow the cheese to brown slightly. Remove from the oven and let stand 15 minutes before removing from the pan. Serve in wedges garnished with guacamole, salsa and sour cream.

Serves 6 to 8.

EGGPLANT AND CHÈVRE GRATIN

. . . .

Accompany this flavourful luncheon dish with thick slices of crusty bread. The recipe is easily converted to a first-course hot appetizer by reducing the size of the portions.

¼ cup balsamic vinegar
¼ cup raspberry vinegar
3 tablespoons granulated sugar
12 thin slices pancetta* or bacon
8 slices eggplant, 3 inches in diameter and
  ½ inch thick
8 slices ripe tomato, 3 inches in diameter and
  ½ inch thick
6 ounces chèvre (soft goat cheese), thinly sliced
Pepper
4 sprigs fresh herbs of choice

In a small saucepan, heat vinegars and sugar over medium-high heat, stirring frequently until reduced to a syrup, about 8 minutes. Reserve and keep warm.

In a skillet over medium heat, fry pancetta until crisp then drain on paper towels. Sauté eggplant in bacon fat until soft and golden brown. To assemble, layer on a baking sheet: 2 slices of eggplant, topped with 3 slices of pancetta and 2 slices of tomato. Bake in a 350°F oven for 5 to 7 minutes, until warmed through. Add cheese and place under the broiler until hot and cheese is soft. Transfer to serving plates, drizzle vinegar reduction over and around gratins. Season with freshly ground pepper and garnish with herb sprigs.

Serves 4.

* Pancetta is a salt-cured unsmoked Italian bacon found in the deli section of most grocery stores. If unavailable, you may substitute regular smoked bacon, but the taste will be slightly different.

GRILLED VEGETABLE
PITA POCKETS

· · · · · · · · · · · ·

Keep in mind that it is difficult to give exact cooking times for grilling foods. Heat will vary according to the size and type of grill, the fuel used and weather conditions. Be prepared to stand over the grill watching the food as it cooks.

⅓ cup mayonnaise

⅓ cup plain Balkan-style yogurt

2 teaspoons grated onion

1 tablespoon chopped fresh dill or ¾ teaspoon dried dill weed

1 medium eggplant, sliced lengthwise ½ inch thick

2 small zucchini squash, sliced lengthwise ½ inch thick

1 sweet red pepper

1 sweet yellow pepper

¼ cup herb- or citrus-infused olive oil or extra-virgin olive oil

Pepper

4 pita breads, cut in half and separated

4 ounces feta cheese, crumbled

In a small bowl, combine mayonnaise, yogurt, onion and dill. Cover and refrigerate.

Brush vegetables with olive oil and set in a grilling basket. Grill over medium heat, turning vegetables occasionally until cooked, about 15 minutes. Eggplant and zucchini will be browned; red and yellow peppers charred. Cool vegetables to room temperature. Cut eggplant and zucchini in broad strips. Peel charred skin from peppers, core and remove seeds, then slice in broad strips. Season vegetables with freshly ground pepper to taste.

Fill pita halves with grilled vegetables. Top with dilled mayonnaise and crumbled feta cheese.

Makes 8 half sandwiches, 4 servings.

GRILLED PORTOBELLO MUSHROOMS WITH MIXED PEPPERS AND CASSIS

ARBOR VIEW INN, LUNENBURG, N.S.

Full of flavour, portobello mushrooms are large and meaty. Cassis is a black currant liqueur.

4 large portobello mushrooms
4 sprigs fresh thyme
½ cup extra-virgin olive oil (approximate)
¼ cup balsamic vinegar (approximate)
Coarse sea salt
Pepper
2 large sweet red peppers
2 large sweet yellow peppers
1 to 2 tablespoons Cassis liqueur

Remove mushroom stems. Clean mushroom caps by brushing lightly. Cut each cap into 3 and arrange in a flat-bottomed baking dish. Tear off the thyme leaves and sprinkle over the mushrooms. Drizzle with enough of the oil and vinegar to lightly coat. Season with salt and pepper. Let stand for 2 hours, turning once.

Quarter red and yellow peppers and remove core and seeds. Carefully shave about half of the inner flesh of the pepper, leaving a thin section of the skin and some flesh.

Slice into a fine julienne. In a small bowl, whisk together enough of the oil and vinegar to coat the peppers. Season with pepper and salt and marinate at least ½ hour.

Heat grill to high setting. Grill mushrooms, turning until cooked, approximately 2 minutes per side.

Spoon pepper mixture into centre of plate and arrange mushrooms over peppers. Serve warm, garnished with additional thyme sprigs and a drizzle of Cassis.

Serves 4 to 6.

PORTOBELLO VEGGIE BURGERS

· · · · · · · · · · ·

Anyone who prefers a vegetarian entrée will find these portobello-mushroom burgers absolutely delicious. Even guests who are beef-burger aficionados won't be able to resist their aroma and flavour.

8 portobello mushrooms, 4- to 5-inch diameter
½ cup extra-virgin olive oil
⅓ cup balsamic vinegar
2 tablespoons fresh thyme leaves, chopped
1 tablespoon minced garlic
8 large burger buns
Toppings: lettuce, tomato slices, avocado slices, green or red pepper slices, mozzarella or Swiss cheese slices, crumbled blue cheese or hummus

Remove stems from mushrooms and carefully wipe the caps with a damp cloth. In a bowl, whisk together oil, vinegar, thyme and garlic. Place mushroom caps in a single layer in large freezer bag. Pour vinegar mixture into the bag, press air out and seal. Turn the bag to distribute marinade over mushrooms and marinate at room temperature for 2 hours.

Remove mushrooms from bag and grill 6 to 8 minutes on greased grill over medium heat, turning once, until mushrooms are cooked. Serve on toasted buns with condiments of choice.

Makes 8.

VEGETABLES AND SIDES

ASPARAGUS WITH ALMONDS

· · · · · · · · · · · · · ·

CATHERINE MCKINNON'S SPOT O'TEA
RESTAURANT, STANLEY BRIDGE, P.E.I.

Choose asparagus spears that have tightly furled tips, and are even in size and colour. Snap off the woody ends and carefully peel away any tough skin with a vegetable peeler.

1 pound asparagus
Salt and pepper to taste
1½ tablespoons slivered almonds, toasted*
2 tablespoons butter

Prepare tender young asparagus as directed above. Place in a large frying pan and pour in boiling water to just cover the vegetables. Add salt. Cover and simmer until barely tender, about 4 minutes. Drain, season with salt and pepper and serve dotted with butter and sprinkled with almonds.

Serves 4.

* To toast almonds, spread almond slivers on a baking sheet and bake at 350°F in toaster oven, watching closely, until light brown, about 4 to 5 minutes.

BEETS DIJONNAISE

· · · · · · · · · · · · · ·

HALLIBURTON HOUSE INN, HALIFAX, N.S.

This is guaranteed to make beet lovers out of the most jaded palate. Try it and you'll agree with his prediction.

½ cup heavy cream (35% mf)
1 heaping teaspoon Dijon mustard
2 cups sliced or halved cooked beets

Mix cream and mustard until well blended, in a medium saucepan. Add beets. Simmer until cream is reduced and sauce has thickened and clings to the beets, about 8 minutes.

Serves 4.

STEAMED CARROTS WITH DILL SAUCE

. . . .

Choose straight carrots of equal size. If fresh dill is not available, substitute ½ teaspoon dried dill.

1½ pounds fresh carrots, trimmed and peeled
3 tablespoons butter
2 teaspoons chopped fresh dill
1½ tablespoons heavy cream (35% mf)
Salt and pepper to taste

Slice carrots into uniform thickness and steam until crisp-tender, about 5 minutes. Melt butter in a saucepan and sauté carrots for 1 minute, tossing to coat. Stir in dill and cream and heat through, about 2 minutes. Season with salt and pepper.

Serves 4.

BRAISED RED CABBAGE WITH APPLES AND ONION

. . . .

DUNCREIGAN COUNTRY INN, MABOU, N.S

Colourful in its presentation, this braised cabbage dish is an excellent accompaniment to roasted pork or turkey.

1 large onion, thinly sliced
1 tablespoon vegetable oil
1 small red cabbage, quartered, cored and very thinly sliced
½ cup chicken stock
2 teaspoons balsamic vinegar
2 firm red cooking apples
2 tablespoons cream sherry
¼ cup pure maple syrup

In a skillet over low heat, sauté sliced onion in oil, stirring frequently until caramelized, about 30 minutes. Set aside.

In a large saucepan over low heat, simmer cabbage in chicken broth and vinegar until tender, about 45 to 50 minutes, stirring occasionally. Core apples and cut, unpeeled, into wedges. Spread onions over cabbage and top with apple wedges. Drizzle with sherry and maple syrup and cook, covered, 15 minutes. To serve, carefully ladle with a slotted spoon onto plates, without disturbing the layers.

Serves 4 to 6.

GRILLED CORN ON THE COB

. . . .

This recipe, with its wonderful smoky flavour, is a summer favourite. To ensure sweet tender corn, cook it as soon after picking as possible. Look for ears of corn with a damp green end, moist silk and plump uniform rows of kernels.

12 ears corn (or more, depending upon appetite level
  of guests)
Butter
Salt and pepper

From each ear of corn, remove all but the last few pale-coloured layers of husk. Without breaking, gently peel back the remaining husk and remove the silk. Rinse the corn and pull the husks back up over the ears. Soak the ears in cold water for 15 minutes.

Shake excess water from ears and grill over medium-high, about 6 inches above the flame. Cook for 15 to 20 minutes, turning frequently to avoid burning the husks. Serve corn with butter, salt and pepper.

Serves 6.

FRESH STEAMED FIDDLEHEADS

. . . .

THE PINES RESORT HOTEL, DIGBY, N.S.

Fiddleheads, the furled fronds of the ostrich fern, are one of the first treats of spring. They are harvested in the wild from the banks of rivers and streams. Raw fiddleheads contain a natural toxin that is destroyed by heat so they should be cooked about 10 minutes before being eaten. Fiddleheads are a good source of potassium and are low in calories and sodium.

1½ pounds fresh fiddleheads
1½ teaspoons fresh lemon juice
I teasoon lemon zest

Remove brown paper-like chaff from fiddleheads. Rinse fiddleheads well and trim ends to no longer than 1 inch. Place in a vegetable steamer over boiling water, being careful that the steamer does not touch the water. Cover and steam fiddleheads for 10 to 15 minutes, or until tender-crisp.

Drain and place in a serving dish. Drizzle with lemon juice. Sprinkle with lemon zest.

Serves 6.

BAKED LEEKS

. . . .

This mild-flavoured member of the onion family is a regular in soups, stews and sauces. The leeks in this recipe are a vegetable side dish that is so good guests might be tempted to take more than their share.

3 medium leeks, 1 to 1½-inch diameter
¼ cup water
1 tablespoon butter
¼ cup freshly grated Parmesan cheese
Pepper, to taste

Remove outer leaves from leeks; trim rootlets and cut tops 1 to 2 inches into the green area. Cut leeks in half from top to bottom and wash thoroughly to remove all soil trapped between the layers. Pat dry. Slice leeks from top to bottom into very thin lengths and place in a microwavable ovenproof dish.

Pour water over leeks, cover and microwave on high for 3 minutes. Drain, dot with butter and sprinkle with Parmesan cheese and pepperCover dish and bake in 350°F oven 20 to 25 minutes until tender. Uncover during last 10 minutes to brown.

Serves 6.

BAKED SWEET ONIONS

. . . .

This is a glamorous way to showcase the often taken-for-granted onion. The recipe works best with large sweet onions such as Spanish, Vidalia, Walla Walla or Mayan.

2 to 3 large sweet onions
Sprigs of fresh herbs (any combination of thyme,
  rosemary, oregano, basil)
½ teaspoon salt
½ teaspoon pepper
3 tablespoons balsamic vinegar
1½ tablespoons water
2 tablespoons extra-virgin olive oil
2 tablespoons brown sugar

Cut off onion tops, peel skin but leave root end intact. Slice onions into wedges, being careful not to cut through the root end. Place onions in baking dish and gently fan out wedges while keeping the root ends intact. Stuff herb sprigs into the wedges and season with salt and pepper. Pour vinegar, water and oil over onions. Cover and bake in 400°F oven 40 minutes, basting once or twice. Remove cover and sprinkle onions with brown sugar. Bake, basting a few times until onions have spread like flower petals, and are soft and browned, about 15 to 20 minutes.

Serves 4 to 6.

FRESH MINTED PEAS

. . . .

This simple-to-prepare recipe combines fresh garden peas and mint in a dish filled with fresh flavour and aroma. It makes a great accompaniment to all summertime seafood and meat entrées but is especially suited to fresh lamb.

3 cups shelled fresh peas
¼ cup unsalted butter
2 tablespoons chopped fresh mint
Pinch of granulated sugar
Salt and ground white pepper to taste

In saucepan of boiling water, lightly cook peas until still firm, about 3 to 4 minutes. Drain peas in colander and chill in cold water to stop cooking then reserve.

In large skillet over medium heat, melt butter. Add peas, mint, sugar and salt and pepper to taste. Sauté until peas are heated and serve immediately.

Serves 6.

ROASTED ROSEMARY POTATOES

. . . .

INN ON THE LAKE, WAVERLEY, N.S.

Crispy, hot red-skinned potatoes with flavour of rosemary and olive oil make a perfect complement to Cedar-Planked Salmon (page 99).

½ cup extra-virgin olive oil
2 tablespoons fresh rosemary leaves, finely chopped
½ teaspoon each salt and pepper
2 pounds small new red potatoes

In a bowl, whisk together oil, rosemary, salt and pepper. Add potatoes and toss to coat.

Place potatoes in a single layer in a roasting pan and bake in a 375°F oven, stirring occasionally, until crispy on the outside and fork-tender inside, about 40 to 45 minutes.

Serves 6.

ROASTED GARLIC, STILTON AND POTATO PAVÉ

GABRIEAU'S BISTRO, ANTIGONISH, N.S.

Potato Pavé is prepared in advance and served in squares. Boil your potatoes up to a day ahead and chill thoroughly before grating.

1½ pounds potatoes
¾ cup blend cream (10% mf)
1 large egg
1 tablespoon roasted garlic*
3½ ounces Stilton or Gorgonzola cheese, cubed
¼ cup grated Parmesan cheese
Pinch of rosemary
Pinch of nutmeg

Boil the potatoes in salted water. Cool and peel the potatoes then grate them into a greased 9-inch square baking dish. Mix remaining ingredients in a blender and pour over the potatoes. Mix together. Bake in a 325°F oven for about 1 hour or until firm and light brown on top.

Serves 6.

* *For a quick method of roasting garlic, steam whole garlic bulbs until tender, about 10 minutes. Toss in extra-virgin olive oil and bake in a toaster oven or regular oven at 400°F until golden brown, about 30 minutes. Squeeze soft garlic from the bulb with your fingers.*

NEW BRUNSWICK POTATO CAKE

THE DUFFERIN INN AND SAN MARTELLO DINING ROOM, SAINT JOHN, N.B.

Easily made ahead, this Potato Cake is delicious served with beef or pork entrées. Saint Marie goat cheese and other chèvres have a mild flavour and similar in texture to cream cheese.

1¼ pounds Yukon Gold potatoes, peeled and thinly sliced
1 leek, white part only, washed and sliced
⅓ pound Saint Marie goat cheese or ¾ cup heavy cream (35% mf)
3 large eggs
Salt and pepper to taste
1 sprig fresh rosemary

PASTRY
¾ cup all-purpose flour
¼ teaspoon salt
⅓ cup unsalted butter
2 tablespoons cold water
1 small egg or 1 large egg yolk

PASTRY
Combine flour and salt in a bowl. Cut in butter until crumbly. In a separate bowl, whisk together water and egg. Drizzle over flour mixture, stirring to combine. Press into disc, wrap and refrigerate 1 hour. Roll out on a floured surface large enough to line a greased 8-inch pie plate. Crimp edge and set aside.

Meanwhile, cook potatoes covered in boiling, salted water for 4 minutes. Add leeks and cook 1 minute. Drain and cool.

Layer potatoes and leeks in pie shell. Cream goat cheese and add eggs, 1 at a time. Season with salt and pepper. Pour over potatoes, being sure to cover completely. Sprinkle with rosemary and bake at 375°F for 50 minutes or until vegetables are soft and golden brown.

Serves 6 to 8.

SWISS PAN POTATO GRATIN

• • • • • • • • • • • • •

This dish is a real treat on buffets or as a pot-luck supper contribution. It's a little addictive, so beware.

½ cup butter
¼ cup extra-virgin olive oil
6 cups sliced onions, about ⅛ inch thick
1 stalk celery, minced
4 cloves garlic, minced
2 teaspoons salt
2 teaspoons pepper
¼ cup all-purpose flour
1 cup chicken or vegetable stock
2 cups milk
¼ cup heavy cream (35% mf)
1 cup shredded Gruyere cheese
1 cup shredded smoked Applewood Cheddar
3 pounds Yukon Gold potatoes, diced, skins on
1 cup breadcrumbs

In a large saucepan, heat ¼ cup of the butter and oil. Add onions, celery, garlic, salt and pepper. Sauté on high heat for 5 minutes then reduce heat to low for the rest of the cooking time. Stir often with a wooden spoon, scraping the caramelized onion bits from the bottom of the pan. The onions should be sweet and sticky and not look wet.

Add the flour to onions, tossing to coat. Add stock, milk and cream, stirring well. Simmer for 10 minutes on low. Add the cheeses. Arrange the potatoes in a casserole dish or large baking pan. Add the onion mixture and stir to combine.

In a small skillet, heat remaining butter and toast breadcrumbs for a few minutes. Sprinkle over potato mixture and bake in a 350°F oven for 40 minutes.

Serves 6 to 8.

SMOKED BACON, OKA CHEESE AND SWEET POTATO GRATIN

• • • • • • • • • • • • •

As Craig Flinn says in his introduction to this recipe in his cookbook Fresh & Local, *"I make this for my mother every Christmas. I never follow a recipe so this one I tested recently and it worked very well, especially with the fantastic Oka cheese. Its flavour is much like a Swiss Alpenzeller or Gruyere: pleasingly nutty and full of robust earthy aroma."*

1 cup diced onion
2 cloves garlic
6 slices smoky bacon, minced
1 tablespoon extra-virgin olive oil
1 cup chicken stock
½ cup heavy cream (35% mf)
2 pounds peeled sweet potato, in lengthwise slices, ⅛ inch thick
1½ cups Oka cheese, shredded
¼ cup butter
1 cup breadcrumbs

In a saucepan, sauté onion, garlic and bacon in oil until onions are slightly browned.

In a separate pot, bring chicken stock and cream to a boil. Set aside.

Meanwhile, grease a casserole dish with butter or oil and layer with sweet potatoes. After each layer sprinkle some bacon and onion mixture and a little cheese. Moisten each layer of potatoes with 2 tablespoons of the stock and cream. Repeat layering until potatoes are about ½ inch from top. In a separate frying pan, melt butter and combine with breadcrumbs. Sprinkle over potatoes.

Bake in a 350°F oven for about 1 hour. Do not cover. If breadcrumbs become too dark, lower the heat to 300°F and cook until a knife is easily inserted through the sweet potatoes.

Serves 4.

THE LAST WORD IN LATKES

. . . .

JUBILEE COTTAGE COUNTRY INN, WALLACE, N.S.

3 large baking potatoes, peeled
1 large onion, grated
1 large egg, beaten
Salt and pepper to taste
2 tablespoons all-purpose flour
½ teaspoon baking powder
Vegetable oil, for frying

For best results, grate potatoes into very cold water, then drain and squeeze out all excess liquid. Drain liquid from onion. In a large bowl, mix together the potato, onion, egg, salt, pepper, flour and baking powder.

Heat a film of oil in a large, heavy nonstick skillet over medium-high heat. Drop 2 heaping tablespoons of potato mixture into the skillet and flatten with a spoon. Fry until golden brown, approximately 4 minutes per side. Drain on paper towel and keep warm.

Makes 12 latkes.

TATTIES AND NEEPS (POTATOES AND TURNIPS)

. . . .

DUNCREIGAN COUNTRY INN, MABOU, N.S.

Tatties and Neeps are a wonderful addition to a roast or meat dish. You can prepare the dish early in the day and reheat at serving time. Variations of this traditional Mabou recipe include using carrots in place of turnips or adding cheese.

1 small turnip, peeled and cubed
1 medium onion, diced
4 large potatoes, peeled and quartered
¼ cup butter
Salt and pepper to taste

Boil turnip and onion in a small saucepan until tender. Drain, reserving cooking liquid. Boil potatoes in a separate saucepan until tender. Drain, then dry potatoes over low heat, breaking up with a fork to allow steam to escape. Mash potatoes and gradually add butter and 1 teaspoon of cooking water to make a stiff mashed potato. Season with salt and pepper and cool slightly.

Place reserved turnip and onion in a food processor and purée. Mash into potatoes and place in a piping bag with a large star tip. Pipe onto a greased cookie sheet. Chill uncovered, until firm.

Bake at 350°F for about 20 minutes.

Serves 6 to 8.

APPLE AND RUTABAGA CASSEROLE

BLOMIDON INN, WOLFVILLE, N.S.

Donna Laceby from Blomidon Inn shared this recipe a number of years ago. It is a great accompaniment for all roasted meat entrées and has become a family favourite. Please note that what some Canadians call turnips are in fact rutabagas. While rutabagas and turnips are from the same family, rutabagas are large with yellowish flesh and turnips are smaller and have white flesh. They are interchangeable in this recipe.

1 large rutabaga, 2½ to 3 pounds
1 teaspoon granulated sugar
1 cup water
2 tart apples, cored and sliced
¼ cup heavy cream (35% mf)
2 tablespoons butter

Peel and cube the rutabaga. Cook covered in boiling salted water until tender, drain and mash. Meanwhile, in a skillet, heat sugar and water and poach apple slices until barely soft. Remove apples with a slotted spoon.

Layer mashed turnip and apples in a small casserole. Top with cream and dot with butter. Bake at 350°F for 30 minutes.

Serves 4 to 6.

CHIARD

MONIQUE AUCOIN, INVERNESS COUNTY, N.S.

Chiard is a simple but delicious potato dish, prepared by Acadian grandmothers with the resources of the area: salted pork fat, potatoes, onions and salted chives, which give it a unique flavour. Chiard remains a popular dish with the younger generations of Cheticamp Acadians. Serve immediately by itself or with cold meats, vegetables or pickled beets.

½ cup salted pork fat, in ½-inch cubes, freshened (soaked in cold water)
1 small onion, chopped
6 medium potatoes, peeled, thinly sliced
2 tablespoons salted chives, chopped
1½ cups water
½ cup green beans
½ cup thinly sliced carrots
Salt and pepper to taste

Fry pork fat until golden. Add onion and sauté until soft, but not brown. Add potatoes and coat with fat. Add chives, water, beans, carrots (if using), salt and pepper. Simmer over medium heat for 15 to 20 minutes, until potatoes are tender.

Serves 4 to 6.

SALTED CHIVES OR HERBES SALÉES

Herbes Salées (herbs preserved with salt) are a staple in Acadian kitchens.

Wash and thoroughly dry herbs, choosing from parsley, thyme, chives, summer savory or chervil. Some cooks add minced carrot, celery and leeks to the mix as well.

Chop herbs finely and place in a large bowl. For each 6 cups chopped herbs, add ¼ to ⅓ cup coarse pickling salt. Toss well. Spoon into a clean jar. Put the top on and refrigerate for about 2 weeks. Turn the jar periodically. Drain off accumulated liquid and repack in sterilized jars.

The Herbes Salées are ready to use, or to refrigerate to enjoy later.

TURNIP SURPRISE

GLORIA LANGLANDS, HALIFAX, N.S.

Food writer, broadcaster and consultant Gloria Langlands was brought up in Moncton, N.B., and though not of French origin, remembers her grandmother and mother making Acadian dishes. Root vegetables were plentiful on Acadian farms. Today's guests will never believe the turnip can be elevated to such culinary heights.

4 small to medium turnips, peeled, sliced and cut in
  strips
1¾ cups soft breadcrumbs
⅓ cup butter
1 cup applesauce, or 2 large apples, finely chopped
4 teaspoons granulated sugar
Salt to taste
½ teaspoon white pepper
2 large eggs, beaten

Cook the turnip covered in boiling salted water until tender. Drain and mash. Toss the breadcrumbs with the butter; reserve ½ cup. Set aside. Stir remaining breadcrumbs into the turnips. Add applesauce, sugar, salt and pepper, and mix well. Beat in the eggs. Pour into a buttered 2-quart casserole and top with reserved breadcrumbs. Bake uncovered at 350°F for 30 minutes.

Serves 8 or more, depending on size of turnips.

OVEN-ROASTED PLUM TOMATOES

THE BLOMIDON INN, WOLFVILLE, N.S.

Fresh from the inn's gardens, these succulent slow-roasted tomatoes add punch to pasta dishes, salads or as an accompaniment to wild game and other meats. They are so good you might just want to pop them in your mouth for a quick, flavourful snack.

2 tablespoons minced garlic
2 teaspoons chopped fresh thyme
1 tablespoon chopped fresh basil
2 teaspoons chopped fresh oregano
3 tablespoons balsamic vinegar
2 tablespoons extra-virgin olive oil
12 Roma plum tomatoes, cut in wedges

In a bowl, mix together all ingredients except tomatoes until blended. Add tomatoes and toss to coat.

  Line a rimmed baking sheet with foil or parchment paper. Arrange tomatoes in a single layer on foil and bake at 275°F for 2 hours, or until tomatoes have lost their moisture.

Makes 1½ cups.

AUTUMN SQUASH CASSEROLE

. . . .

SEAWIND LANDING COUNTRY INN,
CHARLOS COVE, N.S.

*Moist and sweet butternut squash works well for this dish, but other winter squash
such as acorn, buttercup or hubbard are also good. Select squash that are heavy for
their size with deep-coloured skin that is free of blemishes.*

5 cups peeled cubed butternut squash (2 medium)

⅔ cup granulated sugar

½ cup butter

1 large egg

1 teaspoon vanilla extract

¼ cup milk

Pinch of nutmeg

¼ cup packed brown sugar

¼ cup all-purpose flour

½ cup chopped pecans or walnuts

Pinch of cinnamon

Boil squash until soft. Drain thoroughly and mash with sugar and ½ cup of the butter. In a bowl, beat the egg, vanilla, milk and nutmeg. Mix into the squash and pour into a greased 1-quart casserole dish.

Melt remaining butter. Mix with the sugar, flour, nuts and cinnamon. Sprinkle over squash mixture and bake at 350°F for 30 minutes or until topping is golden brown.

Serves 4 to 6.

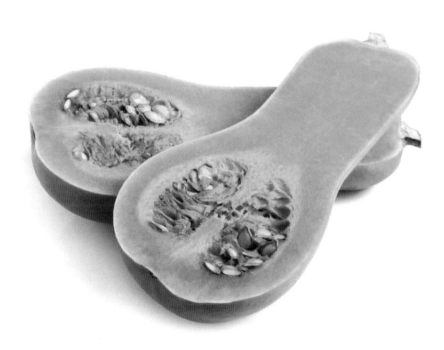

GRAPE TOMATO CLAFOUTI

· · · · · · · · · · · · ·

Grape tomatoes turn a traditional sweet cherry clafouti into a savoury luncheon treat. The concentrated sweet flavour of these tiny tomatoes is the perfect complement to the clafouti's fresh herbs and cheese. Accompany with salad and freshly baked bread or rolls.

2 cups grape tomatoes

¼ cup sliced black olives

2 green onions, sliced

2 tablespoons extra-virgin olive oil

½ teaspoon chopped fresh thyme

½ teaspoon chopped fresh rosemary

2 cloves garlic, minced

½ teaspoon granulated sugar

Pinch of salt and pepper

1 cup light cream (20% mf)

3 large eggs

2 tablespoons all-purpose flour

2 cups shredded melting cheese of choice (mozzarella, Manchego, Swiss)

Spread tomatoes, olives and green onions in a shallow 6-cup baking dish. Drizzle with oil and sprinkle with herbs, garlic, sugar, salt and pepper. Bake at 400°F until tomatoes begin to shrivel, about 10 minutes. Remove from oven and reduce oven temperature to 350°F.

In a bowl, whisk cream, eggs and flour until smooth.

Pour over tomato mixture and sprinkle with cheese. Return to oven and bake until golden and puffed, about 30 minutes.

Cut into wedges.

Serves 4 to 6.

GRILLED VEGETABLE MEDLEY

. . . .

COOPER'S INN AND RESTAURANT, SHELBURNE, N.S.

You are not limited to the vegetables listed in our ingredients. Use your imagination and create your own unique medley.

4 to 6 cups summer vegetables, cut in portions
  suitable for grilling (thick zucchini slices, pattypan
  squash cubes, sweet pepper squares, whole
  mushrooms)
⅓ cup extra-virgin olive oil
3 tablespoons lemon juice
3 tablespoons dry white vermouth
1 tablespoon dried crushed rosemary
1½ teaspoons dried thyme
¼ teaspoon salt
¼ teaspoon granulated sugar
Pepper

Prepare vegetables. In a bowl, whisk together remaining ingredients until well combined. Marinate vegetables in oil mixture for at least 30 minutes. Heat a grill or barbecue. Place vegetables in a grilling basket and grill for 5 minutes on each side until browned and cooked through.

  Marinade is sufficient for 4 to 6 cups of prepared vegetables. Allow 1 cup of prepared vegetables per serving.

Serves 4 to 6.

OVEN-ROASTED CAMPARI TOMATOES

. . . .

Sweet little Campari tomatoes, a gift to North America from Europe, are easy to prepare and provide brilliant colour to your entrée. Depending upon their size, allow 2 to 3 per serving.

8 to 12 Campari tomatoes, stems intact
Extra-virgin olive oil
Freshly ground sea salt

Arrange tomatoes in a baking dish. Drizzle tops with a small amount of oil and lightly sprinkle with sea salt. Bake in a 375°F oven until heated through and skins begin to wrinkle, about 10 to 12 minutes, depending on size.

Serves 4.

FRIED GREEN TOMATO PARMESAN

· · · · · · · · · · · · · ·

This recipe is a fun twist on eggplant Parmesan. Try serving it for lunch with a Caesar salad and a glass of Chianti.

FRIED GREEN TOMATOES

4 medium green tomatoes

½ cup all-purpose flour

2 large eggs, beaten

½ teaspoon salt

½ teaspoon pepper

1½ cups panko or other dried breadcrumbs

½ cup grated Parmesan cheese

1 cup light olive oil or vegetable oil

8 ounces mozzarella, sliced

2 tablespoons chopped flat-leaf parsley, or fresh basil leaves

TOMATO SAUCE

1 shallot, minced

1 clove garlic, minced

2 tablespoons extra-virgin olive oil

1 large ripe red tomato, chopped

½ cup red wine (optional)

1 cup passatta (ground tomatoes available in jars)

½ teaspoon chili flakes

¼ cup chopped sundried tomatoes

1 teaspoon granulated sugar

1 teaspoon red wine vinegar

Salt and pepper to taste

TOMATO SAUCE

In a 10-inch frying pan, sauté the shallot and garlic in the oil for 3 minutes, then add the chopped tomato. Cook over high heat for 3 minutes and deglaze with red wine. Reduce the heat and simmer the sauce until the wine is completely evaporated. Add the passatta, chili flakes, sundried tomatoes, sugar, vinegar, salt and pepper. Bring the sauce to a boil. Reduce the heat to low and simmer for 20 minutes or until the sauce is thick like tomato paste rather than a loose pasta sauce. This prevents the crispy fried green tomatoes from going soggy.

FRIED TOMATOES

Remove about ⅛ inch from the bottom and the stem end. Cut each tomato into 3 slices about ½-inch thick. To bread the tomatoes set out 3 shallow bowls: the first contains the flour, the second the beaten eggs seasoned with the salt and pepper and the third the panko and half of the Parmesan cheese. Dredge each slice in flour first, then the egg mixture and finally the panko-Parmesan mixture. Set on rimmed baking sheet.

Heat the oil in a steep-sided skillet over medium heat. Add the tomato slices, one at a time, and fry until golden and crispy, about 3 minutes. Remove from the hot oil and drain on paper towels. Move the slices to a rimmed baking sheet and put a small slice of mozzarella cheese on each one. Broil for 20 or 30 seconds to melt the cheese.

PRESENTATION

Place 3 pieces of tomatoes slightly overlapping each other on a plate, ensuring the cheese is visible on each one. Spoon a little sauce on top of each one, sprinkle liberally with the remaining Parmesan cheese and the chopped parsley and serve immediately.

Serves 4.

GRILLED VEGETABLE PAQUETS

. . . .

Heat the barbecue and pop these packets of veggies over the coals before you cook your main course. Always a crowd pleaser, these crisp vegetables will keep warm when transferred to an upper rack on the grill.

4 to 6 medium potatoes, scrubbed and thinly sliced
1 small onion, diced
4 to 6 mushrooms, cleaned and sliced
½ cup grated Parmesan cheese
¼ cup vegetable oil
Paprika, salt and better to taste

Using heavy-duty aluminum foil, cut 4 18- by 24-inch pieces. Place 2 layers together and coat generously with vegetable oil spray. Wash and dry potatoes, then thinly slice into a large bowl. Add onion and mushrooms. Sprinkle with Parmesan cheese. Drizzle with oil and toss to coat vegetables, then spoon out onto prepared sheets of foil. Sprinkle with paprika, salt and pepper. Fold, envelope-style, into 2 packets, crimping edges to form a tight seal. Grill over medium-low heat, turning regularly until vegetables are tender, about 20 to 25 minutes.

Serves 6 to 8.

RICE PILAF

. . . .

THE PINES RESORT HOTEL, DIGBY, N.S.

This dish can be made ahead of time. To reheat, simply place the rice in a buttered casserole, cover and bake in a 350°F oven for about 20 minutes.

1 tablespoon extra-virgin olive oil
1 clove garlic, minced
½ sweet red pepper, finely chopped
½ cup finely diced onion
1½ cups long-grain rice
1 teaspoon salt
Pepper, to taste
3 cups boiling water
2 tablespoons chopped parsley

Heat oil in a large saucepan over medium-low heat. Add garlic, red pepper and onion. Sauté until slightly softened, about 2 minutes. Add rice, salt and pepper and cook, stirring constantly, for 1 minute. Add boiling water, reduce heat to minimum, then cover and cook until rice is tender and liquid is absorbed, about 20 minutes. Remove from heat and let stand, covered, for 5 minutes. Stir in parsley.

Serves 6.

RATATOUILLE

. . . .

BLOMIDON INN, WOLFVILLE, N.S.

The gardens of Blomidon Inn supply the chefs with an abundance of summer vegetables. This ratatouille, served to rave reviews, is best when tomatoes are at their peak and zucchini threaten to take over the vegetable plot!

1 small onion, chopped

1 cup chopped sweet peppers, red, green or yellow

2 cloves garlic, minced

2 tablespoons extra-virgin olive oil

1 small zucchini, chopped

½ medium eggplant, diced

3 large tomatoes, chopped

½ to ⅓ cup tomato juice

1 tablespoon balsamic vinegar

1 tablespoon chopped fresh basil,
  or ½ tablespoon dried

1 teaspoon chopped fresh oregano,
  or ½ teaspoon dried

1 teaspoon chopped fresh thyme, or ½ teaspoon dried

1 tablespoon tomato paste

Salt and pepper to taste

Fresh basil leaves

In a large saucepan over medium heat, sauté onion, peppers and garlic in oil, stirring frequently. Add zucchini, eggplant and tomatoes, and sauté until all vegetables are tender. Stir in tomato juice, vinegar and herbs. Bring to a boil and stir in tomato paste. Simmer until sauce has thickened. Season with salt and pepper and serve in individual dishes with fresh basil leaves.

Serves 4 to 6.

CREAMY CARROTS AND PARSNIPS

. . . .

THE WHITMAN INN, KEMPT, N.S.

This is a busy cook's dream recipe! Easy to prepare, it can be popped in the oven at a moment's notice.

4 cups sliced carrots

2 cups sliced parsnip

1 medium leek, white part only, cleaned and chopped

1 cup mayonnaise

2 tablespoons chopped parsley

2 tablespoons prepared horseradish

¼ teaspoon salt

¼ teaspoon pepper

1 cup cracker crumbs

2 tablespoons butter, melted

In a large saucepan, cover carrots, parsnip and leek with water and bring to a boil. Reduce heat and simmer until vegetables are crisp-tender. Drain and place in a large bowl.

In a separate bowl, whisk together the mayonnaise, parsley, horseradish, salt and pepper. Toss mixture with vegetables and transfer to a greased ovenproof baking dish, sprinkle with cracker crumbs and drizzle with butter. Bake at 350°F until bubbly and browned, about 25 minutes.

Serves 6.

HODGE PODGE

. . . .

FISHERMAN'S LIFE MUSEUM, JEDDORE, N.S.

Hodge Podge is a traditional Maritime summer dish of new vegetables cooked together and served with cream and butter. This recipe comes from the curator of the Fisherman's Life Museum in Jeddore, N.S. Hodge Podge is prepared on site using vegetables from the museum's garden and is usually served to museum visitors during one weekend each year. The museum consists of the small home, gardens and outbuildings of an inshore fisherman, his wife and 13 daughters. It has been preserved as it was over a century ago.

1½ cups green beans in 1-inch pieces

1½ cups yellow beans 1-inch pieces

1½ cups sliced baby carrots

1½ cups tiny new potatoes, scrubbed and quartered

1 medium onion, diced

1½ cups freshly shelled peas

½ cup blend cream (10% mf)

2 tablespoons butter

White pepper to taste

In a large saucepan of unsalted boiling water, bring beans and carrots to a boil over medium-high heat. Cover and simmer for 7 minutes, until tender. Add potatoes and onion, and cook 10 minutes. Add peas and cook 5 minutes.

Drain all but ¼ cup of water from saucepan. Add cream and butter to saucepan, gently stirring, to avoid breaking up the vegetables. Season with pepper and serve immediately.

Makes 4 servings, about ½ cup each.

SALADS

BROCCOLI SALAD

. . . .

THE MURRAY MANOR BED AND BREAKFAST,
YARMOUTH, N.S.

*Broccoli is an excellent vegetable to serve as a side
salad. Its bright green colour and crisp texture
complement a variety of other dishes.*

1 large head fresh broccoli
½ cup sultana raisins
½ cup sunflower seeds or chopped walnuts
2 tablespoons finely diced candied ginger
½ cup mayonnaise
Salt and pepper to taste

Cut broccoli into bite-size florets and blanch in
boiling, salted water for 2 minutes. Immediately
drain broccoli and chill in ice water to stop the
cooking process. Drain.

Combine broccoli, raisins, sunflower seeds and
ginger in a bowl. Toss with mayonnaise and season
with salt and pepper. Serve chilled.

Serves 4.

OLD-FASHIONED CABBAGE SALAD

. . . .

SANDRA NOWLAN, HALIFAX, N.S.

*An old recipe adapted from early German settlers to
Nova Scotia results in a salad that's tangy, refreshing
and low in calories. Unlike conventional coleslaw,
it can be prepared well in advance of serving and
will stay crunchy in the fridge for several days. The
Germans and Pennsylvania "Deutsch" immigrants
prepared a similar salad in which they added ½ cup
of heavy cream instead of oil, and they increased the
sugar.*

⅓ cup white vinegar
2 tablespoons vegetable oil
1 tablespoon granulated sugar
½ to 1 teaspoon celery seeds
½ teaspoon dry mustard
¾ teaspoon salt
½ teaspoon pepper
3 cups finely shredded cabbage
1 tablespoon finely chopped green onion or chives
2 tablespoons chopped sweet red pepper (optional)
Parsley, for garnish
Cherry tomatoes, for garnish

Mix the vinegar, oil, sugar and seasonings to make
a dressing. Stir in the prepared vegetables and mix
well. Cover and refrigerate. Garnish with fresh
parsley and tomatoes.

Serves 6.

TILLY'S COLESLAW

. . . .

LINDY GUILD, MAHONE BAY, N.S.

When a cook "from away" doesn't have family in rural Nova Scotia, she adopts a grandmother. Tilly Hiltz, who listened patiently to laments on the lack of fresh green vegetables during the winter months, gave this recipe to Heritage Contest finalist Lindy Guild to help her through the "saladless season." Now it's made each year after Christmas and it does justice to the fine cabbages grown in Lunenburg County. Tilly says it has been made and served regularly by the ladies of the Lutheran Church in Mahone Bay at their church suppers. The recipe is undoubtedly German in origin and survives without changes over the years.

2 pounds fresh green cabbage, finely shredded
½ pound onions, thinly sliced
¼ pound carrots, grated
¼ cup plus 2 tablespoons granulated sugar
1 tablespoon salt
1 cup white or cider vinegar
2 teaspoons mustard seeds
2 teaspoons celery seeds
¾ cup vegetable oil

Toss cabbage, onions, carrots, ¼ cup of the sugar and salt in a large basin. Let stand for half an hour. Mix vinegar, mustard seeds, celery seeds and the remaining sugar in a saucepan. Bring to a boil, remove from the heat and add vegetable oil. Pour over cabbage mixture and toss thoroughly. Ladle into containers, cover and refrigerate. Let mellow one day. Stir before serving as the juices settle to the bottom. It keeps for up to 6 weeks in the refrigerator.

Serves 8.

MARITIME CAESAR

. . . .

THE ACTOR'S RETREAT CAFÉ, VICTORIA, P.E.I.

Erskine Smith, artistic director of P.E.I.'s Victoria Playhouse shared this Maritime Caesar recipe with innkeeper Pam Stevenson. It became a house favourite.

1 large head romaine lettuce
2 large egg yolks
3 ounces smoked herring fillet
2 cloves garlic, crushed
1 tablespoon Worcestershire sauce
Juice of ½ small lemon
⅓ cup balsamic vinegar
⅔ cup extra-virgin olive oil, green coloured preferred
½ cup grated Parmesan cheese
Toasted croutons, for garnish
Parmesan cheese, for garnish

Tear romaine lettuce into bite-size pieces. Place in a large salad bowl.

In a separate bowl, blend together egg yolks, herring fillet and garlic with wooden spoon. Whisk in Worcestershire sauce, lemon juice, vinegar and oil and blend well. Stir in cheese, mixing until fully blended.

Drizzle lettuce with dressing and serve with garnished with toasted croutons and additional cheese.

Serves 4.

GREEN SALAD WITH "TIDE'S TABLE" DRESSING

. . . .

INN ON THE COVE, SAINT JOHN, N.B.

Willa and Ross Mavis, innkeepers in Saint John, are also authors of the cookbook Tide's Table. *Ross states that honey and cider vinegar are the perfect foil for the salty bite of anchovy paste in this unique dressing.*

6 cups fresh salad greens
¼ cup liquid honey
¼ cup apple cider vinegar
2 teaspoons dry mustard
1 tablespoon grated onion
4 teaspoons anchovy paste
¼ teaspoon salt
⅔ cup extra-virgin olive oil
2 teaspoons poppy seeds
1 small red onion, finely sliced

In a blender or food processor combine honey, vinegar, mustard, onion, anchovy paste and salt. With blender running add oil in a thin stream until well mixed. Add poppy seeds, stir to incorporate and refrigerate for about 30 minutes before using.

Toss salad greens and red onion with just enough dressing to lightly coat. Pile salad decoratively on plate.

Serves 4 to 6.

ORGANIC GREENS WITH ORANGE-SHALLOT VINAIGRETTE

. . . .

CHIVES CANADIAN BISTRO, HALIFAX, N.S.

To provide contrast, mix mild and bitter salad greens, such as arugula, oak leaf, mâche and radicchio. The salad is topped with a drizzle of vinaigrette bursting with the flavour of shallots.

Organic field greens to serve 4
⅔ cup crumbled Danish blue cheese
½ cup smoked almonds
1 Granny Smith apple, cored and julienned

ORANGE SHALLOT VINAIGRETTE

1 cup orange juice
Zest of 1 orange, minced
2 small shallots, finely minced
1 tablespoon honey vinegar, or 2 teaspoons white
  vinegar and 1 teaspoon liquid honey
¾ cup light olive oil
Salt and pepper
1 teaspoon granulated sugar (optional)

VINAIGRETTE

In a saucepan over medium-high heat, boil the orange juice until reduced to ¼ cup. Add zest, shallots and vinegar. Pour into a blender and, with motor running, add oil in a slow, steady stream until emulsified. Adjust seasoning with salt and pepper. Add sugar, if using, then refrigerate.

Makes 1 cup.

SALAD

Arrange greens on 4 chilled plates. Sprinkle with cheese, almonds and apple. Drizzle with enough of the Orange Shallot Vinaigrette to coat the greens lightly.

Serves 4.

MURRAY MANOR POLISH ONIONS

THE MURRAY MANOR BED AND BREAKFAST, YARMOUTH, N.S.

This recipe is for the busy cook who appreciates a dish that can be prepared in advance. Similar to the cucumber salads made famous on Nova Scotia's South Shore, Polish Onions are delicious and easy to prepare.

½ cup water
½ cup vinegar
⅓ cup granulated sugar
1 teaspoon salt
1 large Spanish onion, thinly sliced
1 cup sour cream
Celery seed and pepper

In a deep bowl, stir water and vinegar with sugar and salt until dissolved. Place onion in a bowl and cover with vinegar solution. Refrigerate 8 hours.

At serving time, drain onion and toss with sour cream. Garnish with a sprinkling of celery seeds and freshly ground pepper.

Serves 4.

TOMATO AND BASIL SALAD WITH BALSAMIC VINAIGRETTE

THE INN AT SPRY POINT, SPRY POINT, P.E.I.

In the season for eating outdoors, set the table on the verandah or under the canopy of a shade tree. The ingredients featured in this salad flourish during summer, making it easy to prepare and a perfect part of your al fresco meal.

BALSAMIC VINAIGRETTE

3 tablespoons balsamic vinegar
1 tablespoon sherry vinegar
¼ teaspoon salt
Pinch white pepper
1 garlic clove, minced
¾ cup extra-virgin olive oil

SALAD

8 cups field greens (any combination of arugula, lamb's lettuce, pea shoots, red chicory, escarole, red oakleaf or green leaf salad greens)
1 small red onion, cut in thin rings
4 tomatoes, cut in wedges
2 cups loosely packed fresh basil, shredded

BALSAMIC VINAIGRETTE

In medium bowl, whisk together balsamic vinegar, sherry vinegar, salt, pepper and garlic. Add oil in a steady stream and continue to whisk until vinaigrette is thick and creamy. Adjust seasoning if necessary and refrigerate.

Makes ¾ cup.

SALAD

Combine greens, onion, tomatoes and basil in large bowl. Drizzle with vinaigrette and toss to coat.

Serves 6.

GRILLED ASPARAGUS WITH
TOMATO VINAIGRETTE

. . . .

This great vegetable side dish works as well chilled as it does warm. As a salad, it goes well with cold meats and cheese, crusty French bread and a cold Pinot Grigio. Served just off the grill it is perfect with barbecued salmon or pork chops. The vinaigrette is a great go-to recipe as you can use jarred or dried sundried tomatoes from your pantry.

ASPARAGUS

2 pounds asparagus
3 tablespoons extra-virgin olive oil
½ teaspoon salt
½ teaspoon pepper
Fresh basil leaves, for garnish

TOMATO VINAIGRETTE

½ cup sundried tomatoes
1 shallot, minced
1 clove garlic, minced
½ cup white balsamic vinegar
1 teaspoon granulated sugar
½ teaspoon dried basil
½ teaspoon salt
1 teaspoon hot sauce, such as Tabasco
1 cup extra-virgin olive oil

ASPARAGUS

Clean asparagus and snap off woody bottoms. Toss in oil, salt and pepper. It is important that the asparagus is kissed with the oil but not drowning in it, as that will cause flare-ups. Grill asparagus on a greased grill over high heat for about 5 to 6 minutes, turning constantly while grilling.

Set asparagus on a platter with all tips in the same direction. Drizzle with ¾ cup of Tomato Vinaigrette and garnish with basil.

Serves 4 to 6.

TOMATO VINAIGRETTE

If using dried tomatoes, soak tomatoes in water to soften. Most jarred tomatoes are packed in oil and will be soft enough already. Drain off oil (for added flavour reserve some of the tomato oil to use instead of olive oil).

Pulse tomatoes in a food processor. Add shallot, garlic, vinegar, sugar, basil, salt and hot sauce and purée until smooth. Slowly add oil in a steady stream until vinaigrette emulsifies. Store in a sealed jar in the refrigerator for up to a month.

Makes 1¼ cups, enough to make the salad twice.

WARM POTATO SALAD

. . . .

LIBERTINE CAFÉ AND KITCHEN, HALIFAX, N.S.

Chef Peter Woodworth credited this recipe to his wife Sandra who brought this family favourite from her home in Germany. Cornichons used in the recipe are tiny tart pickles like gherkins, but not sweet.

5 medium russet potatoes
5 large eggs, hardcooked
8 cornichons, chopped into small dice
Small bunch chives, chopped
1 tablespoon Dijon mustard
½ cup vegetable oil
¼ cup white wine vinegar
Salt and pepper to taste

Scrub potatoes and place in a pot of cold water. Bring to a boil, cover, reduce heat and cook until potatoes are barely fork-tender. Remove from heat, drain and cut into bite-size pieces. Return to pot, cover to keep warm.

Meanwhile, shell hard-cooked eggs and slice in half. Remove yolks and set aside. Chop egg whites into bite-size pieces and add to potatoes with cornichons and chives.

Place mustard in a large salad bowl. Press egg yolks through a sieve and add to the mustard. Using a whisk, gradually blend in oil, then vinegar. Add potato mixture to dressing and toss lightly. Serve warm.

Serves 4.

HEIRLOOM TOMATO SALAD WITH BOCCONCINI, BASIL, AGED BALSAMIC VINEGAR AND OLIVE OIL

Heirloom tomatoes are locally produced, non-hybrid varieties traditionally not commercially produced in large quantities. Using beautiful heirloom tomatoes in this salad adds tremendous colour and a sweetness that you do not get with most mass-produced tomatoes. This salad is inspired by the traditional Insalate Caprese of Italy.

2 pounds heirloom tomatoes (mixed varieties)
3 2-ounce balls fresh bocconcini (fresh baby mozzarella)
30 leaves fresh basil
2 tablespoons chopped chives
6 tablespoons aged balsamic vinegar (minimum 10-year)
½ cup extra-virgin olive oil
2 tablespoon coarse sea salt, such as fleur de sel
Several grindings of pepper

Slice, quarter or halve the different tomato varieties. This will add texture and visual appeal. On 6 small plates, assemble tomatoes. Tear bocconcini cheese into small pieces and arrange over tomatoes, 1 ounce per plate. Add fresh basil leaves, about 5 per plate. Garnish each salad with a sprinkle of chopped chives, 1 tablespoon balsamic vinegar and 2 tablespoons oil, and season with fleur de sel and pepper.

Serves 6.

SPINACH AND ORANGE SALAD WITH POPPY SEED DRESSING

. . . .

CHARLOTTE LANE CAFÉ & CRAFTS,
SHELBURNE, N.S.

Owner-chef Roland Glauser of the Charlotte Lane notes that this is a very versatile salad. The apple and orange segments may be replaced by mango chunks, peach or plum slices, and toasted almonds or pine nuts may be sprinkled on top.

SALAD

12 ounces spinach, large stems removed
1 large Granny Smith apple, diced
1 orange, peeled and sliced

POPPY SEED DRESSING

½ cup liquid honey
½ cup extra-virgin olive oil
½ cup fresh orange juice
¼ cup balsamic vinegar
1 teaspoon Dijon mustard
2 teaspoons poppy seeds
¼ teaspoon ground sage

POPPY SEED DRESSING

Whisk together all ingredients.

Makes 1½ cups.

SALAD

Tear prepared spinach leaves into bite-size pieces and place in a large salad bowl. Top with apple and orange slices, drizzle with enough dressing to coat leaves and toss. Refrigerate any remaining dressing for up to 5 days.

Serves 4 to 6.

SUMMER VEGETABLE PASTA SALAD

. . . .

Pasta salads should be invigorating and made with slightly crunchy, bright vegetables. Experiment with your own vegetable selection using the choicest types available.

5 cups assorted summer vegetables, such as
  green beans, cut in 2-inch lengths
Broccoli florets
Cauliflower florets
Carrot, cut in ¼-inch slices
Zucchini, cut in ¼-inch slices
Sugar snap peas
Grated zest from 1 lemon
¼ cup lemon juice
1 clove garlic, minced
4 teaspoons salt
½ cup vegetable oil
½ pound short pasta, such as penne, fusilli or farfalle
10 cherry tomatoes
20 brine-cured olives, pitted and sliced
12 large fresh basil leaves, chopped
¼ cup chopped fresh parsley

In a large pot of boiling water, blanch all vegetables but tomatoes for 1 minute. Drain in colander and chill in cold water to stop cooking. Drain well.

In a medium bowl, whisk zest, juice, garlic and ¼ teaspoon of the salt. Whisk in oil in a slow steady stream until emulsified. Set aside.

In a large pot of boiling water, add remaining salt and pasta. Boil until pasta is al dente, about 7 minutes. Drain, reserving ½ cup of the liquid.

In a large serving bowl, combine pasta, blanched vegetables, cherry tomatoes, olives, basil, parsley and two-thirds of the vinaigrette. Toss to coat, cover and refrigerate. Bring to room temperature before serving, adding reserved pasta water or additional vinaigrette if necessary.

Serves 8.

DILLED SHRIMP AND PASTA SALAD

. . . .

ACTON'S GRILL AND CAFÉ, WOLFVILLE, N.S.

The dressing in this recipe, featuring lemon and fresh dill, makes the salad a favourite at this popular restaurant. Serve either warm or chilled.

3 tablespoons lemon juice
2 or 3 large cloves garlic, crushed
1½ teaspoons Dijon mustard
1 teaspoon anchovy paste
½ teaspoon salt
½ teaspoon pepper
½ teaspoon granulated sugar
¼ cup vegetable oil
⅓ cup grated Parmesan cheese
5 cups small pasta shells
¼ cup finely chopped fresh dill
¾ pound small cooked shrimp

In a medium bowl, stir together the juice, garlic, mustard, anchovy paste, salt, pepper and sugar. Gradually whisk in the oil, then the Parmesan cheese and set aside.

Boil pasta in a large pot of boiling salted water. Drain and place in a large bowl. Pour dressing over pasta, tossing to coat. Stir in dill and shrimp. Serve either warm or chilled.

Serves 6 to 8.

LOBSTER POTATO SALAD SUPREME

. . . .

MARY MOUZAR, HALIFAX, N.S.

Atlantic Canadians are specialists in the cuisine of potatoes and lobster. And many dishes derived from this combination are indeed memorable. Lobster chowder, rich with lobster meat and cubes of potatoes is enjoyed by thousands of visitors each year. Another ritual is the lobster salad supper held in communities where people earn their living by lobster fishing. The trick with this salad is to keep it moist but not to allow the mayonnaise and onion to overpower the lobster. This flavourful lobster potato salad has a little apple to enhance the taste as well as the texture. The recipe serves four, but can be halved, doubled or tripled. Save some extra lobster claw pieces to garnish with the apple slices.

1 cup chopped cooked lobster
1 tablespoon green relish or chopped sweet pickles
¼ teaspoon pepper
½ teaspoon white wine vinegar
1 teaspoon Dijon mustard
2 tablespoons finely chopped parsley
½ cup mayonnaise or salad dressing
½ cup diced unpeeled apple
2 cups diced cooked potatoes
1 cup cooked peas
Lettuce
1 apple, cored and sliced, unpeeled
½ cup water
1 teaspoon lemon juice

In a small bowl, combine lobster, pickles, pepper and vinegar. Let stand for 5 minutes. Drain and reserve any juice. In a medium bowl, combine mustard, parsley and mayonnaise. Fold in diced apple, potato and peas. If more moisture is desired, add some of the reserved juice. Line a salad bowl with lettuce and fill with the salad. Garnish with a pinwheel of apple slices that have been dipped in a mixture of the water and lemon juice.

Serves 4.

ROASTED BEET, WALNUT AND GOAT CHEESE SALAD

· · · · · · · · · · · ·

For a beautiful colour, try to get some golden or candy cane (chioggia) beets along with the more common red ones for this simple salad. Other than roasting the beets, there is very little to do here but to assemble.

3 medium red beets
3 medium yellow beets
½ cup walnut halves
1 head of Boston or Bibb lettuce, cleaned
1 stalk celery, thinly sliced on an angle
½ cup crumbled soft goat cheese
2 green onions, thinly sliced
Half an orange
2 tablespoons aged sherry vinegar (or good-quality wine vinegar)
3 tablespoons extra-virgin olive oil
Salt and pepper

Place the beets on a baking sheet and bake in a 350°F oven until tender, about 45 minutes. Cool on a board and, when you can handle them, slip skins off or peel with a paring knife. Cut into sixths or eighths depending on size and set aside until ready to assemble the salads. While roasting the beets, toast the walnuts on a baking tray for about 7 or 8 minutes, and cool.

In the centre of 4 plates, place a couple of whole lettuce leaves. Arrange the beets on top along with the walnuts, celery, cheese and onions. Using a micro-planing tool or a zester, grate a small amount of orange zest on each salad. Dress each with vinegar and oil, and season with salt and pepper.

Serves 4.

FRUITS DE MER SALAD WITH
SAUCE MARIE ROSE

. . . .

Sauce Marie Rose is the European equivalent of North America's cocktail sauce. In this salad appetizer its smoothness enhances the different textures and flavours of the seafood more than the sharp horseradish heat of a traditional seafood sauce. You can serve this dish as a salad on some Boston lettuce leaves, in a martini glass or on a large platter garnished with watercress or fresh basil leaves. Use only the very freshest seafood from your local fishmonger.

SALAD

6 cups water

3 cups dry white wine

1 medium onion, coarsely chopped

1 carrot, coarsely chopped

1 stalk celery, coarsely chopped

1 lemon, halved

3 bay leaves

3 sprigs fresh thyme

1 2-pound live lobster

12 sea scallops

18 tiger prawns

12 choice oysters, shucked

1 pound calamari sliced into ¼-inch rings

¼ cup sliced chives

SAUCE MARIE ROSE

1 cup mayonnaise

½ cup tomato ketchup

1 teaspoon lemon juice

¼ teaspoon salt

1 tablespoon Worcestershire sauce

1 teaspoon hot sauce, such as Tabasco

1 tablespoon brandy or dry sherry

SALAD

In a stockpot, bring water, wine, onion, carrot, celery, lemon, bay leaves and thyme to a boil. As soon as the liquid boils, drop in the live lobster and cook, covered, for 12 minutes. Remove lobster and refrigerate until cool. Lower the temperature of the cooking liquid to a simmer and poach each type of seafood until just cooked but not rubbery. Depending on the size of the ingredients, each should take between 1 and 3 minutes. The calamari will take the shortest time and the scallops will take the longest. Remove seafood from cooking liquid and spread out on a rimmed baking sheet. Refrigerate right away to prevent residual cooking as much as possible.

SAUCE MARIE ROSE

Meanwhile, combine all ingredients in a bowl and whisk until smooth.

When ready to serve, clean lobster and cut tail meat and claws into 1-inch pieces. Toss lobster and chilled seafood with Sauce Marie Rose and garnish with sliced chives.

Serves 6.

POTATO AND MUSSEL SALAD

. . . .

STRATHGARTNEY COUNTRY INN,
CORNWALL, P.E.I.

This is an innovative combination that uses two of Prince Edward Island's best known ingredients — fresh mussels and potatoes.

1½ to 2 pounds potatoes
¾ cup extra-virgin olive oil
¼ cup white wine vinegar
¼ cup white wine
3 tablespoons chopped fresh basil
Salt and pepper to taste
24 cultivated mussels, steamed and shucked
Fresh salad greens
8 cherry tomatoes
Edible flowers, for garnish

Boil potatoes in a covered saucepan of boiling salted water until tender. Drain and let dry and begin to cool.

Meanwhile, prepare vinaigrette. Combine oil, vinegar, wine, basil, salt and pepper in a blender and whirl until well blended.

Peel and cut warm potatoes into generous ¼-inch slices. In a bowl, gently toss with half of the vinaigrette and cool to room temperature. In a separate bowl, toss mussels with the remaining vinaigrette.

To assemble, line plates with salad greens. Add a circle of potato slices, overlapping slightly. Arrange mussels in the centre of each plate with tomatoes. Garnish with flowers.

Serves 4.

HONEY MUSTARD DRESSING

. . . .

THE GARRISON HOUSE INN,
ANNAPOLIS ROYAL, N.S.

Honey and Dijon mustard combine to produce a sweet yet tangy dressing.

3 tablespoons raspberry vinegar
1½ tablespoons honey
6 tablespoons mayonnaise
1 tablespoon Dijon mustard
1 tablespoon minced onion
1½ tablespoons chopped fresh parsley
Pinch of salt
¾ cup oil (olive, vegetable or combination)

Combine all ingredients, except oil, in a blender. Add oil in a slow stream, processing only until blended.

Makes 1½ cups.

SMOKED MACKEREL, APPLE AND CELERY ROOT SALAD

. . . .

There are many places in Nova Scotia where locals sell smoked fish by the side of the road, making this salad easy for locals to make. However you can make this salad wherever smoked mackerel is available. You can eat it hot by flashing it in the microwave, but as a salad it is wonderful chilled and accompanied by some crunch. This dish is more of a luncheon or brunch choice and wonderful served with buttered bread and some thinly sliced English cucumbers. When preparing the vegetables for this salad, a julienne or matchstick cut is nicest for appearance.

SALAD

2 fillets smoked mackerel (about 6 ounces each)
2 apples, cored, peeled and julienned
½ small celery root, peeled and julienned
¼ fennel bulb, cored and sliced very thin
2 fennel bulb tops (fronds), coarsely chopped
  (optional)
2 green onion tops, sliced on the bias
1 English cucumber, sliced ⅛ inch thick
Pepper (optional)
Lemon wedges (optional)

DRESSING

½ cup mayonnaise
1 tablespoon granulated sugar
1 tablespoon white vinegar
2 tablespoons water
1 tablespoon Dijon mustard
1 teaspoon celery seeds
Salt and pepper to taste

DRESSING

Combine all the ingredients in a bowl and whisk until smooth. Set aside.

SALAD

Using your fingers, pick the smoked mackerel meat from the skin, being careful to remove any bones. The fish should be in medium-size flakes; if they are too small the salad will have a mushy texture. Combine the fish in a bowl with the apples, celery root, sliced fennel, fennel fronds, green onions and dressing. Gently fold together, being careful not to break apart the flakes of fish and vegetables. Refrigerate.

PRESENTATION

Divide the slices of cucumber onto 6 plates, laying them in a circle and overlapping a bit. Make a small pile of salad in the centre of each plate, allowing the edges of the cucumber slices to be seen. Garnish with some freshly ground pepper and lemon wedges, if desired.

Serves 6.

CRANBERRY JELLY MOULD

. . . .

VIRJENE COLE, LARRY'S RIVER, N.S.

A sparkling jelly mould is a welcome addition to any buffet table. It's no surprise that its origin is based on the wild cranberries growing on a farm near the sea.

1 package red jelly powder
1 cup boiling water
½ cup cold water
2 cups raw cranberries, roughly chopped
½ cup granulated sugar
2 apples, cored, peeled and finely chopped
2 small oranges, peeled, sectioned and finely chopped

In a bowl, dissolve the jelly powder with the boiling water; stir in the cold water. Refrigerate until lightly set. Add cranberries, sugar, apples and oranges. Refrigerate until completely set.

Serves 6 to 8.

EAST COAST LOBSTER SALAD

. . . .

MRS. JOHN MEISNER, UPPER BLANDFORD, N.S.

A traditional Nova Scotia dish that is light despite the richness of locally caught lobster. Family and guests always have good comments when this great-grandmother from the sea-swept Blandford Peninsula serves her lobster salad. It was always part of holiday fare for Mrs. John Meisner. She found it handwritten in an old recipe scribbler.

3 lobsters, freshly boiled and shelled
3 large eggs, hard cooked, peeled and chopped
½ cup chopped sweet pickles
½ cup mayonnaise
½ small onion, finely chopped
½ teaspoon salt and a few grains of pepper
Lettuce leaves

Cut the lobster into bite-size pieces. Add the remaining ingredients and toss together. Serve on lettuce leaves.

Serves 4.

YEAST BREADS

STONEGROUND WHOLE WHEAT BREAD

· · · · · · · · · · · · ·

ACTON'S GRILL AND CAFÉ, WOLFVILLE, N.S.

In our grandparents' day the flour they bought came from small mills where grain was ground between large stones. The flour contained all the goodness of the whole grain: the germ, fibre, starch, minerals and vitamins. The bakers at Acton's are committed to making the same high-quality bread daily using stoneground whole wheat flour.

2 fresh yeast cakes or 2 packages active dry yeast
2 cups warm water
1 tablespoon granulated sugar
½ teaspoon salt
1 tablespoon extra-virgin olive oil or vegetable oil (approximate)
3 cups whole wheat flour, preferably stoneground
2 to 2½ cups all-purpose flour

In a large bowl, dissolve the yeast in the warm water along with the sugar, salt and oil. Add 1 cup of all-purpose flour and whisk well. Let this "sponge" proof for 45 minutes in a warm place.

Add remaining flours and knead into a soft but not sticky dough. Depending on the quality of the flour, you may need a little more to get desired consistency. Place dough in a greased bowl, turning to grease surface. Cover and let rise in a warm place, until double in volume, about 1 hour.

Punch down dough, divide in half and shape into 2 free-form oval loaves. Place on a greased cookie sheet, cover and let rise again, until doubled, about 45 minutes. Bake in preheated 400°F oven for 25 to 30 minutes, or until hollow-sounding when tapped on bottom. Brush tops with additional oil, if desired.

Makes 2 large loaves, about 20 slices.

OLD-FASHIONED MOLASSES BROWN BREAD

· · · · · · · · · · · ·

Freshly baked brown bread brings memories of mother's kitchen — a treat not often found in today's busy lifestyles. This is a simple recipe requiring a little time, but the results are marvellous.

2 tablespoons active dry yeast
1 cup lukewarm water
3 cups hot water
1 tablespoon salt
3 tablespoons butter
1 cup fancy molasses
2 cups large-flake rolled oats
8 cups all-purpose flour

Sprinkle dry yeast over lukewarm water and stir to dissolve. Let stand 10 minutes or until mixture doubles in size. Meanwhile, in a large bowl, place hot water, salt, butter, molasses and rolled oats. Beat mixture and let cool. Stir in the yeast mixture and add flour, a cupful at a time, mixing until well incorporated. Turn onto a floured board and knead until smooth, about 7 to 10 minutes. Shape into a ball and place in a greased bowl, turning to grease surface. Cover and let rise in a warm place until double in volume, about 1 hour.

Punch down dough, divide in half and shape into 2 loaves. Place in 2 greased 9- by 5-inch loaf pans. Cover and let rise 1 hour.

Bake in a 350°F oven for 1 hour or until golden brown and loaf sounds hollow when tapped on the bottom. Remove from pans and cool on racks.

Makes 2 loaves, about 20 slices.

BLOMIDON INN BREAD

. . . .

BLOMIDON INN, WOLFVILLE, N.S.

Dining at the Blomidon Inn would not be complete without a slice of this delicious bread. The combination of oats, cornmeal and molasses give it a rich and dense flavour with stick-to-the-ribs goodness.

1 cup large-flake rolled oats
½ cup cornmeal
1¼ cups fancy molasses
½ teaspoon salt
2 cups hot water
¼ cup butter
1 cup warm water
3 tablespoons active dry yeast
½ tablespoon granulated sugar
7 cups all-purpose flour

Stir together oats, cornmeal, molasses, salt, hot water and butter and let mixture cool to a lukewarm temperature. In a separate bowl, stir together the warm water, yeast and sugar. Let yeast soften until slightly foamy then stir to ensure that it is properly dispersed.

In a heavy stand mixer, combine oat mixture and yeast mixture and mix at lowest speed until blended. Remove bowl from stand and add flour 1 cup at a time to make a firm — but not dry or sticky — dough that comes clean from the side of the bowl. Turn dough out onto work surface and knead for 3 to 5 minutes until the flour has been worked in uniformly and the dough is more elastic.

Divide dough in half and shape into loaves. Place in well-greased large loaf pans. Cover and let rise until the dough rises about 1 inch above the pan. This usually takes about 60 to 75 minutes. Bake at 350°F until loaves sound hollow when tapped, about 25 to 30 minutes. Remove from pans and cool on a rack.

Makes 2 loaves, about 20 slices.

POTATO BRAN BREAD

. . . .

SANDRA NOWLAN, HALIFAX, N.S.

Sandra Nowlan's grandmother Smith in French Lake, N.B. made bread daily to feed her family of eight. Her secret for moist flavourful loaves was to add mashed potatoes and potato water to the dough.

4 medium potatoes, peeled and diced

4 cups water

½ cup butter

½ cup granulated sugar

1 tablespoon salt

1½ cups buttermilk

Pinch of ginger

2 packages active dry yeast (2 tablespoons)

2 cups wheat bran

12 cups all-purpose flour

1½ teaspoons caraway seeds (optional)

Oil

In a saucepan, cook potatoes in 3 cups of the water until tender. Drain off the water into a large measuring cup, adjusting the volume to 3 cups. Pour into a large bowl. To the hot potato water add butter, all but 1 teaspoon of the sugar, salt and buttermilk. Mash the potatoes and add to the bowl. Cool.

Meanwhile, warm remaining water to lukewarm, add remaining sugar, ginger and yeast. Stir and let stand 10 minutes to froth. Add to potato mixture. Stir in the bran and 4 cups of the flour. Add the caraway seeds, if using. Beat with a heavy stand mixer on high speed for 1 minute. Mix in the remaining flour, 1 cup at a time, using a wooden spoon. You may not need all the flour.

When dough is stiff enough to handle, turn out onto a floured work surface and knead 10 to 12 minutes until dough is smooth and elastic. Place in a greased bowl. Brush oil over the top of the dough and cover with waxed paper and a tea towel. Let rise for about 1 hour in a warm place until doubled in bulk. Punch down. Divide into 8 pieces and shape into 4 double loaves. Place in 4 well-greased 9- by 5-inch pans. Let rise until doubled, about 50 minutes, in a warm place. Bake at 425°F for 15 minutes, reducing heat to 375°F for 25 minutes until well browned and hollow sounding when tapped on the bottom. Remove from pans at once and cool on a rack.

Makes 4 double loaves.

CHALLAH

· · · · · · · · · · · ·

FREIDA PERLIN AND BETTE TETRAULT,
HALIFAX, N.S.

The major Jewish festivals that celebrate the seasons of the year are multi-purpose, with an historical, religious element and a secular side. During all of them, special foods are prepared. Freida Perlin of Halifax has been recognized throughout the local Jewish community as a cook without equal. Challah is usually braided in three. Freida braids her bread in a complicated six-strand pattern, where the outer pieces are rhythmically brought into the centre.

½ cup lukewarm water
¼ cup granulated sugar
1 tablespoon active dry yeast
4 cups all-purpose flour
2 teaspoons salt
⅓ cup oil
½ cup water
4 large eggs
Sesame seeds

Mix lukewarm water, 1 tablespoon of the sugar and yeast and let proof for 10 minutes. Combine flour, remaining sugar and salt in a large bowl. Make a well in the centre and pour in the yeast mixture, water, oil and 3 of the eggs. Knead, either by hand or by machine, for about 10 minutes until the dough is smooth and elastic. Let rise for 1½ to 2 hours in a clean, greased bowl. Shape or braid the bread and place it on a lightly greased cookie sheet. Let rise again for 1 hour. Beat the remaining egg and brush overtop. Sprinkle on sesame seeds. Bake at 350°F for 35 to 40 minutes or until golden and loaf sounds hollow when tapped on bottom.

Makes 1 loaf, about 12 slices.

LEBANESE BREAD (HOBUS LUBANY)

· · · · · · · · · · · ·

VALERIE MANSOUR, HALIFAX, N.S.

When Alexandra Mansour arrived in Amherst, N.S. in 1948 as a newlywed from Lebanon, her native food was a little too exotic for local taste buds, and ingredients, unless homegrown, had to be brought in with relatives from Montreal or the United States. Today, Mansour's recipes are in a cookbook and her home is a stopping-off point for her daughter's friends who just happen to arrive at mealtime. Chickpeas, lentils and bulgar wheat, the staples of Lebanese cooking, are now readily found in large grocery stores.

4 teaspoons granulated sugar
½ cup warm water
1 tablespoon active dry yeast
1 cup milk
1 tablespoon vegetable oil
6 to 8 cups all-purpose flour
1 teaspoon salt
1 cup water (approximate)

Dissolve 1 teaspoon of the sugar in the warm water and add the yeast. Let stand for 10 minutes; then stir well. Warm the milk, oil and remaining sugar over medium heat. Meanwhile, mix the flour and salt in a large bowl. Add the yeast and milk mixtures and mix well. Knead until you have a soft dough that sticks to your fingers. Add water if the dough seems too stiff. (You may need about a cup.) Form into a ball. Cover the bowl, wrap in towels and let rise in a warm place for at least 2 hours, although overnight is preferable.

Divide into 8 pieces and form each into a smooth ball. Set on a lightly floured surface and cover with a towel. Let rest for 20 minutes. Roll each ball into a ¼-inch-thick round. Bake 2 at a time on a cookie sheet at 500°F for 7 to 10 minutes or until golden and puffed. Let cool on a rack.

Makes 8 loaves.

GLAZED CINNAMON BUTTER ROLLS

· · · · · · · · · · ·

MARY MOUZAR, HALIFAX, N.S.

Many of us from time to time have tasted baked goods that seemed almost fresher than fresh because they were so light and moist with the most wonderful texture and flavour. One of the treasured baking secrets passed on to Mary Mouzar by her late mother, Mabel Henderson of Liverpool (who probably learned it from her mother), was to use mashed potato or the water in which potatoes were cooked. Added to breads, biscuits, doughnuts and other such goodies, mashed potato or cooking liquid greatly enhances the flavour, texture and keeping qualities.

½ cup hot mashed potatoes
½ cup warm water or potato water
½ cup scalded milk
4 cups all-purpose flour (approximate)
½ cup granulated sugar
¼ cup lukewarm water
1 package active dry yeast (1 tablespoon)
¼ cup butter
¾ teaspoon salt
2 large eggs
½ cup softened butter, for spreading
1 cup packed brown sugar
2 teaspoons cinnamon
Chopped nuts (optional)

GLAZE

2 teaspoons softened butter
1 tablespoon milk
¼ teaspoon vanilla extract
⅔ cup icing sugar

In a large mixing bowl, use a whisk to beat the potatoes, warm water, milk and ½ cup of the flour until well blended. Set aside to cool to lukewarm. Meanwhile, mix ½ teaspoon of the sugar in the ¼ cup lukewarm water and stir in the yeast. Set aside until it doubles in bulk. Stir yeast into potato batter. Cover and let rise until light.

In a medium bowl, cream butter and remaining granulated sugar. Add salt and eggs and beat until well blended. Stir into the yeast mixture. Stir in the remaining flour. Knead about 100 times, adding more flour to board as needed to keep dough from sticking. Place in a greased bowl. Turn to grease all over and let rise until double in bulk. Punch down.

On a floured surface, roll dough to form a rectangle about 16 by 20 inches wide. Spread with softened butter, sprinkle with brown sugar, cinnamon and chopped nuts, if using. Roll as for a jelly roll and cut into 1-inch slices. Place the slices, ½ inch apart, in a greased baking pan with sides. Let rest until double in size. Bake in a 375°F oven for about 16 to 20 minutes or until nicely browned. While rolls are still hot, use a pastry brush to spread the glaze over the top of each.

GLAZE

In a small bowl, blend all ingredients in the order given.

Makes about 18 rolls.

QUICKBREADS

BUTTERMILK BISCUITS

. . . .

CHIVES CANADIAN BISTRO, HALIFAX, N.S.

Sweet or savoury, the choice is yours! At Chives Canadian Bistro, the chefs serve their warm biscuits as a savoury appetizer base for foie gras and chutney. We have included this versatile recipe because the biscuits are equally delicious served as a bread accompaniment or, without the chives, as the base for a sweet dessert, such as Old-Fashioned Shortcake (page 251).

2 cups all-purpose flour
1 tablespoon baking powder
2 teaspoons granulated sugar
¼ teaspoon salt
½ cup butter, cubed
1 large egg
1 cup buttermilk
¼ cup chopped chives

In a mixing bowl, combine flour, baking powder, sugar and salt. Using a pastry blender, cut in butter until mixture resembles coarse crumbs. Whisk together the egg and buttermilk, mix in the chives and add to dry mixture, stirring lightly with a fork to make a soft dough. Turn out onto a floured board and gently knead 2 or 3 times. Form each biscuit by dropping a tablespoon of dough onto a lightly greased baking sheet and bake in 400°F oven until golden, approximately 15 minutes. For large biscuits, roll 1 inch thick, cut with a 2-inch cutter and bake 30 to 35 minutes.

Makes 36 tiny or 10 large biscuits.

BANANA FLAX MUFFINS

. . . .

Flax seeds are being touted as one of the top-10 foods that are good for you. Rich in omega-3 fatty acids, they also contain high-quality protein, phytonutrients and soluble fibre. Flax flour is made from finely ground flax seeds and should be refrigerated or frozen to keep it fresh. These moist fruit-studded muffins, high in fibre and potassium, are excellent for breakfast or a tasty snack.

3 medium bananas
1 large egg
1 cup buttermilk
¼ cup granulated sugar
¼ cup packed brown sugar
3 tablespoons canola oil
1 teaspoon vanilla
1 cup flax flour
1 cup whole wheat flour
1 cup all-purpose flour
1 tablespoon baking powder
½ teaspoon baking soda
½ to 1 teaspoon cinnamon
½ cup raisins
½ cup chopped dates

Mash bananas in a large bowl and beat in the egg, buttermilk, sugars, oil and vanilla. In a separate bowl, mix together flours, baking powder, soda and cinnamon. Add banana mixture and stir just until evenly moistened. Stir in raisins and dates.

Spoon batter into paper-lined or greased muffin tins, filling each almost full. Bake in 400°F oven for 20 to 25 minutes or until firm to the touch. Cool on a rack. These muffins freeze well.

Makes 14 large muffins.

PEERLESS CRANBERRY MAPLE SUGAR SCONES

· · · · · · · · · · · · ·

WICKWIRE HOUSE BED AND BREAKFAST,
KENTVILLE, N.S.

Maple sugar, which is about twice as sweet as white sugar, is made by boiling down the maple sap until the liquid has almost completely evaporated. At Wickwire House, the scones are served with jam or English Double Devon Cream.

1½ cups all-purpose flour
⅓ cup maple sugar
1 teaspoon baking powder
¼ teaspoon salt
¼ teaspoon baking soda
⅓ cup dried cranberries
Zest of 1 orange
⅓ cup butter, cubed
½ cup sour cream

In a mixing bowl, combine flour, ¼ cup of the maple sugar, baking powder, salt and baking soda. Stir in dried cranberries and orange zest. Cut in butter until mixture resembles coarse crumbs. Stir in sour cream.

Shape dough into a ball and pat into an 8-inch round on a lightly greased cookie sheet. Cut dough into 8 wedges and sprinkle with remaining maple sugar. Bake in 400°F oven for 18 to 20 minutes or until lightly browned.

Makes 8 scones.

STRAWBERRY PECAN MUFFINS

· · · · · · · · · · · · ·

Serve these muffins warm from the oven. It is doubtful that any will be left over, but they reheat beautifully in a microwave.

¾ cup all-purpose flour
¾ cup whole wheat flour
2 teaspoons baking powder
½ teaspoon ground cinnamon
½ teaspoon salt
½ cup finely chopped pecans
1 large egg
½ cup packed brown sugar
1 cup milk
¼ cup vegetable oil
1 teaspoon vanilla extract
1 cup chopped strawberries

Combine flours, baking powder, cinnamon and salt in a large bowl. Add the pecans and mix well. In a separate bowl, whisk together the egg, brown sugar, milk, oil and vanilla. Add the egg mixture to the flour mixture and stir gently until well blended. Fold in strawberries. Fill paper-lined or greased muffin tins three-quarters full. Bake in 375°F oven for 20 to 25 minutes, or until lightly golden brown and a toothpick inserted in the centre comes out clean.

Makes 12 muffins.

BLUEBERRY SCONES

. . . .

Buttery, warm and slightly sweet, these easy-to-prepare breakfast treats are guaranteed to start your day on a happy note.

2¼ cups all-purpose flour
½ cup granulated sugar
4 teaspoons baking powder
½ cup butter, cubed
¾ cup dried blueberries
⅔ cup buttermilk
2 large eggs

In a large bowl, combine flour, sugar and baking powder. Cut in butter until mixture resembles coarse crumbs. Add blueberries, stirring to combine.

In a small bowl, whisk together buttermilk and eggs. Add to dry mixture stirring with a fork until just combined. Spoon dough into 12 individual portions on a parchment paper–lined baking sheet. Bake in 375°F oven until firm to touch and golden brown on top, about 15 to 18 minutes. Serve warm or at room temperature.

Makes 12 scones.

BERRY LAYER MUFFINS

. . . .

AUBERGE LE HERON COUNTRY INN,
NEW MILLS, N.B.

You can use whatever fruit is in season to give these wonderful little muffins a change of flavour. Make a double batch and freeze half to enjoy later.

⅓ cup butter, softened
⅔ cup packed brown sugar
2 large eggs
¾ cup milk
½ teaspoon vanilla extract
2 cups all-purpose flour
4 teaspoons baking powder
½ teaspoon salt
¾ cup whole berries (blueberries, raspberries)
2 tablespoons granulated sugar
1 teaspoon cinnamon

In a large bowl, cream together butter and brown sugar until fluffy. Beat in eggs, milk and vanilla. Don't be alarmed if mixture curdles.

In a separate bowl, sift together flour, baking powder and salt. Add to egg mixture all at once, stirring just enough to dampen dry ingredients.

Fill 12 paper-lined or greased muffin tins halfway with batter. Place a spoonful of berries in centre of batter and fill tins with remaining batter. Combine granulated sugar and cinnamon and sprinkle over muffins. Bake in 375°F oven for 20 to 25 minutes.

Makes 12 muffins.

CRANBERRY ORANGE MUFFINS

. . . .

MOUNTAIN GAP INN AND RESORT,
SMITHS COVE, N.S.

This is a delightfully tart muffin thanks to the orange juice concentrate and cranberries. You can double the recipe and freeze half.

1 cup coarsely chopped cranberries
1 large egg, beaten
⅔ cup milk
⅓ cup butter, melted
3 tablespoons orange juice concentrate
½ teaspoon vanilla extract
Zest of 1 orange
1¾ cups all-purpose flour
⅓ cup granulated sugar
2½ teaspoons baking powder
1 teaspoon salt

Mix together cranberries, egg, milk, butter, orange juice concentrate, vanilla and zest.

In a separate large bowl, sift together flour, sugar, baking powder and salt. Add the milk mixture to the dry ingredients, stirring just enough to blend. Spoon into paper-lined or greased muffin tins and bake in 400°F oven until golden, 20 to 25 minutes.

Makes 12 muffins.

PUMPKIN CREAM CHEESE MUFFINS

. . . .

EVANGELINE INN AND CAFÉ, GRAND PRÉ, N.S.

These little muffins with their surprise filling will delight both young and old.

1 large egg
½ cup milk
½ cup pumpkin purée
⅓ cup vegetable oil
1¾ cups all-purpose flour
½ cup granulated sugar
1 tablespoon baking powder
½ teaspoon cinnamon
½ teaspoon nutmeg
¼ teaspoon ginger
¼ teaspoon salt
4 ounces cream cheese

TOPPING
¼ cup packed brown sugar
½ teaspoon cinnamon
1 tablespoon butter

In a large bowl, whisk together the egg, milk, pumpkin and oil. In a separate bowl combine the flour, sugar, baking powder, spices and salt. Add wet ingredients to dry ingredients, stirring until blended.

TOPPING

In a small bowl, mash together brown sugar, cinnamon and butter until crumbly.

Fill paper-lined or greased muffin tins half full. Divide cream cheese into 12 equal pieces and place one piece on batter in each cup. Top with remaining batter and sprinkle with topping. Bake in 400°F oven until domed and firm to touch, about 20 minutes.

Makes 12 muffins.

LEMON POPPY SEED MUFFINS

. . . .

Light and airy, these muffins have just enough zest to add zing to the palate.

½ cup butter, softened

1¼ cups granulated sugar

2 large eggs

Zest of 2 lemons

Juice of 1 lemon

2¼ cups all-purpose flour

1 tablespoon poppy seeds

1 teaspoon baking powder

½ teaspoon salt

½ cup milk

LEMON GLAZE

Juice of 1 lemon

2 tablespoons granulated sugar

1 teaspoon poppy seeds

Using a mixer, cream butter and sugar until fluffy. Beat in eggs, one at a time, beating until well combined. Stir in lemon zest and juice.

In a separate bowl, mix together the flour, poppy seeds, baking powder and salt. Add to egg mixture a third at a time alternately with milk half at a time. Fill paper-lined or greased muffin tins two-thirds full and bake in 375°F oven until a toothpick inserted in the centre comes out clean, about 25 to 35 minutes.

LEMON GLAZE

Meanwhile, in a small bowl, stir lemon juice, sugar and poppy seeds until sugar dissolves.

Turn muffins out onto a rack and brush with glaze.

Makes 12 muffins.

CARROT PINEAPPLE MUFFINS

• • • • • • • • • • • • •

VIRJENE COLE, KENSINGTON, P.E.I.

Growing up on a farm meant using garden produce, carrots included. Instead of cooking them just as a vegetable, this Heritage Recipe Contest finalist decided to try carrots in her favourite muffin recipe, and she's been doing it ever since.

1½ cups all-purpose flour
1 cup granulated sugar
1 teaspoon baking powder
1 teaspoon baking soda
1 teaspoon cinnamon
½ teaspoon salt
2 large eggs
⅔ cup vegetable oil
1 teaspoon vanilla extract
1 cup grated carrot
½ cup crushed pineapple, undrained

In a large bowl, whisk together the flour, sugar, baking powder, baking soda, cinnamon and salt.

In a separate bowl, whisk the eggs, oil and vanilla. Add the carrot and pineapple. Pour over the dry ingredients and stir just until wet and dry ingredients are combined.

Fill paper-lined or greased muffins tins almost full. Bake in 400°F oven until domed and firm to the touch, about 20 minutes.

Makes 12 large muffins.

BLUEBERRY LEMON MUFFINS

• • • • • • • • • • • • •

If you want to keep some of these muffins for breakfast, you would be well advised to hide them.

2 cups all-purpose flour
¾ cup granulated sugar
1 tablespoon baking powder
½ teaspoon salt
1 large egg
Zest of 1 lemon
1 cup milk
¾ cup butter, melted
1¼ cups fresh or frozen blueberries
1 tablespoon lemon juice

Sift flour, ½ cup of the sugar, baking powder and salt into a large bowl. Whisk egg, zest, milk and ½ cup of the melted butter, and stir into dry ingredients until just blended. Stir in blueberries. Fill paper-lined or greased muffin tins two-thirds full. Bake in 400°F oven until firm to the touch, about 20 minutes.

While muffins are baking, combine remaining melted butter and lemon juice in a small bowl. Spoon remaining sugar into a separate bowl. When muffins are slightly cooled, dip tops first in lemon butter and then in sugar.

Makes 18 muffins.

RAISIN GINGER BRAN MUFFINS

· · · · · · · · · ·

Moist and flavourful, these muffins have been a family favourite. The crystallized ginger imparts an exotic taste, but if you're not crazy about it, just leave it out.

1 cup all-purpose flour
1½ cups bran
1½ teaspoons baking powder
¾ teaspoon salt
½ teaspoon baking soda
½ cup packed brown sugar
2 large eggs
1 cup milk
¼ cup vegetable oil
¼ cup fancy molasses
½ cup raisins
¼ cup finely diced crystallized ginger

In a large bowl, combine flour, bran, baking powder, salt and baking soda. Blend in brown sugar.

In a separate bowl, beat eggs. Add milk, vegetable oil and molasses. Whisk to combine. Pour egg mixture over dry ingredients, stirring just until moistened. Stir in raisins and crystallized ginger.

Spoon batter into large paper-lined or greased muffin tins and fill just to the top of paper. Bake in a 400°F oven until domed and firm to the touch, about 18 to 20 minutes.

Makes 12 muffins.

CORN BREAD

· · · · · · · · · ·

JOAN NEVERS, PLASTER ROCK, N.B.

Joan Nevers has warm memories of sharing corn bread with her family: "Almost every Saturday night we had beans and corn bread. On our farm, where the meals were large, we always had a pan of corn bread ready for when the men came in from the woods. It saved on homemade bread, which took much longer to make. I still live in the country and whenever I can I make my corn bread with buttermilk from a farm."

1 cup cornmeal
1 cup all-purpose flour
¾ cup granulated sugar
½ teaspoon salt
½ teaspoon baking soda
1 cup buttermilk
2 large eggs
1 tablespoon butter, melted

In a large bowl, whisk the cornmeal with the flour, sugar and salt. In a separate bowl, whisk the baking soda into the buttermilk. Whisk in the eggs and butter. Pour the wet ingredients over the dry and stir just to combine.

Scrape into a well greased 8-inch square pan. Bake in 350°F oven until golden brown, about 30 minutes.

Makes 1 pan of corn bread, about 9 pieces.

CHOCOLATE CHIP LOAF

. . . .

ANNE MARIE CURRIE, SYDNEY, N.S.

Some people love to make cookies and some don't, but everyone loves chocolate chips. Anne Marie Currie reports that this recipe is her own invention.

2 cups all-purpose flour

⅔ cup granulated sugar

4 teaspoons baking powder

1 teaspoon salt

1 cup chocolate chips

½ cup walnut pieces

½ cup chopped dates

1 large egg

1 cup strong, cold coffee

½ teaspoon baking soda

1 tablespoon vegetable oil

Blend the first 4 ingredients in a large bowl. Add chocolate chips, walnuts and dates and stir until well coated. In a separate bowl, whisk the egg with the coffee, baking soda and oil. Pour over the dry ingredients and stir just enough to combine. Pour into a 9- by 5-inch greased loaf pan and let stand for 20 minutes. Bake at 325°F until a toothpick inserted into the centre comes out clean, about 1 hour. Cool before slicing.

Makes 1 loaf, 10 to 12 slices.

GRANDMOTHER'S CRANBERRY LOAF

. . . .

DONNA GOODWIN, LARRY'S RIVER, N.S.

A recipe that's been in the family for many years won a place as finalist in an Atlantic Insight Heritage Recipe Contest for Donna Goodwin. As a child, she visited her grandmother and together they would go out picking wild cranberries sprayed by the ocean nearby. Then she watched the baking of a cranberry loaf moist with orange juice. Donna's family enjoys it and they feel fortunate to be able to gather cranberries today.

2 cups all-purpose flour

1 cup granulated sugar

1½ teaspoons baking powder

½ teaspoon salt

½ teaspoon baking soda

½ cup butter, cubed

1 large egg

1 teaspoon orange zest

¾ cup orange juice

1½ cups golden raisins

1½ cups whole cranberries

Sift flour, sugar, baking powder, salt and baking soda into a large bowl. Cut in butter until mixture is crumbly. Whisk egg, zest and juice and add all at once. Stir just enough to moisten mixture. Fold in raisins and cranberries. Spoon into a greased 9- by 5-inch loaf pan. Bake at 350°F until a toothpick inserted into the centre comes out clean, about 70 minutes. Cool on a rack.

Makes 1 loaf, 10 to 12 slices.

PUMPKIN BREAD

· · · · · · · · · ·

Spread with softened cream cheese, pumpkin bread is a breakfast comfort food. The recipe can be doubled — allowing one for immediate consumption and one that can be tucked away in the freezer for a busy morning treat.

1½ cups all-purpose flour
1 cup granulated sugar
1 teaspoon baking powder
1 teaspoon baking soda
1 teaspoon cinnamon
½ teaspoon salt
2 large eggs
½ cup vegetable oil
1 cup pumpkin purée
½ cup raisins

In a large bowl, whisk together the flour, sugar, baking powder, baking soda, cinnamon and salt. In a separate bowl, whisk eggs and oil. Stir in pumpkin and raisins. Pour over the dry ingredients, stirring until combined. Pour into a greased 9- by 5-inch loaf pan. Bake in 350°F oven for 1 hour or until a toothpick inserted in the centre of the loaf comes out clean. Let cool in pan for 10 minutes, remove and cool on a rack.

Makes 1 loaf, 10 to 12 slices.

NUT AND SEED BREAD

· · · · · · · · · ·

BLUENOSE LODGE, LUNENBURG, N.S.

This loaf keeps very well, wrapped and refrigerated. It is delicious served with cream cheese.

2¼ cups all-purpose flour
¾ cup whole wheat flour
1½ teaspoons baking powder
1½ teaspoons baking soda
¾ teaspoon salt
1½ cups lightly packed brown sugar
½ cup chopped nuts
3 tablespoons wheat germ
3 tablespoons sesame seeds
3 tablespoons poppy seeds
2 large eggs
1½ cups buttermilk
⅓ cup vegetable oil

In a large bowl, combine all dry ingredients, from flour to poppy seeds, and mix thoroughly. In a separate bowl, beat together eggs, buttermilk and oil. Add wet to dry ingredients and stir until just mixed. Pour batter into a greased and floured 9- by 5-inch loaf pan. Bake in a 350°F oven for 55 to 60 minutes or until a toothpick inserted in centre of loaf comes out clean. Cool a few minutes and then turn out onto a rack.

Makes 1 large loaf, 10 to 12 slices.

CRANBERRY LEMON LOAF

. . . .

JENNIFER WADE, VANCOUVER, B.C.

Jennifer Wade says, "When my mother first returned to Canada from India, she felt sure she had never tasted anything so delicious as the wild cranberries and blueberries of Nova Scotia. By experimenting and combining many recipes, she developed this cranberry loaf, which has become a favourite on our table."

¼ cup butter, softened

¾ cup granulated sugar

2 large eggs

2 teaspoons lemon zest

2 cups sifted all-purpose flour

2½ to 3 teaspoons baking powder

1 teaspoon salt

¾ cup milk

1 cup chopped fresh cranberries

½ cup chopped walnuts

½ cup mixed peel

TOPPING

1 tablespoon lemon juice

2 tablespoons granulated sugar

Cream butter and sugar well. Add eggs and zest. Beat well. Sift the dry ingredients separately and add to the creamed mixture in 3 additions alternately with milk in 2 additions. Beat well. Gently fold in the cranberries, walnuts and peel. Scrape into a greased 9- by 5-inch loaf pan and bake at 350°F until a toothpick inserted into the loaf comes out clean, about 55 minutes. Let stand for 10 minutes and then remove from the pan.

TOPPING

Combine the lemon juice and sugar and drizzle slowly over the top of the loaf. Let cool. Serve with a dollop of whipped cream.

Makes 1 loaf, 10 to 12 slices.

GRAHAM BREAD

. . . .

DAWN BREMNER, JEMSEG, N.B.

Sarah Emily Dykeman gave this recipe to her daughter, Charity, who gave it to her daughter, Myrtle, who shared it with her cousin and his wife, who were the grandparents of the present custodian of the recipe. That's a genealogy to be admired as much as a baked loaf of graham bread. It's a basic, quick bread that would have cooked in a Dutch oven over an open fireplace. This substantial bread now cooks as well in a modern oven. The honey came from Sarah Dykeman's bees, and molasses would have been used when honey wasn't available. Over the years, the amount of honey is reduced to make the bread lighter and the leavening has been adjusted. The mixture of whole wheat and white flours was also a later adaptation. Children particularly like slices spread with crunchy peanut butter.

⅓ cup liquid honey
1½ cups milk
2 teaspoon baking soda
2 cups graham flour or any whole wheat flour
1 cup all-purpose flour
1 teaspoon salt

Warm the honey, if necessary, so it will blend with the milk. Dissolve the soda in the milk and honey, then add the dry ingredients. Mix well and place in a greased 9- by 5-inch loaf pan. Cover with a tea towel and let rise in a warm place for 30 minutes. Bake at 350°F until a toothpick inserted into the centre of the loaf comes out clean, about 50 minutes.

Makes 1 loaf, 10 to 12 slices.

FRESH STRAWBERRY BUTTER

. . . .

What better way to start the day than with a freshly baked muffin or bagel topped with delicious Strawberry Butter? Keep any unused butter in the freezer, where it will keep for several months.

½ cup fresh strawberries, rinsed, hulled and patted dry
1 cup unsalted butter
2 tablespoons icing sugar

Blend together all ingredients in food processor until the mixture is pale pink. Use immediately or store in the freezer in an airtight container.

Makes 1¼ cups.

CAKES

APPLE NUT POUND CAKE

. . . .

An ample cake that is easy to prepare, this recipe is sure to become a family favourite. Serve it by the slice at room temperature, or warmed and accompanied by ice cream.

1 teaspoon cinnamon
2¼ cups granulated sugar
1 cup butter, softened
4 large eggs
1 teaspoon vanilla extract
2⅔ cups all-purpose flour
1 tablespoon baking powder
¼ teaspoon salt
¼ cup apple juice
4 apples, cored, peeled and sliced
⅓ cup chopped walnuts or pecans

Grease and flour a 10-inch tube pan.

In a small bowl, combine cinnamon and 3 tablespoons of the sugar, and reserve.

With a mixer, cream butter and remaining sugar until light and fluffy. Add eggs, one at a time, beating well after each addition then add vanilla. Sift together flour, baking powder and salt, and add to batter alternately with the apple juice, making 3 additions of dry ingredients and 2 of juice, mixing just until the batter is smooth.

Pour half of the batter into the tube pan. Arrange half of the apple slices and all of the nuts on top of the batter. Sprinkle half of the cinnamon sugar over the nuts and apples. Pour remaining batter in pan; top with remaining apples and sprinkle with remaining cinnamon sugar mixture.

Bake in 325°F oven for 75 to 80 minutes or until a toothpick inserted in centre of the cake comes out clean. Cool for 15 minutes on a rack and then invert and cool completely.

Serves 12.

SCANDINAVIAN APPLE CAKE

. . . .

SEVEN RESTAURANT & WINE BAR, HALIFAX, N.S.

This is a delicious treat in autumn, when freshly picked apples are abundant.

¾ cup butter, melted
1 cup granulated sugar
2 large eggs
2 teaspoons vanilla extract
2¼ cups all-purpose flour
2 teaspoons baking soda
2 teaspoons baking powder
2 teaspoons cinnamon
2 teaspoons allspice
1½ teaspoons cardamom
½ teaspoon salt
5 apples, peeled, cored and chopped

Grease and line the bottom of a 10-inch springform pan.

In a large bowl, beat the butter and sugar until light in colour. Mix in eggs one at a time and add vanilla.

In a separate bowl, whisk together the flour, baking soda, baking powder, spices and salt until blended. Add to butter mixture and fold in the apples. Pour into prepared pan and bake in 350°F oven for 50 to 65 minutes or until a toothpick inserted into the centre comes out clean.

Remove pan from oven and let cool for 15 minutes on a rack. Remove side of pan.

Let cool completely or serve warm with a dollop of whipped cream.

Serves 12.

DOWN EAST APPLE CAKE

. . . .

THE OLD FISH FACTORY RESTAURANT,
LUNENBURG, N.S.

Bake the cake a day ahead and store it in a cake container. This dense, moist cake is the ideal finish to a day of vigorous summer activity!

1 large egg
½ cup granulated sugar
⅓ cup vegetable oil
3 tablespoons orange juice
1 teaspoon vanilla extract
¾ cup all-purpose flour
1¼ teaspoons baking powder
¼ teaspoon salt
3 apples, peeled and sliced
⅓ cup packed brown sugar
1 teaspoon cinnamon
¼ teaspoon ginger
2 teaspoons lemon juice
2 teaspoons liquid honey

With an electric mixer, beat egg with granulated sugar until light and fluffy. Beat in oil, orange juice and vanilla. In a separate bowl, combine flour, baking powder and salt. Add to egg mixture, stirring only until blended. Peel apples and slice into a bowl. Sprinkle with brown sugar, cinnamon and ginger, and arrange in a greased 9-inch round cake pan. Pour cake batter over apples and bake in a 350°F oven for 35 to 40 minutes or until a toothpick inserted into the centre comes out clean. Cool on a rack, then loosen sides and turn out onto a serving plate. Whisk together lemon juice and honey, and brush apples to form glaze.

Serves 8.

APPLESAUCE CAKE

. . . .

CARRIE ALBERT, GRAND FALLS, N.B.

When Carrie Albert submitted this recipe to Atlantic Insight *magazine, it was already 100 years old. Her grandparents were Danish, and emigrated to New Brunswick. Carrie said she used it a lot when she cooked for lumberjacks, woodsmen and farmers.*

½ cup lard and butter mixed
1 cup granulated sugar
1 large egg
1 teaspoon baking soda
1 cup of applesauce
2 cups sifted all-purpose flour
1 teaspoon ginger
1 teaspoon cinnamon

SAUCE
1 cup granulated sugar
1 heaping teaspoon cornstarch or potato flour
Pinch of salt
Cold water
Boiling water
1 tablespoon butter
Vinegar or lemon extract to taste

In a large bowl with a mixer, beat lard, butter, sugar and egg until smooth. In a bowl, combine baking soda and applesauce. In a separate, combine dry ingredients. Add to butter mixture alternately with the applesauce mixture.

Bake in a greased 9-inch square pan in a 350°F oven until a toothpick inserted into centre comes out clean. Serve with sauce.

SAUCE

Mix sugar, cornstarch and salt in a saucepan. Stir in enough cold water until mixture has the consistency of cream. Gradually add boiling water, stirring constantly over medium heat until the mixture is smooth and has consistency of maple syrup. Remove from heat, add butter and a little vinegar.

Serves 8.

HOT APPLE CAKE WITH CARAMEL PECAN SAUCE

· · · · · · · · · · · · ·

ST. MARTINS COUNTRY INN, ST. MARTINS, N.B.

Desserts that have fruit or vegetables as ingredients, such as apple, zucchini or carrot, have a delicious flavour that improves if left for a day or two. This recipe with its accompanying pecan sauce will not likely survive that long.

1 cup unsalted butter, softened
1 cup granulated sugar
2 large eggs
1 teaspoon vanilla extract
1½ cups all-purpose flour
1½ teaspoons cinnamon
1 teaspoon baking soda
¼ teaspoon salt
4 medium tart apples, peeled, cored and finely chopped
¾ cup coarsely chopped pecans

CARAMEL PECAN SAUCE

2 tablespoons unsalted butter
¼ cup pecan halves
½ cup packed dark brown sugar
½ cup heavy cream (35% mf)
1 tablespoon rum or bourbon

In a bowl, cream butter and sugar until fluffy, approximately 3 minutes. On low speed, beat in eggs, one at a time and add vanilla.

Sift together dry ingredients and stir into the batter, stirring just until mixed. Blend in apples and pecans.

Spoon batter into a greased 7 by 11-inch cake pan and bake in a 350°F oven for 35 to 45 minutes, until top is golden and a toothpick inserted in centre of cake comes out clean. Cool in pan for 10 minutes before turning out on a rack.

Serve cake warm with vanilla ice cream on the side and topped with Caramel Pecan Sauce.

CARAMEL PECAN SAUCE

In a small saucepan, over moderately-high heat, melt butter. Add nuts and cook, stirring constantly, until nuts are toasted and butter is light brown. Add sugar and cream. Continue to stir as sugar dissolves and the sauce boils, turning a deep golden brown. Remove from heat, add rum and cool.

Makes 12 servings.

CHOCOLATE BEET CAKE

. . . .

SANDRA NOWLAN, HALIFAX, N.S.

Disguising beets for children and people who don't like them in a moist chocolate cake is almost as shocking as the magenta colour of the batter. But this cake is such a favourite in the Nowlan family that it usually gets eaten before it's iced. The beets are homegrown on a farm in Musquodoboit Harbour, N.S., and each year the crop is expanded so that some can be put away in the freezer just for winter cakes. During baking the colour of the cake is transformed to a glorious dark brown.

3 large eggs
1¼ cups granulated sugar
⅞ cup vegetable oil
1½ cups cooked, puréed beets
2 squares unsweetened chocolate, melted and cooled
½ teaspoon vanilla extract
1¾ cups all-purpose flour
1½ teaspoons baking soda
½ teaspoon salt
½ teaspoon baking powder

In a mixer, beat the eggs and sugar at top speed until light and fluffy. Reduce speed to low and gradually add the oil. Add beets, chocolate and vanilla. Sift flour, soda, salt and baking powder. Add to beet mixture and mix at low speed until no traces of flour remain. Pour batter into a greased and floured 9-inch square pan. Bake at 350°F until firm to the touch and a toothpick inserted into the centre comes out clean, about 50 to 60 minutes.

Serves 9.

CARROT CAKE SURPRISE

. . . .

This recipe has won numerous prizes at fairs and events — in addition to endless compliments.

2 cups all-purpose flour
1½ cups granulated sugar
2 teaspoons each cinnamon and baking soda
½ teaspoon each salt, ginger, nutmeg and mace
3 large eggs
¾ cup mayonnaise
2 cups grated carrots
1 cup crushed pineapple, undrained
1 cup raisins
¾ cup chopped walnuts

CREAM CHEESE ICING

8-ounce package cream cheese, softened
¼ cup butter, softened
1 tablespoon milk
2 cups icing sugar

In a large bowl, whisk together the flour, sugar, cinnamon, baking soda, salt, ginger, nutmeg and mace. In a separate bowl, whisk the eggs. Whisk in the mayonnaise. Scrape over the dry ingredients. Top with the carrots, pineapple, raisins and walnuts. Beat together. Scrape into greased 9- by 13-inch pan and bake at 350°F for about 35 to 45 minutes. Cool before icing.

CREAM CHEESE ICING

Beat all ingredients until light and very fluffy, and then ice the cake. This icing will keep for weeks if tightly covered in the fridge.

Serves 12.

BLUEBERRY CINNAMON COFFEE CAKE

INN ON THE LAKE, FALL RIVER, N.S.

During the blueberry season at the Inn on the Lake just outside Halifax, the chefs adapt a variety of different recipes to include blueberries.

1 cup blueberries
1 teaspoon cinnamon
½ cup butter, softened
1 cup granulated sugar
2 large eggs
1½ teaspoon vanilla extract
1½ cups all-purpose flour
2 teaspoons baking powder
¼ teaspoon salt
⅔ cup milk
Whipped cream (optional)

BLUEBERRY SAUCE

1 cup blueberries
1 cup granulated sugar
1 tablespoon cornstarch
¼ cup cold water

Toss blueberries with cinnamon and set aside. Cream butter and sugar together until fluffy. Beat in eggs, one at a time, then add vanilla. Sift together flour, baking powder and salt. Add to butter mixture in 3 additions, alternately with milk, in 2 additions. Fold in blueberry mixture. Pour batter into a greased 10-inch round springform pan and bake in 350°F oven for 40 to 45 minutes or until a toothpick inserted into the centre comes out clean. Let cool for 20 minutes, unmould and serve with warm blueberry sauce and whipped cream, if using.

BLUEBERRY SAUCE

Combine all ingredients in a saucepan, bring to a boil and simmer until thickened. Serve warm with coffee cake.

Serves 10 to 12.

CRANBERRY BLUEBERRY STREUSEL CAKE

JENNY MACDONALD, NEW GLASGOW, N.S.

There's always company at Christmastime and hostesses like to have something not too sweet, but Christmassy just the same. Most people like cranberries and most like blueberries. But at short notice, baking supplies are not always at hand. Combining several ideas into one produced a new taste.

STREUSEL

½ cup chopped nuts
⅓ cup packed brown sugar
¼ cup flour
½ teaspoon cinnamon
3 tablespoons butter

CAKE

⅓ cup soft butter
¾ cup granulated sugar
1 large egg
2 cups flour, ½ all-purpose, ½ whole wheat
1 tablespoon baking powder
1 teaspoon salt
1 cup milk, soured if available
½ cup fresh or frozen cranberries
½ cup fresh or frozen blueberries
Whipped cream

STREUSEL

Using fork, combine all ingredients and set aside.

CAKE

Cream the butter and sugar. Beat in the egg. Combine the flour, baking powder and salt. Add alternately with milk. Spread half of the batter in a greased 9-inch square pan. Sprinkle with cranberries and half of the streusel mixture. Add the remaining batter. Sprinkle with blueberries and the remaining streusel mixture. Bake at 350°F until a toothpick inserted into the centre comes out clean, about 45 to 50 minutes. Serve warm with whipped cream.

Serves 9.

188   BEST RECIPES OF THE MARITIME PROVINCES

BLUEBERRY CAKE

. . . .

ANN AMES-WARMAN, TRURO, N.S.

Farmers' markets are not only the source of fresh fruit and vegetables in season. Many stall-holders are cooks who bring the best from their home kitchens. The Tatamagouche Farmers' Market is located in a formerly abandoned train station in the Nova Scotia town. Most of the customers are local people and cottagers.

½ cup butter, softened
2 cups granulated sugar
2 large eggs
3½ cups all-purpose flour
1 teaspoon baking soda
1 teaspoon salt
1 cup milk
1½ teaspoons lemon extract
4 cups blueberries

TOPPING

2 tablespoons granulated sugar
1 teaspoon cinnamon
½ cup butter, melted
1 tablespoon fresh lemon juice

Beat together the butter and sugar, and beat in the eggs. Sift together flour, baking soda and salt. Mix milk with lemon extract. Mix dry ingredients in 3 additions and milk mixture alternately in 2 additions into creamed mixture. Fold in the blueberries and pour into a greased 9- by 13-inch pan.

TOPPING

Mix sugar with cinnamon and sprinkle on batter. Bake at 350°F for 1 hour. Combine butter with the lemon juice. Prick the warm cake with a fork and drizzle the mixture over.

Serves 12 to 16.

GRANDMA'S GUMDROP CAKE

. . . .

BILLIE MCFETRIDGE, VANCOUVER, B.C.

When Billie McFetridge visited her grandmother, the biggest treat was her gumdrop cake, which was kept in a crock in the basement and only served for "special." Billie loved this cake so much her grandmother finally gave her the recipe. She have kept it in the family and it has been a special treat to many over the years. The significant thing Billie remembers Grandma doing before putting the cake in the oven was making the sign of the cross on it. Billie always does the same thing!

3 cups all-purpose flour
1 teaspoon baking powder
Salt to taste
1 cup sliced gumdrops
1 cup light raisins
A little minced peel
1 cup butter, softened
1½ cups granulated sugar
3 large eggs
½ cup cold water
Juice of 1 orange

Sift flour with baking powder and salt. Mix together gumdrops, raisins and peel and add ½ cup of the flour mixture. In bowl, cream butter and sugar thoroughly. Add eggs, one at a time, and beat until light and fluffy. Mix water and orange juice. Add dry ingredients to butter mixture, making 3 additions of dry ingredients and 2 of liquid. Lastly, add floured gumdrop mixture. Put in a 10- by 6-inch loaf pan lined with well-greased paper. Bake at 300°F for 2 hours or until cake springs back when pressed lightly. Cool in pan.

Makes 1 large loaf, 12 slices.

BLUEBERRY ORANGE CAKE

· · · · · · · · · · · · ·

Blueberry cakes are special favourites in the Maritimes and Newfoundland. Cookbooks by local authors can be counted on to include at least one version of this classic. This recipe shows off the berries baked in a layer running through the centre of an orange Bundt cake. (Westerners can substitute saskatoons).

BATTER

½ cup butter, softened
1 cup granulated sugar
1 large egg
2 teaspoons orange zest
2 cups all-purpose flour
1 tablespoon baking powder
½ teaspoon salt
1 cup blueberries
½ cup orange juice
½ cup milk

ICING

3 tablespoons packed brown sugar
1 teaspoon orange zest
3 tablespoons orange juice
1 tablespoon orange liqueur, gin or extra orange juice

Butter a 9-inch tube or Bundt pan. Dust with flour and tip out the excess.

BATTER

Cream the butter, add the sugar and beat until light and fluffy. Add the egg and zest. Beat well.

Sift together the flour, baking powder and salt. Spoon out 1 tablespoon, toss with berries, and set aside. Stir a third of the dry ingredients into the creamed mixture, then the orange juice, followed by a second portion of dry ingredients, then the milk and the last third of the dry ingredients.

Spoon half the batter into the prepared pan. Distribute the berries over the batter, keeping them centred ½-inch from the edges of the pan. Spoon the rest of the batter over the berries. Tap the pan once lightly on the counter.

Bake in a 350°F oven for 45 minutes, or until a toothpick inserted in the middle of the cake comes out clean. Cool 10 minutes in the pan on a rack, then turn out onto a flat serving plate.

ICING

Combine all the icing ingredients and drizzle over the cake while it is still slightly warm.

Serves 12.

SPIRITED PUMPKIN MOUSSE CAKE

· · · · · · · · · · · ·

This dessert, which is not quite a cheesecake and not quite a pumpkin pie, has a wonderful flavour and is a nice alternative to traditional Thanksgiving desserts.

VANILLA WAFER CRUST

2 cups vanilla wafer crumbs (or graham cracker crumbs)

¼ cup granulated sugar

6 tablespoons butter, melted and cooled

FILLING

1½ cups pumpkin purée

½ cup heavy cream (35% mf)

¾ cup granulated sugar

3 large egg yolks, beaten

¾ teaspoon cinnamon

½ teaspoon ginger

¼ teaspoon nutmeg

¼ teaspoon allspice

¼ teaspoon salt

¼ cup orange flavoured liqueur (Grand Marnier or Cointreau)

4 teaspoons unflavoured gelatin

3 large egg whites

Pinch of cream of tartar

Pinch of salt

Whipped cream

Orange zest, for garnish

VANILLA WAFER CRUST

In a bowl, combine vanilla wafer crumbs, sugar and melted butter. Pour into 9-inch springform pan and press into bottom and sides. Bake in 400°F oven for 10 minutes. Cool completely before filling.

FILLING

In a saucepan, whisk together the pumpkin, cream, ½ cup of the sugar, egg yolks, cinnamon, ginger, nutmeg, allspice and salt until smooth. Cook over medium heat, stirring occasionally, for 10 minutes. Meanwhile, pour the liqueur into the top pan of a double boiler, sprinkle the gelatin overtop and let it rest 5 minutes. Place top of double boiler over simmering water and stir until gelatin has dissolved. Transfer pumpkin mixture to a bowl, add gelatin and stir to combine. Let cool.

With a mixer, beat egg whites and cream of tartar until soft peaks form. With mixer running, add remaining sugar, 1 tablespoon at a time, and beat until stiff peaks form. Fold egg whites into pumpkin mixture and pour into prepared Vanilla Wafer Crust. Cover and refrigerate at least 6 hours.

To serve, slide cake off base onto serving plate. Remove sides of pan. Cut cake into wedges, top with whipped cream and garnish with orange zest.

Serves 8 to 10.

CHEESECAKE WITH RHUBARB IN ROSÉ WINE SYRUP

· · · · · · · · · · · ·

Cheesecake is a bistro classic. The cheesecake itself is absolutely delicious, but the tart rhubarb is exactly what the recipe needs to cut through the creaminess of the dessert's foundation. The rhubarb takes a bit of planning, but the beautiful rose-coloured syrup and tangy fruit will leave your guests gasping with delight.

CHEESECAKE

1½ cups graham cracker crumbs

1 cup granulated sugar

1 teaspoon cinnamon

6 tablespoons butter, melted

1 pound cream cheese

3 large eggs

1 teaspoon lemon juice

2 teaspoons vanilla extract

TOPPING

2 cups sour cream

3 tablespoons granulated sugar

1 teaspoon vanilla extract

RHUBARB IN ROSÉ WINE SYRUP

2 cups Canadian rosé wine

1 cup granulated sugar

3 tablespoons grenadine

1 tablespoon rosewater

1 cinnamon stick

1 pod star anise

1 pound fresh rhubarb

Mint leaves, for garnish

CHEESECAKE

In a bowl, combine graham cracker crumbs, ¼ cup of the sugar, cinnamon and melted butter and mix well. Press mixture into the bottom of a 9-inch springform pan to a ¼ inch thickness.

In a large bowl, beat cream cheese until light and smooth (about 10 minutes), scraping down the sides of the bowl and the beaters once or twice during that time. Add eggs one at a time, followed by lemon juice, remaining sugar and vanilla. Beat until all ingredients are incorporated and mixture is smooth.

Pour onto graham cracker crust and bake in 375°F oven for 25 to 30 minutes, until set but still with a bit of movement in the centre of the filling. Let cool on the counter for at least 30 minutes or until cool.

TOPPING

Whisk sour cream together with sugar and vanilla until smooth. Once cheesecake has cooled, pour sour cream mixture over top. Bake for 5 minutes in a 475°F oven. Let cool at room temperature for 1 hour, then refrigerate for at least 6 hours before removing cake from the pan.

SYRUP

Combine wine, sugar, grenadine, rosewater, cinnamon stick and star anise in a saucepan and bring to a boil. Reduce liquid by half and allow to cool completely.

Trim rhubarb and cut into batons about 3 inches long. Remove star anise pod and cinnamon from syrup and place the rhubarb in the saucepan. Bring to a boil and immediately remove from the heat, allowing fruit to steep in syrup. This will prevent rhubarb from turning mushy. If syrup looks a little thin, simply remove rhubarb and boil down again

Serve about 3 batons of rhubarb on the top (or the side) of each slice of cheesecake and drizzle a tablespoon or so of the syrup over it. Garnish with a few mint leaves.

Serves 12.

Tip: When slicing cheesecake, dip a knife into hot water, dry it quickly on a towel, and make your slice. Repeat for every slice to ensure clean cuts and a neat presentation. Another trick is to use a length of dental floss that can cut through the entire diameter of the cake at one time, and is then pulled out through the side.

PEERLESS CRANBERRY CARROT CAKE

. . . .

WICKWIRE HOUSE, KENTVILLE, N.S.

After many variations, this recipe was perfected by innkeeper Darlene Peerless.

4 cups grated carrots

2 cups granulated sugar

1 cup butter, cut in pieces

1 14-ounce can crushed pineapple in
   unsweetened juice,

3 cups all-purpose flour

1 tablespoon cinnamon

2 teaspoons baking soda

2 teaspoons cloves

1 teaspoon allspice

1 teaspoon nutmeg

½ teaspoon baking powder

½ teaspoon salt

1 cup dried cranberries

2 large eggs

CREAM CHEESE ICING

8 ounces cream cheese, softened

½ cup butter, softened

2 cups icing sugar, sifted

½ cup pecans, chopped

½ cup crushed pineapple, well drained

¼ cup chopped dried cranberries

In a medium saucepan, bring carrots, sugar, butter and pineapple with juice to a simmer, then cook 5 minutes, stirring occasionally. Remove from heat and cool completely.

Combine flour, cinnamon, baking soda, cloves, allspice, nutmeg, baking powder and salt in a large bowl. Stir in cranberries.

In a separate large bowl beat eggs until lemon-coloured, then add carrot mixture and stir to combine. Add flour mixture, stirring only until batter is combined. Pour into a greased and floured 10-inch Bundt or tube pan and bake in a 350°F oven about 45 minutes or until a toothpick inserted into the centre comes out clean. Remove from oven and let stand 10 minutes before turning out onto a serving plate to cool. Cover with cream cheese icing.

ICING

Beat cream cheese, butter and icing sugar until light and fluffy. Stir in remaining ingredients.

Serves 10 to 12.

RED RIBBON CRANBERRY COFFEE CAKE

CRANBERRY COVE INN, LOUISBOURG, N.S.

Guests at the Cranberry Cove Inn, which overlooks Louisbourg Harbour, are often served this layered cranberry cake warm from the oven.

TOPPING

¼ cup all-purpose flour
2 tablespoons granulated sugar
1 tablespoon butter

CRANBERRY SAUCE

2 cups cranberries
1 cup granulated sugar
½ cup water

BATTER

2 cups all-purpose flour
¾ cup granulated sugar
1½ teaspoons baking powder
½ cup butter, cubed
1 large egg
1 teaspoon vanilla extract
¾ cup milk

TOPPING

Place topping ingredients in a small bowl and, using a fork, mash until ingredients are the size of small peas. Set aside.

CRANBERRY SAUCE

Combine cranberries, sugar and water in a saucepan over medium-high heat. Bring to a boil, reduce heat and simmer until berries are tender and sauce has thickened, approximately 20 minutes. Cool and purée. Transfer to a bowl.

BATTER

Combine flour, sugar and baking powder in a large bowl. Cut in butter with a pastry blender until mixture resembles coarse meal.

In a separate bowl, whisk together egg, vanilla and milk. Add to flour mixture, stirring only until batter is moist.

Spread half the batter over the bottom of a greased 9-inch quiche pan.

Beat cranberry with a fork until smooth. Spread evenly over batter in pan. Top with remaining batter, spreading with a spatula to avoid disturbing the cranberry sauce. Sprinkle with topping and bake at 350°F 20 minutes or until a toothpick inserted into the centre comes out clean.

Serves 8.

FRESH-GINGER GINGERBREAD, BUTTERSCOTCH APPLES AND CINNAMON CRÈME ANGLAISE

. . . .

Hot gingerbread cake means winter. In the Maritimes everyone has a recipe, but most people would agree that the cake should be dark and moist. This version features the heat of fresh ginger. It gives a "snap" and spiciness in balance with the more subtle warmth of the powdered ginger.

GINGERBREAD

1 cup butter, softened
1 cup packed brown sugar
6 large eggs
2½ cups fancy molasses
3 tablespoons grated fresh gingeroot
4 cups all-purpose flour
¼ cup cinnamon
3 tablespoons ginger
1½ tablespoons baking powder
2 teaspoons baking soda
2 teaspoons cloves
½ whole nutmeg, grated (1 teaspoon)
2 cups boiling water

BUTTERSCOTCH APPLES

4 pie apples (Spy, Granny Smith or Jonagold)
2 tablespoons granulated sugar
1 teaspoon cinnamon
½ cup packed brown sugar
¼ cup butter
¾ cup golden corn syrup
1 small can evaporated milk
2 tablespoons Bailey's Irish Cream liqueur

CRÈME ANGLAISE

4 large egg yolks
¼ cup granulated sugar
1 teaspoon cinnamon
1 vanilla bean, split, with seeds scraped from pod
⅔ cup heavy cream (35% mf)
⅔ cup milk

GINGERBREAD

Cream butter and brown sugar until light and fluffy. Gradually add eggs, then molasses and beat until smooth. Stir in the fresh gingeroot. In a separate bowl, sift together the dry ingredients. Fold into the wet ingredients and pour the batter into a large greased 9- by 13-inch pan. Add the boiling water to this mixture and mix until just combined. It may be necessary to use 2 smaller pans as this recipe is quite large. Bake at 350°F for 45 minutes or until a toothpick inserted into the centre of the cake comes out clean.

BUTTERSCOTCH APPLES

Peel and core apples; cut into eighths. Toss in granulated sugar and cinnamon. Bake in a 400°F oven for 10 minutes, or until lightly browned. Let cool. In a heavy saucepan, cook brown sugar, butter, corn syrup and evaporated milk to the soft ball stage, 230°F on a candy thermometer. Add liqueur and stir in apples. Set aside.

CRÈME ANGLAISE

Whisk egg yolks, sugar and cinnamon in a bowl. In a saucepan, combine vanilla seeds and pod with cream and milk and heat to just below boiling. Remove from the heat and stir one ladle at a time into egg mixture. Pour mixture back into the saucepan and cook over very low heat stirring constantly, about 10 minutes, or until it coats the back of a spoon. Strain through a fine sieve into a clean bowl set in a larger bowl of ice and water. Stir often as it cools. Refrigerate in a sealed container for up to 1 week.

To serve, warm the cake in a microwave for 20 to 30 seconds for each portion. Top with the apples and drizzle Crème Anglaise on the plate.

Serves 12.

ATLANTIC MAPLE SYRUP CAKE

JOAN NEVERS, PLASTER ROCK, N.B.

New Brunswick has an abundance of maple trees. Years ago making the syrup was all done by hand. Joan Nevers always had lots of syrup and loved it on oatmeal, pancakes and ice cream. Now she uses it in her recipes. Her granny made this cake, even when she was well up in years.

½ cup butter, softened
¼ cup granulated sugar
2 large eggs
2¼ cups all-purpose flour
1 tablespoon baking powder
¾ teaspoon baking soda
½ teaspoon ginger or mace
1 cup pure maple syrup
½ cup hot water

MAPLE ICING

2 large egg whites
¾ cup granulated sugar
½ cup maple syrup
¼ teaspoon cream of tartar

Cream together butter and sugar. Beat in eggs, one at a time. Sift dry ingredients together and add to butter mixture a third at a time alternately with mixture of maple syrup and hot water. Beat until smooth. Bake in a greased 9-inch square pan at 350°F for 25 to 30 minutes or until a toothpick inserted into the centre of the cake comes out clean. Allow to cool in the pan.

ICING

Put all the ingredients in top of a double boiler. Cook over boiling water, whipping constantly for 7 to 9 minutes, until stiff peaks form. Cool and spread on cake.

Serves 8.

MAPLE SYRUP GINGERBREAD

LISCOMBE LODGE, LISCOMB MILLS, N.S.

Savour this cake warm from the oven over a fresh cup of coffee. This old-time favourite takes on a new flavour with the addition of maple syrup.

1⅓ cups all-purpose flour
1 teaspoon baking powder
1 teaspoon ginger
½ teaspoon baking soda
½ teaspoon salt
¾ cup pure maple syrup
½ cup vegetable oil
1 large egg
⅓ cup warm water

Mix together the dry ingredients in a large bowl. In a separate bowl, beat the maple syrup, oil and egg until smooth. Blend in warm water. Make a well in the dry ingredients and add the syrup mixture, stirring until flour mixture is moistened. Pour into greased 8-inch square pan and bake in 350°F oven 30 minutes or until cake springs back in the centre when lightly touched.

Serves 8.

MAPLE APPLE COFFEE CAKE

INN ON THE LAKE, WAVERLEY, N.S.

This moist cake combines the wonderful flavours of tart Nova Scotia apples and pure maple syrup.

½ cup butter, softened
3 large eggs
½ cup pure maple syrup
2 teaspoon vanilla extract
2 cups all-purpose flour
2 teaspoons baking powder
1 teaspoon cinnamon
¼ teaspoon nutmeg
⅛ teaspoon salt

TOPPING

3 large tart apples, peeled, cored and sliced
¼ cup granulated sugar
½ teaspoon cinnamon
¼ teaspoon nutmeg
2 tablespoons butter, softened

Beat butter with mixer until light and fluffy. Add eggs one at a time, beating well after each addition. Add maple syrup and vanilla and beat until mixture is fully combined.

In a separate bowl, sift together flour, baking powder, cinnamon, nutmeg and salt. Fold dry ingredients into butter mixture and spoon the batter into a greased 9-inch round cake pan.

TOPPING

Toss apples with sugar, cinnamon, nutmeg and butter. Arrange decoratively on top of batter and bake at 375°F until the apples are tender and a toothpick inserted into the centre of the cake comes out clean, about 50 to 60 minutes. Remove to a rack and let cool 10 minutes before removing from the pan. Serve warm, sliced in wedges.

Serves 8.

BERRY LAYER CAKE

ANNE MARIE CURRIE, SYDNEY, N.S.

The jars of sweet berry jams stored away deserve more than toast and muffins for company. An old Cape Breton recipe, a very simple one, is a reminder that cakes didn't require hours of preparation in the days when homemakers were often farm wives with more important things to do. The addition of homemade jam to a layer cake makes Sunday special.

2 cups all-purpose flour
1 tablespoon baking powder
½ teaspoon salt
½ cup butter, softened
1¼ cups granulated sugar
2 large eggs
1 teaspoon vanilla extract
1 cup milk
1 cup jam (strawberry or raspberry)
Whipped cream

Combine flour, baking powder and salt. Cream butter and sugar until fluffy. Beat in eggs one at a time, beating well after each addition. Stir in vanilla. Add dry ingredients to creamed mixture a third at a time alternately with 2 additions of milk ending with dry ingredients. Pour into 2 greased 8- or 9-inch round layer pans and bake at 325°F until firm to the touch, about 20 minutes. Cool on a rack. Spread jam between cooled layers of cake and top generously with whipped cream.

Serves 8 to 12.

LEMON ROULADE

Family and friends will love this light lemon cake. It's great for a summer picnic.

ROULADE SPONGE

¼ cup all-purpose flour
1 tablespoon cornstarch
4 large egg whites
⅓ cup granulated sugar
8 large egg yolks
Pinch of salt
Zest of ½ lemon

FILLING

3 large egg yolks
½ cup white wine
½ cup granulated sugar
Zest of 1 lemon
Juice of 2 lemons
1 envelope unflavoured gelatin powder (1 tablespoon)
½ cup heavy cream (35% mf), whipped
Raspberry purée, for garnish

Line a 12- by 16-inch baking sheet with parchment paper and spray with baking spray.

In a small bowl, mix flour and cornstarch together and set aside.

In another bowl, whip the egg whites and ¼ cup of the sugar, until soft peaks form.

In a third bowl, stir yolks, remaining sugar, salt and zest together. Carefully fold egg whites into the yolk mixture. It is best to do this in 3 batches so as not to deflate the volume of the whites. Sift the flour mixture over the batter and carefully fold until just combined.

Pour the batter onto the prepared pan, spread evenly with a spatula and bake in a 425°F oven for 7 to 10 minutes, or until the sponge springs back when lightly touched. Remove from the oven and turn out onto a clean damp towel. Roll on the long side, like a jellyroll. Set aside.

FILLING

Meanwhile, in a large bowl over a pot of simmering water, whisk yolks, wine, sugar, zest and juice until light and fluffy, about 110°F. Add gelatin, remove from heat and the heat until the gelatin has dissolved.

Place over a bowl of ice and water and whisk until just cooled. Take care not to cool too much, or the gelatin will set. Gently fold the whipped cream into the lemon mixture.

Unroll the sponge and spread the filling over it, leaving a 1-inch border.

To roll the cake, lift the towel evenly and keep pulling in an upward motion, keeping it as even as possible. Set on a tray and let it set seam down in the refrigerator for 40 minutes. Dust with icing sugar, slice and serve with a small pool of raspberry purée.

Serves 12.

CAPTAIN BURGESS RUM CAKE

. . . .

BLOMIDON INN, WOLFVILLE, N.S.

This has long been a Blomidon Inn favourite dessert. Store your syrup-drenched cake for a day or two to let the rum flavour mellow.

¾ cup butter, softened

1½ cups granulated sugar

4 large eggs

3 cups all-purpose flour

4½ teaspoons baking powder

¼ teaspoon salt

1 cup milk

½ cup dark rum

1 cup raisins

1 cup chopped pecans

¼ cup pecan halves

GLAZING SYRUP

¼ cup butter, melted

¼ cup water

1 cup granulated sugar

¼ cup dark rum

Grease a 10-inch tube pan and line with waxed paper.

Cream together butter and sugar until fluffy. Add eggs, one at a time, beating after each addition.

In a separate bowl, combine flour, baking powder and salt. Add dry ingredients to creamed mixture, alternately with milk and rum, being careful to mix only until batter is smooth. Fold in the raisins and chopped pecans.

Place pecans halves on the bottom of the tube pan. Spread the cake batter evenly over the nuts and bake at 350°F for 55 to 60 minutes, or until a toothpick inserted into centre of the cake comes out clean. Let cake cool for 10 minutes in the pan on a rack. Turn the cake out onto a rack to cool before glazing.

GLAZING SYRUP

In a small saucepan, combine butter, water, sugar and rum and place over medium heat until sugar is dissolved. Prick the top of the cake at 1-inch intervals with a small skewer and drizzle the syrup over the cake, repeating until all is absorbed. Store in a tightly sealed container at a cool temperature to mellow before serving.

Serves 12 to 14.

WICKWIRE HOUSE PEACH CARDAMOM CAKE

· · · · · · · · · · · · ·

WICKWIRE HOUSE, KENTVILLE, N.S.

This is a wonderfully moist cake flavoured with cardamom, an aromatic spice of the ginger family. Serve it with coffee in the morning, in the afternoon with a pot of tea, or simply enjoy as dessert.

1¼ cups packed brown sugar

1 tablespoon cinnamon

½ cup chopped pecans

3 or 4 peaches, peeled, pitted and thinly sliced

1 cup butter, softened

2 large eggs

1 teaspoon vanilla extract

2 cups all-purpose flour

1¼ teaspoons baking soda

1 teaspoon baking powder

¾ teaspoon cardamom

¼ teaspoon salt

1 cup sour cream

Icing sugar

In a small bowl, combine ¼ cup of the brown sugar, cinnamon and pecans and set aside. Prepare peaches and set aside in a separate bowl.

With a mixer, cream butter and remaining brown sugar until light and fluffy. Add eggs and vanilla and beat well.

In a separate bowl sift together the flour, baking soda, baking powder, cardamom and salt. Fold flour mixture into butter mixture a third at a time alternately with half of the sour cream at a time, beginning and ending with flour and being careful not to overmix.

Grease and flour a 10-inch Bundt pan. Spoon a third of the batter into the pan, add half the nut mixture and half the peach slices. Add another third of the batter, then the remaining nuts and peaches. Top with remaining batter and bake at 350°F until brown on top and a toothpick inserted into the centre comes out clean, 1½ hours.

Remove from oven and let stand in a pan 10 minutes before turning out on a serving plate to cool. Dust with icing sugar.

Serves 8.

HARVEST PUMPKIN CHEESECAKE

. . . .

FIRESIDE CAFÉ, CANNING, N.S.

Absolutely delicious! This cheesecake is so moist and light it is like eating a cloud of pumpkin mousse. Though this makes 12 to 16 servings, you must allow for seconds.

CRUST

3 tablespoons granulated sugar
1½ cups graham cracker crumbs
⅓ cup butter, melted

CHEESECAKE

4 large eggs, separated
1 pound cream cheese
¾ cup granulated sugar
1 cup pumpkin purée
1 teaspoon vanilla extract
3 tablespoons all-purpose flour
1 teaspoon cinnamon
½ teaspoon ginger
½ teaspoon nutmeg
¼ teaspoon salt
1 cup blend cream (10% mf)

TOPPING

1 cup sour cream
2 tablespoons granulated sugar
½ teaspoon vanilla extract
Freshly grated nutmeg

CRUST

In a bowl, combine dry ingredients. Mix in melted butter. Press crumbs over the bottom and up the sides of a 10-inch springform pan. Reserve.

CHEESECAKE

Beat egg whites until light and fluffy. Reserve. Beat cream cheese until smooth. Stir in sugar, egg yolks, pumpkin and vanilla. Sift together flour, spices and salt. Add to pumpkin mixture alternately with the cream, mixing until combined. Gently fold in reserved egg whites.

Pour into prepared crust. Place pan on a baking sheet and bake at 350°F for 60 to 70 minutes, until cheesecake is just set into the centre and the edges are starting to crack. Cool on rack 5 minutes. (Leave oven on.)

TOPPING

In a bowl, whisk together sour cream, sugar and vanilla. Pour over cheesecake, return to oven and bake 6 minutes. Remove from oven and grate nutmeg over the top.

Run a knife around the edge of the cheesecake to loosen from the side of the pan. Cool on a rack. Refrigerate, loosely covered, 4 to 5 hours before serving.

Serves 12 to 16.

PIES, TARTS AND PASTRIES

DUTCH APPEL TAART

. . . .

BLOMIDON INN, ANNAPOLIS VALLEY, N.S.

At the Blomidon Inn, only Annapolis Valley Red Delicious apples are used for this wonderful tart. We're sure that you won't compromise the results if you choose another variety of apple, but don't alter the sugar or the spices. They serve it garnished with whipped cream and toasted almond slices.

PASTRY

1 cup cold butter, cubed
2 cups all-purpose flour
1 cup granulated sugar
1 teaspoon baking powder
1 large egg, beaten

FILLING

3 pounds Red Delicious apples, peeled and cored and
   diced in ¼-inch pieces
1 cup granulated sugar
2 tablespoons cinnamon
2 teaspoons nutmeg
Pinch of cloves
3 tablespoons sherry
1 tablespoon lemon juice

PASTRY

In a large mixing bowl, cut together butter, flour, sugar and baking powder. Incorporate beaten egg. While this pastry mixture is still coarse and crumbly, reserve ½ cup for topping. Mix remainder into a ball, press gently over the bottom and halfway up the side of a greased and floured 10-inch springform pan. The pastry should be of uniform thickness, just over ¼ inch.

FILLING

Mix together the apples, sugar, spices, sherry and lemon juice and spoon into pastry-lined pan. The level of filling will exceed the height of the pastry, but baking will compensate. Sprinkle with reserved topping and bake on the middle rack in a 375°F oven until top is a rich golden brown, about 1 hour. Let cool and refrigerate. Unmould and cut into wedges.

Serves 12.

APPLE PIE

An apple pie to make Mum proud! The Manor Inn's version with early Gravenstein apples was tested with excellent results.

PASTRY FOR A DOUBLE-CRUST PIE OR TWO SINGLE-CRUST PIES

1¾ cups all-purpose flour

¾ teaspoon salt

¾ cup lard

4 to 5 tablespoons cold water

FILLING

4 cups peeled, cored and sliced apples

1 cup granulated sugar

¼ cup all-purpose flour

1 teaspoon cinnamon

½ teaspoon nutmeg

PASTRY

Combine flour and salt in a mixing bowl. Cut in lard with a pastry blender until mixture is the size of large peas. Sprinkle water over the surface, a little at a time, tossing lightly. Form the dough into a ball, handling it as little as possible.

Use a lightly floured surface, or preferably a pastry cloth and a covered rolling pin. Divide pastry in half and flatten each half into a disc. Roll lightly from the centre until the pastry is about 1 inch larger than a 9-inch pie plate.

Roll pastry over rolling pin and transfer to a greased pie plate. Unroll and ease into place, being careful not to stretch the pastry. Moisten pastry on the rim.

FILLING

Toss all ingredients together in a bowl. Place in pie shell. Roll out remaining pastry and cover the apple filling. Trim pastry off at the rim and flute the edges. Cut 4 steam holes in the centre of the top pastry. Bake at 375°F for 35 to 40 minutes, until apples are tender, juices are bubbling and the pastry is browned. Cool on a rack.

Serves 6 to 8.

HAZEL HASKELL'S BLUEBERRY PIE

. . . .

ALICE LEDUC, WATERVILLE, N.S.

Hazel Haskell of Berwick, N.S., is a champion pie-maker who knows what it's like to handle lots of fruit. Her father and two brothers were instrumental in introducing cultivated blueberries to the Annapolis Valley. "At one time we had 4,000 blueberry bushes on our farm in Morristown," she says. The berries had to be packaged, then were shipped to Boston, New York and Montreal. "Mom used to make blueberry pie and blueberry pudding with berries freshly picked from the fields," she recalls. "The aroma was irresistible." Her secret for making fruit and berry pies is to add a little molasses or tapioca.

3 cups blueberries
1⅓ cups granulated sugar
¼ cup all-purpose flour
1 tablespoon butter
1 tablespoon fancy molasses
Pastry for Double-Crust Pie (page 205)

Mix the berries with the sugar and flour. Cut the berries with 2 knives or a pastry cutter and toss all together with a fork. Let stand while rolling out the pastry for a double-crust pie. Fill the unbaked pie shell with the berry mixture. Dot with butter and drizzle with molasses. Add top crust, flute the edges and slash in 4 places. Bake at 425°F for 10 minutes. Reduce heat to 350°F and bake until nicely browned and the juice barely begins to bubble through the slits in the crust.

Serves 6 to 8.

ACADIAN SUGAR PIE

. . . .

This recipe is remarkable for its heritage, flavour and significance to the history of Canadian cooking. Except for the lemons and vanilla, these ingredients would have been available to our ancestors in the depths of winter.

Pastry for single-crust pie (page 205)
2 large eggs
2 large egg yolks
1 cup packed brown sugar
1 cup dark corn syrup or golden syrup
½ teaspoon fine sea salt
1 tablespoon vanilla extract
Juice of ½ lemon
⅔ cup unsalted butter
Whipped cream
Toasted nuts, such as pecans, walnuts or hazelnuts

Grease a 10-inch diameter tart pan with removable bottom and dust with flour, tapping out any excess. Roll the pastry into a circle no more than ⅛ inch thick. Ease into the pan and press the dough into the scalloped edges of the tart pan. Cut away any overhanging dough. Using a fork, prick the pastry on the bottom of the pan. Refrigerate.

In a bowl, beat eggs and egg yolks until slightly frothy. Add brown sugar, syrup, salt, vanilla and juice, and stir until well mixed and smooth. Melt butter in a microwave or small saucepan and add while hot to egg mixture.

Pour filling into prepared tart pan. Bake at 350°F for 35 to 40 minutes or until crust is brown and custard has set. The custard will move as a semi-molten mass when the pan is agitated. Cool tart for 1 hour on a rack to allow residual heat to finish cooking the centre, then refrigerate for a minimum of 3 hours before cutting.

Serve with a good dollop of unsweetened whipped cream and a few toasted nuts to balance the dish — as the name implies, sugar pie is a very sweet dessert.

Serves 10.

ACADIAN APPLE PIE

. . . .

DELTA BEAUSEJOUR HOTEL, MONCTON, N.B.

Chef Denis Bettinger of Moncton's Delta Beausejour Hotel with its long-established fine-dining Windjammer Room provided the recipe for this delicious and decadent dessert.

SWEET DOUGH

⅓ cup granulated sugar
⅓ cup butter, softened
1 small egg, beaten, or 1 large egg yolk
1 cup all-purpose flour

FILLING

½ cup raisins
¾ cup apple juice
⅓ cup water
½ cup granulated sugar
4 medium-large apples, peeled and sliced
1 tablespoon butter
1 teaspoon grated lemon zest
½ teaspoon lemon juice
¼ teaspoon salt
¼ teaspoon cinnamon
2 tablespoons cornstarch
⅓ cup cold water
¾ cup walnut halves, chopped

TOPPING

¼ cup butter, melted
½ cup granulated sugar
½ cup all-purpose flour
½ cup rolled oats
¼ cup maple syrup

SWEET DOUGH

With a mixer, whip sugar and butter until light and fluffy. Add egg and continue to beat. Mix in flour and form into a ball. Roll the dough on a floured surface to fit into a shallow 9-inch pie plate.

FILLING

In a saucepan, combine raisins, apple juice, water and sugar. Add apples, butter, zest, juice, salt and cinnamon. Bring to a boil, reduce heat and simmer over medium heat for 5 minutes. Dissolve cornstarch in cold water and stir into raisin mixture. Bring to a boil, then simmer 3 minutes. Remove from heat and stir in walnuts. Spoon into pie plate lined with Sweet Dough.

TOPPING

Mix the butter and sugar, flour and oats and sprinkle over pie. Bake in 350°F for 35 to 45 minutes until crust is golden brown. Serve warm or chilled, drizzled with maple syrup.

Serves 6 to 8.

TORTA DI MELE ALLA PANNA
(APPLE CREAM PIE)

. . . .

LA PERLA, DARTMOUTH, N.S.

At La Perla they garnish this flan with a dusting of cinnamon, lemon zest and fresh mint leaves.

PASTRY

1¼ cups all-purpose flour

¼ cup granulated sugar

1 teaspoon baking powder

2 teaspoons lemon zest

½ teaspoon salt

½ teaspoon cinnamon

½ cup unsalted butter, at room temperature

1 large egg yolk

2 tablespoons sherry

FILLING

2 large apples, peeled, cored and sliced

2 large eggs

½ cup granulated sugar

2 tablespoons all-purpose flour

¼ teaspoon salt

8 ounces cream cheese, softened and cubed

¼ cup raisins

½ cup heavy cream (35% mf)

1 tablespoon mixed peel

2 teaspoons lemon zest

Whipped cream, for garnish

Cinnamon, for garnish

PASTRY

Combine the flour, sugar, baking powder, lemon zest, salt and cinnamon in a large bowl. Cut in butter with a pastry blender. Beat egg yolk and sherry. Drizzle over flour mixture and stir with a fork to incorporate. Gather dough into a ball and roll between 2 pieces of waxed paper to form an 11-inch circle.

Fit pastry into a 10-inch tart or flan pan with removable bottom and trim edges.

FILLING

Arrange apples, overlapping slightly, on the pastry. Beat eggs and sugar until thick and lemon-coloured. Gradually blend in flour and salt. Add cream cheese and beat until smooth. Stir in cream, mixed peel, raisins and lemon zest. Pour over apples.

Bake in a 375°F oven until the apples are tender and the crust golden brown, about 45 to 55 minutes. Cool, then refrigerate.

Serves 6 to 8.

PRIZE-WINNING BLUEBERRY PIE

. . . .

MARILYNN RUDI, SACKVILLE, N.B.

The tiny hamlet of Elgin, N.B., nestled in the rolling hills that stretch from Moncton to Sussex, is blessed with two of nature's delectable treats — blueberries and maple syrup. Years ago for a summer festival competition Erna Faye Steeves baked this prize-winning blueberry pie.

1 quart blueberries
Pastry for 9-inch Double-Crust Pie, rolled (page 205)
1 cup granulated sugar
3 tablespoons all-purpose flour
Pinch of cinnamon or nutmeg
3 to 4 teaspoons butter

Pour blueberries into a pastry-lined pie plate. Mix sugar, flour and cinnamon, and pour evenly over the berries. Dot with butter. Cover with top pastry, trim and flute edge and cut steam holes in several places in the centre. Bake at 450°F for 10 minutes then at 350°F until juice bubbles up in the steam holes, about 45 minutes.

Serves 6 to 8.

BLUEBERRY FLAN

. . . .

AMHERST SHORE COUNTRY INN, LORNEVILLE, N.S.

Donna Laceby, who developed this recipe at the Amherst Shore Country Inn, suggested adding a little tapioca to absorb some of the juices if you are using frozen blueberries.

PASTRY

1½ cups all-purpose flour
½ cup granulated sugar
1½ teaspoon baking powder
½ cup butter, softened
1 large egg, beaten
½ teaspoon almond extract

FILLING AND TOPPING

5 cups fresh or frozen (thawed) blueberries
2 tablespoons orange liqueur
1 teaspoon lemon zest
4 teaspoons minute tapioca, if using frozen berries
2 cups sour cream
½ cup granulated sugar
2 large egg yolks
½ teaspoon almond extract
⅔ cup heavy cream (35% mf), whipped

PASTRY

Blend flour, sugar, baking powder and butter in a mixing bowl. Combine egg and almond extract. Drizzle over butter mixture, stirring to combine. Pat over the base of a greased 10½-inch springform pan.

FILLING AND TOPPING

In a bowl, mix together blueberries, liqueur, zest and minute tapioca, if using frozen berries. Spoon onto pastry-lined pan.

Mix sour cream, sugar, yolks and almond extract. Spoon evenly over blueberry filling. Bake at 350°F for 1¼ hours or until crust is golden and berries are bubbling and tender. Let cool, then refrigerate. Serve with whipped cream.

Serves 10 to 12.

POUTINES À TROU (DUMPLINGS WITH A HOLE) WITH RUM BUTTER SAUCE AND VANILLA BEAN CRÈME ANGLAISE

· · · · · · · · · · ·

This dessert is well known and well loved by Acadians all over southeastern New Brunswick. Poutines à trou are essentially little apple, cranberry and/or raisin pies formed into balls, with a hole cut in the top to act as a vent during cooking. They are usually served still warm from the oven with a brown sugar sauce poured into the hole. This version is an interpretation of the old Acadian classic, served with warm rum butter sauce and a vanilla bean Crème Anglaise. It is a late-summer version that uses pear and apple combined, but it can be made with whichever orchard fruit you desire.

PASTRY

2½ cups all-purpose flour

2 tablespoons granulated sugar

4 teaspoons baking powder

½ teaspoon salt

¼ cup unsalted butter, cubed

¾ cup milk

1 tablespoon granulated sugar, for dusting

FILLING

1 large egg, beaten

1 tablespoon water

4 cooking apples, peeled, cored and diced small

2 cooking pears, peeled, cored and diced small

½ cup golden raisins

½ cup dried cranberries

2 tablespoons brown sugar

¼ teaspoon cloves

Pinch of salt

PASTRY

Sift together flour, sugar, baking powder and salt. Cut butter into flour mixture until it is well coated and broken down into pea-sized pieces. Add milk and mix together to form dough. Wrap and refrigerate for at least 1 hour.

FILLING

In a small bowl, beat egg and water for eggwash. Reserve. Combine all remaining ingredients in a bowl.

Roll out pastry on a lightly floured surface to a ¼ inch thickness. With a 5-inch-diameter round pastry cutter, cut out 12 disks. Divide filling evenly onto centres of disks. Moisten edge of pastry lightly with eggwash. Carefully bring edges of pastry up to meet and fully close in the filling, creating a ball. Invert poutines onto a parchment-covered cookie sheet. Cut a ½-inch round hole in top centre of each poutine, brush with a light coating of eggwash and dust entire surface with sugar. Bake for 30 to 35 minutes in a 375°F oven until golden brown and crisp with juicy tender fruit filling. Serve with a warm Rum Butter Sauce poured into the hole in the top of each poutine and set on a pool of Vanilla Bean Crème Anglaise (recipes follow).

Serves 12.

RUM BUTTER SAUCE

¾ cup butter
1 cup packed brown sugar
¼ cup spiced rum

RUM BUTTER SAUCE

Melt butter and brown sugar together over medium-high heat until sugar is dissolved. Remove far from heat and carefully add rum (use caution — the rum may ignite if added close to or on heat). Return the pan to the heat and cook out until sauce has a clear, amber appearance. Serve warm.

VANILLA BEAN CRÈME ANGLAISE

1 vanilla bean pod
1 cup heavy cream (35% mf)
3 large egg yolks
¼ cup granulated sugar

CRÈME ANGLAISE

Slit vanilla pod in half lengthwise. Using the back of a paring knife, scrape out seeds and add pods and seeds to cream in a saucepan. Bring to a simmer, remove from the heat, cover and let steep for 20 minutes. Remove pods. In a separate bowl, mix egg yolks and sugar until smooth. Gradually whisk in warm cream. Place in the top of a double boiler over simmering water, and stir constantly until it thickens enough to coat the back of a wooden spoon. Pass through a fine-meshed sieve into a bowl in a larger bowl of ice and water to chill. Refrigerate, cover surface and serve cold.

BLACKAPPLE PIE

· · · · · · · · · · · ·

LINDY GUILD, MAHONE BAY, N.S.

A traditional English dessert that translates well to the Atlantic region, for it contains apples and the berries that grow wild at the roadsides. When Lindy Guild was growing up in England, she wasn't keen on picking fruit from prickly bushes and the brambles were the worst.

But when her mother said the blackberries were ripe for a pie, there were instant volunteers. They simply couldn't pass up the chance to tell their school friends they had eaten "black" apple pie for supper. The recipe is exactly as Lindy's mother made it, except she always served it with thick Cornish cream poured on each slice. Here, it's best with maple cream yogurt. The pastry recipe makes three double-crust pies, handles well and freezes well, and while there may be similar recipes around, none call for lemon juice — most include vinegar. The pastry tastes good eaten cold or warm.

PASTRY

5½ cups all-purpose flour
1 teaspoon granulated sugar
1 teaspoon salt
1 pound lard, cubed
1 large egg
1 tablespoon lemon juice or vinegar
Cold water

FILLING

2 cups blackberries
2 cups peeled, cored and sliced tart apples
1 cup granulated sugar
3 tablespoons all-purpose flour
¼ teaspoon cloves
¼ teaspoon nutmeg
1 teaspoon lemon juice
2 tablespoons butter

PASTRY

Put flour, sugar and salt into a bowl. With a pastry blender, mix and cut in lard until the mixture is like coarse meal. In an 8-ounce liquid measuring cup beat the egg with a fork, and add juice and water to make up ¾ cup of liquid. Mix with a fork and add it to the dry mixture gradually, using just enough to make the dough stick together. Knead a few times and shape into 6 equal discs. Wrap each in foil refrigerate for up to a week, or freeze for later use. Bring to room temperature before rolling.

Makes 3 double-crust pie shells, 6 single-crust pies.

FILLING

Put the fruit in separate bowls. Combine sugar, flour and spices. Add half of this mixture to the blackberries and the other half to the apples. Stir to coat the fruit. Roll out 1 disc to 10-inch circle. Fit without stretching into a 9-inch pie plate. Put a layer of apples into the pastry-lined pie plate, then the blackberries, alternating until the dish is filled. Sprinkle with juice, dot with butter. Roll out a second disc of pastry and place over the fruit. Trim the edges, seal and crimp the pastry. Make a pattern on top with a fork or cut slits to allow the steam to escape. Bake in a 400°F oven at for 45 to 50 minutes. Cool to room temperature and serve with fresh thick cream or maple cream yogurt.

Serves 6 to 8.

RASPBERRY PIE

The addition of orange juice adds extra tartness to this fruit pie you can counteract with a good dollop of whipping cream.

5 cups fresh or frozen raspberries
1 tablespoon orange juice
1 cup granulated sugar
⅓ cup all-purpose flour
½ teaspoon salt
Pastry for 9-inch Double-Crust Pie, rolled (page 205)
Granulated sugar, for sprinkling

Mix together raspberries, juice, sugar, flour and salt. Pour into a pastry-lined pie plate. Cover with top pastry. Trim and flute edge, sprinkle crust with water and shake a small amount of sugar over the pie. Cut steam holes into several places in the centre of pastry. Bake in 400°F oven 40 to 50 minutes or until crust is golden brown and raspberry juices are bubbling up through the steam holes.

Serves 6 to 8.

ACADIAN WILD BLUEBERRY PÂTÉ

• • • • • • • • • • • •

MARY JANE LOSIER, BATHURST, N.B.

La Fine Grobe sur Mer, literally translated as "fine food by the sea," has won international acclaim as a restaurant since it opened in Nigadoo, N.B. Chef Georges Frachon, the owner, offers fine Acadian and French cuisine prepared with local ingredients. In good French tradition, many of the vegetables, herbs and spices are grown on the property. As if the "fine food" isn't attraction enough to draw people to the restaurant, the outdoor cafe-terrasse overlooks the Baie des Chaleurs where diners can also enjoy ocean breezes and a magnificent view.

PASTRY

5 cups all-purpose flour
3 tablespoons granulated sugar
Pinch of salt
1 pound butter, at room temperature
1 large egg
1 cup ale

FILLING

3 to 4 pounds wild blueberries
2 cups sugar, approximate
¼ cup butter, cut into pieces and softened
1 large egg
1 tablespoon water
Cream

PASTRY

Combine flour, sugar and salt in a bowl. Cut in butter with a pastry blender or forks until mixture is crumbly. Do not use fingers. Beat egg in a separate bowl. Stir in ale. Gradually add liquid to the dry ingredients tossing to make a ragged dough that holds together. Form 5 rectangles of dough and moisten them with water without letting them become sticky. Wrap and refrigerate for 1 hour.

FILLING

Combine the berries with some of the sugar, adding just enough to sweeten. Roll out 1 rectangle of cold dough on a lightly floured board to make a thin rectangle large enough to cover the bottom and sides of a well-buttered and floured 9- by 5-inch glass loaf pan. Add a layer of about a quarter of the blueberry filling. Dot with small pieces of butter. Continue rolling dough and layering until the dish is filled, ending with dough. Crimp the edges. Cut small vent holes on top of the dough with a knife. Mix the egg with water and brush gently over the top of the pie.

Bake in a 350°F oven until the first sign of bubbling berry juice, about 20 minutes. Continue baking until the bottom pastry layer is golden brown. The time depends on the size of the pie and the number of layers. Place a large jellyroll pan on the rack below the pie to catch any juicy overflow. Cool on a rack. Serve warm with cream.

This recipe can be cut in half.

Serves 12 to 14.

BUMBLE BERRY PIE

. . . .

INVERARY INN, BADDECK, N.S.

You can use almost any combination of fruit in Bumble Berry Pie, but you may have to adjust the sugar if you use rhubarb.

½ cup blueberries
½ cup quartered strawberries
½ cup raspberries
½ cup blackberries
½ cup thinly sliced apple
½ to ¾ cup granulated sugar
1 tablespoon cornstarch
¼ teaspoon cinnamon
Pastry for 9-inch Double-Crust Pie, rolled (page 205)

In a bowl, toss together the berries, apple, sugar, cornstarch and cinnamon. Pour into a pastry-lined 9-inch pie plate. Cover with top pastry. Trim and flute edges. Cut steam holes in several places in the centre.

Bake at 350°F until golden brown and filling is bubbling up through the steam holes, about 40 to 45 minutes.

Serves 6 to 8.

PRIZE BUTTER TARTS

. . . .

THE WEST POINT LIGHTHOUSE, WEST POINT, P.E.I.

These tasty little tarts store well and are delicious with a freshly brewed pot of tea.

1 cup packed brown sugar
⅓ cup butter, melted
1 teaspoon vanilla extract
1 large egg, beaten
2 tablespoons milk
Pastry for Double-Crust Pie, rolled (page 205)

Mix together sugar, butter and vanilla. Stir in the egg and milk. Cut out 10 to 12 rounds of pastry to fit tart or muffin tins. Pour filling into pastry-lined tart tins and bake 400°F for 15 minutes.

Makes 10 to 12 tarts.

BUTTERSCOTCH PIE

· · · · · · · · · · · · ·

STEAMERS STOP INN, GAGETOWN, N.B.

This recipe makes a luscious, tall butterscotch pie.

Pastry for single-crust pie (page 205)
4 cups milk
2 cups packed brown sugar
¼ cup butter
½ cup cornstarch
Pinch of salt
2 large eggs
1 teaspoon vanilla extract
1 cup heavy cream (35% mf)

Prepare prebaked pie shell according to instructions on page 311.

In a large saucepan over medium heat, bring 3 cups of the milk, sugar and butter to a boil, stirring constantly.

In a bowl combine cornstarch, salt, remaining milk and eggs. Stir in ½ cup of the hot milk mixture. Whisk back into the hot milk mixture. Simmer until thickened, stirring often. Remove from heat and stir in vanilla. Pour into baked pie shell. Refrigerate. Serve with whipped cream.

Serves 6 to 8.

MAPLE SYRUP PIE

· · · · · · · · · · · · ·

MARILYNN RUDI, SACKVILLE, N.B.

Elgin is in the heart of New Brunswick's maple syrup producing countryside — a rural community between Moncton and Sussex. Roger Steeve's sugar bush is reputedly the largest in the world and his company is a major producer of maple syrup. This recipe is a prize-winner from a summer festival competition in Elgin.

Pastry for single-crust pie (page 205)
2 cups milk
1 cup pure maple syrup
2 heaping tablespoons cornstarch
Pinch of salt
2 large eggs
Whipped cream

Prepare prebaked pie shell according to instructions on page 311.

Scald 1¾ cups of milk and the maple syrup in the top of a double boiler. In a bowl, combine the remaining milk, cornstarch and salt. Whisk into the hot mixture gradually. Cook for 10 minutes or until smooth and thickened (do not overcook or the mixture will break down). In a bowl, whisk eggs and whisk in a quarter of the hot maple syrup mixture; return to pan. Cook, stirring occasionally for 3 minutes. Pour into pie shell. When cold, top with whipped cream.

Serves 6.

DUNDEE MAPLE BUTTER TARTS WITH MARITIME MAPLE SAUCE

THE DUNDEE ARMS, CHARLOTTETOWN, P.E.I.

Maple flavour at its best, at the Dundee Arms the chef often decorates his plate with a maple sauce, Crème Anglaise (page 196) and a real maple leaf. Spectacular and delicious.

PASTRY

1¼ cups all-purpose flour
Pinch of salt
½ cup butter, cubed
2 to 3 tablespoons ice water

FILLING

⅓ cup butter
⅓ cup pure maple syrup
½ teaspoon vanilla extract
1 cup packed brown sugar
Pinch of salt
2 large eggs

SAUCE

2 large egg yolks
⅔ cup pure maple syrup
¼ cup brown sugar
Ice cubes
½ cup heavy cream (35% mf), whipped
¼ cup heavy cream (35% mf), unwhipped

PASTRY

Combine flour and salt in a mixing bowl. Cut in butter with a pastry blender until mixture is the size of large peas. Do not overmix. Sprinkle ice water over mixture and blend with a fork until absorbed. Form into a ball and roll out on a floured surface. Cut into 8 rounds 3½ inches in diameter and place in muffin tins. Set aside.

FILLING

Melt butter in a saucepan over medium heat. Remove from heat. Add syrup, vanilla, sugar and salt. Mix well. Beat eggs in a separate bowl and add to mixture. Fill tart shells. Bake in 375°F oven about 15 minutes, until pastry is browned and filling is bubbly. Remove from oven and set aside 10 minutes.

SAUCE

Meanwhile, in a double boiler, over simmering but not boiling water, heat yolks, syrup and sugar stirring often until mixture thickens and coats the back of a spoon. Cool pot in bowl of water and ice cubes, stirring sauce constantly until cold. Fold in whipped cream, then unwhipped cream. Refrigerate.

To serve, spread a little sauce on a dessert plate and top with tart.

Serves 8.

MAPLE SYRUP PIE

. . . .

AUX ANCIENS CANADIENS, QUEBEC CITY, QUE.

Elaine Elliot coaxed this recipe out of Dominique Nourry of Quebec City's Aux Anciens Canadiens restaurant for her book Maple Syrup. *Dominique serves this traditional pie accompanied by a spoonful of whipped cream.*

Pastry for 8-inch single-crust pie (page 205)
1½ cups packed brown sugar
½ cup heavy cream (35% mf)
⅓ cup pure maple syrup
1 large egg, at room temperature
2 teaspoons butter, softened
Whipped cream, for garnish

Prepare 8-inch prebaked pie shell according to instructions on page 311.

In a large bowl, beat together sugar, cream, syrup, egg and butter until smooth and creamy. Pour into prepared pie shell and bake in 350°F oven for 45 minutes. Cool to room temperature. Serve garnished with freshly whipped cream.

Serves 6.

MAPLE SYRUP TARTE

. . . .

MARY JANE LOSIER, BATHURST, N.B.

Roswitha Derbuch specialized in baking European desserts at her café, catering and food consultation service in Bathurst, N.B. The Café Rosana was like a small, peaceful oasis in the busy supermall. Roswitha used no preservatives or flavour enhancers and insisted on only fresh foods and vegetables.

⅓ cup unsalted butter
⅓ cup granulated sugar
3 large eggs
1 cup pure maple syrup
Pastry for 9-inch single-crust pie (page 205)
1 cup chopped pecans

Beat butter, sugar and eggs together. Beat in maple syrup. Fill the unbaked pie shell. Sprinkle pecans on top and bake at 375°F for 40 minutes.

Serves 6.

BRANT'S PIE

At the Charlotte Lane Café, Chef Glauser prepares this pie with a lattice topping.

1 cup orange juice
⅔ cup granulated sugar
2 cups fresh cranberries
½ large pear, finely diced
½ large McIntosh apple, finely diced
1 tablespoon cornstarch dissolved in 2 tablespoons
  cold water
Pastry for Double-Crust Pie (page 205)
Icing sugar, for dusting
Whipped cream or crème fraîche, for garnish

Combine juice, sugar, cranberries, pear and apple in a large saucepan and bring to a boil over medium-high heat. Reduce temperature and simmer until fruit is soft and cranberries have popped, stirring often. Dissolve cornstarch in cold water and stir into cranberry mixture. Cook until filling has thickened. Remove from the heat, cool, then refrigerate until cold.

Roll out half of the pastry to line a shallow 8-inch pie plate. Pour in pie filling.

Roll out the second half of pastry. Cut in ¾- by 12-inch strips and lay these on pie at 1-inch intervals. Fold back alternate strips to weave crosswise strips over and under for a lattice top. Bake in 350°F oven until lightly brown, approximately 35 to 40 minutes. Cool and dust with icing sugar.

Serve with a dollop of whipped cream or crème fraîche.

Serves 6.

LEMON ALMOND TART

The sharp lemon flavour of this tart is a nice alternative to the sweetness of most desserts.

PASTRY

1 cup all-purpose flour
3½ tablespoons granulated sugar
⅓ cup butter, softened
1 large egg

FILLING

3 large eggs
½ cup granulated sugar
Zest of 1½ lemons
½ cup lemon juice
¾ cup finely ground almonds
⅓ cup butter, melted and cooled
Sliced almonds, toasted, for garnish

PASTRY

Combine flour and sugar. Add butter and mix until crumbly. Beat egg and mix into the pastry. Form into a disk. Chill for at least 30 minutes. Roll out to 10-inch round and fit into a 9-inch tart tin with removable bottom. Line pastry shell with foil and fill with pie weights or beans, or prick bottom of shell with a fork.

Partially bake the tart shell in a 375°F oven for 8 minutes.

FILLING

Meanwhile, with a whisk, beat together the eggs, sugar, zest, juice and ground almonds. Beat in melted butter. Pour into the tart shell and bake at 375°F until pastry is golden and filling has lost its sheen, about 25 to 30 minutes. Cool on a rack. Garnish with toasted sliced almonds.

Serves 8.

STRAWBERRY RHUBARB PIE

. . . .

MOUNTAIN GAP INN AND RESORT,
SMITHS COVE, N.S.

*Heralding the beginning of summer, the combination
of strawberries and rhubarb in this pie offers diners a
taste of the best from Mountain Gap's kitchen.*

Pastry for 9-inch Double-Crust Pie (page 205)
1 cup granulated sugar
3 tablespoons all-purpose flour
Generous pinch nutmeg
3 cups chopped rhubarb
1 cup halved and hulled strawberries
1 tablespoon butter, melted

Roll half of the pastry and fit into a 9-inch pie plate.
In a large bowl, combine sugar, flour and nutmeg.
Add rhubarb and strawberries and toss to coat. Spoon
into the pie shell. Roll top crust and place over filling.
Trim and flute edges to seal and cut slits in top. Brush
with butter. Bake in 350°F oven for 45 to 60 minutes
until fruit is tender and bubbling and pie is golden
brown.

Serves 6 to 8.

LISCOMBE LODGE FRESH STRAWBERRY PIE

. . . .

LISCOMBE LODGE, LISCOMB MILLS, N.S.

*When it was operated by the Nova Scotia government,
Liscombe Lodge made a point of serving Nova Scotian
fruits and produce at their peak.*

Pastry for 9-inch single-crust-pie (page 205)
4 cups strawberries, hulled and halved
1 cup granulated sugar
1 cup cold water
3 tablespoons cornstarch
1 teaspoon lemon juice
Whipped cream (optional)

Prepare prebaked pie shell according to instructions
on page 311.

Crush 1 cup of the strawberries and place in a
saucepan. Stir in sugar, water and cornstarch.
Cook over medium heat, stirring occasionally, until
thickened and clear, about 25 minutes. Remove
from heat, stir in juice and set aside to cool. Spread
remaining berries in pie shell, cover with cooked
berries and refrigerate several hours. Serve with
whipped cream, if desired.

Serves 6 to 8.

PUMPKIN PIE

· · · · · · · · · · · ·

EVANGELINE INN AND CAFÉ, GRAND PRÉ, N.S.

Fresh pumpkins abound in Nova Scotia's Annapolis Valley during autumn harvest.
This small café's chef created a pumpkin pie to rival any you have tried.

2 large eggs
⅔ cup packed brown sugar
1½ cups pumpkin purée
1 teaspoon cinnamon
½ teaspoon ginger
¼ teaspoon cloves
¼ teaspoon nutmeg
½ teaspoon salt
2 tablespoons fancy molasses
1¼ cups blend cream (10% mf)
Pastry for 9-inch single-crust-pie (page 205)

Combine all ingredients, except the pie shell, using an electric mixer, and pour into prepared pie shell. Bake 15 minutes in a 400°F oven, then reduce temperature to 350°F and bake 35 minutes or until a knife inserted in the centre comes out clean. Let cool on a rack and refrigerate.

Serves 6 to 8.

RUSTIC PLUM TART

. . . .

Plums are grown around the world and come in a variety of sizes, colours and sweetness levels. In the Maritime region of Canada, they are one of summer's great eat-out-of-your-hand treats. For this recipe, use sweet plums that are firm but yield slightly when pressed.

TART PASTRY

1¼ cups all-purpose flour
1 tablespoon granulated sugar
¼ teaspoon salt
½ cup unsalted butter, chilled and cubed
⅓ cup ice water

FILLING

¼ cup finely crushed cookie crumbs, such as biscotti, amaretti or graham cracker
1 tablespoon all-purpose flour
1 pound plums
1 tablespoon unsalted butter, melted
Granulated sugar
½ cup berries of choice, such as raspberry, blackberry or blueberry

TART PASTRY

In a bowl, mix together flour, sugar and salt. With a pastry blender, cut butter into flour mixture until crumbly but butter is still in pea-size pieces. Do not overblend. Add ice water all at once and mix just until the pastry begins to come together. Form pastry into a disc, wrap in plastic wrap and refrigerate for 1 hour.

FILLING

In a bowl, mix together crumbs and flour, then reserve. Slice plums in half, remove pits and cut halves into ¼-inch slices.

On a lightly floured surface, roll Tart Pastry into a 15-inch round. Transfer pastry to a large rimless parchment-lined baking sheet or pizza pan. Sprinkle cookie crumbs over dough, leaving a 2-inch border without crumbs. Arrange the plum slices, overlapping slightly, in concentric circles up to the edge of the border. Lift and pleat pastry border inward and over the fruit. Brush the pleated border with melted butter and sprinkle sugar over whole tart.

Bake in a 400°F oven for 30 minutes. Remove from oven and sprinkle exposed plum area with berries. Return to oven and bake for 15 minutes or until fruit is tender and crust is browned. Remove from oven and immediately slide tart onto cooling rack. Serve warm or at room temperature.

Serves 8 to 10.

PUDDINGS: BAKED, CHILLED, STEAMED AND FROZEN

APPLESAUCE

· · · · · · · · · · · · · · ·

DAWN BREMNER, JEMSEG, N.B.

12 cooking apples such as McIntosh, Empire, or
  Gravenstein
¼ cup water
½ cup granulated sugar (approximate)
1 teaspoon cinnamon (approximate)

Core and quarter the apples, but do not peel. Cook,
covered, in a heavy saucepan with the water over
medium to low heat until the apples are soft. Remove
from the heat, cool slightly and put them through a
food mill or press through a sieve. Add the sugar and
cinnamon according to taste. Stir well and cool.

Makes about 4 cups.

MAPLE-BAKED APPLES

· · · · · · · · · · · · · · ·

*Not all apples are created equal; some are ideal for
eating fresh, some make delicious pies and sauces,
while others are perfect for baking. This recipe works
well with Cortland, Jonagold, Rome, Northern Spy
and Granny Smith varieties.*

6 baking apples (about 2½ to 3 pounds total)
⅓ cup packed brown sugar
2 tablespoons chopped walnuts or pecans
2 tablespoons chopped raisins
Pinch each of cardamom, nutmeg and cinnamon
1 tablespoon butter
2 tablespoons water
⅓ cup pure maple syrup
Vanilla ice cream or whipped cream (optional)

Wash, dry and core apples leaving a thin base at the
bottom of the core cavity. With a paring knife, make
a shallow cut around the middle of each apple; place
apples in a shallow baking dish that holds them
comfortably.

  In a bowl, mix together brown sugar, nuts, raisins
and spices. Portion equal amounts of sugar mixture
in apple cavities. Dab apples with butter and pour
water around apples.

  Bake in 400°F oven for 35 minutes. Drizzle maple
syrup over apples and bake until apples are very
tender, about 10 minutes longer.

  Place a warm or cooled apple in an individual
serving bowl and serve with vanilla ice cream or
whipped cream, if desired.

Serves 6.

CLASSIC APPLE CRISP

MOUNTAIN GAP INN AND RESORT,
SMITHS COVE, N.S.

This easy-to-prepare dessert from the Mountain Gap Inn is a traditional Maritime favourite. Serve it with a wedge of Cheddar cheese, a scoop of vanilla ice cream or whipped cream.

6 to 8 apples, peeled, cored and sliced
2 tablespoons lemon juice
¼ cup granulated sugar
¾ cup all-purpose flour
½ cup packed brown sugar
½ teaspoon cinnamon
½ cup butter, softened

Toss apples with lemon juice and granulated sugar and spread in a 9-inch square pan.

In a bowl, combine flour, brown sugar and cinnamon. Add butter and mix in until crumbly. Sprinkle evenly over apples and bake in a 350°F oven until apples are very tender and the top is crisp and golden brown, about 30 to 45 minutes.

Serves 4.

APPLE CRISP

Fruit-crisp desserts appeal to just about everyone in every season. Use rhubarb with extra sugar to sweeten its tartness early in the summer season, blueberries or peaches in mid-summer and apples such as Gravenstein, Jonagold or McIntosh in late summer or fall. Crisps are perfect for large gatherings because you can easily increase the ingredients to feed a crowd.

8 cups peeled, cored and thinly sliced apples
½ cup granulated sugar
2 tablespoons lemon juice
1 cup packed brown sugar
1 cup all-purpose flour
1½ teaspoons cinnamon
¼ teaspoon nutmeg
1½ cups large-flake rolled oats
¾ cup butter, at room temperature, cubed
Vanilla ice cream

In a medium bowl, toss apple, sugar and juice. Spread apple mixture over bottom of greased 9- by 13-inch baking dish.

In a bowl, using your fingertips, mix together sugar, flour, cinnamon and nutmeg. Mix in rolled oats, then butter until crumbly. Sprinkle over apples and bake in a 375°F oven for 40 minutes or until top is golden and apples are soft and bubbly. Serve warm with vanilla ice cream.

Serves 10.

CLASSIC ENGLISH TRIFLE

. . . .

GARRISON HOUSE INN, ANNAPOLIS ROYAL, N.S.

Patrick Redgrave of the Garrison House Inn prepares his trifle using many seasonal fruits. Blueberries and bananas are a winning combination.

8 to 10 ladyfingers, or 1 sponge cake
½ cup Blueberry Jam (page 280)
¼ cup sherry
1½ cups sliced bananas
1½ cups blueberries
½ cup heavy cream (35% mf)
½ teaspoon vanilla extract
¼ cup sliced almonds

CUSTARD

¼ cup granulated sugar
3 tablespoons all-purpose flour
3 large egg yolks
2 cups milk
2 teaspoons lemon zest
1 teaspoon vanilla extract

Split ladyfingers and spread cut sides with thick layer of jam. Arrange pieces jam side up over the bottom of a shallow, clear glass bowl. Sprinkle with sherry. Add fruit.

CUSTARD

In a heavy saucepan, whisk together the sugar, flour, yolks, milk and zest. Cook, stirring over medium heat until mixture is smooth and thick, and begins to boil. Remove from heat, add vanilla and cover surface with waxed paper. Let cool until barely warm.

Pour over trifle. Let stand at room temperature until cool, then cover and refrigerate.

To serve, whip cream until stiff and add vanilla. Spread over custard and top with almonds.

Serves 6 to 8.

CORIANDER FRUIT CRUMBLE

. . . .

MERLIN BIRDSALL, MAHONE BAY, N.S.

Coriander fruit crumble is a slight departure from traditional fruit crumble in its seasoning. Try it with layers of local berries and apples.

FILLING

9 to 10 medium Cortland or McIntosh apples, peeled, cored and sliced into half-moons
8 ounces fresh or frozen blueberries
8 ounces fresh or frozen raspberries
⅓ cup packed brown sugar
2 teaspoons coriander
1 teaspoon cinnamon

TOPPING

¾ cup all-purpose flour
½ cup packed brown sugar
¼ cup large-flake rolled oats
¼ cup unsalted butter
2 teaspoons coriander
Whipping cream or sour cream, for garnish

FILLING

Arrange layers of apples, blueberries and raspberries in greased 9-inch square baking dish and sprinkle with sugar, coriander and cinnamon. Set aside.

TOPPING

Put flour and sugar and oats in medium mixing bowl. Add butter and cut into small pieces with table knife. With fingertips, rub in butter until mixture looks like coarse breadcrumbs. Mix in coriander. Sprinkle over fruit and score topping with fork. Bake for 30 minutes at 350°F. Serve with whipping cream or sour cream.

Serves 8.

BREAD AND APPLE CUSTARD PUDDING

SANDRA NOWLAN, HALIFAX, N.S.

"My mother made bread pudding when she wanted to use up scraps of homemade bread. I remember digging out plump raisins from the soft, custardy pudding," remembers Sandra Nowlan. For best results, it is important to use bread with a good texture. Homemade bread is best, but French, Italian or cracked wheat bread will do.

¼ cup dried currants
2 tablespoons orange juice or orange liqueur
1 large tart cooking apple or 2 medium
2 tablespoons butter, melted
2 cups cubed stale bread, crust removed
4 large eggs
⅓ to ½ cup granulated sugar
2 cups milk
½ cup blend cream (10% mf) or heavy cream (35% mf)
Pinch of salt
1 teaspoon vanilla extract
⅓ cup sliced almonds
2 to 3 tablespoons brown sugar
Cream

Soak currants in juice. Peel, score and cut apple into thin slices. Melt butter in a heavy frying pan and cook apples until translucent. Combine apples and their juices, bread cubes and currant mixture in a 1½-quart greased casserole or baking dish. Beat eggs and add sugar, milk, cream, salt and vanilla. Pour egg mixture over bread mixture. Stir and let soak for 20 minutes. Sprinkle with almonds and brown sugar and place in a large baking pan containing about 1 inch of hot water. Bake for 45 to 60 minutes at 350°F or until a knife comes out clean 2 inches from the edge. Serve warm or cold with cream.

Serves 8.

BLUEBERRY ROLY-POLY

MRS. WANDA ROBSON, NORTH SYDNEY, N.S.

"I remember picking cherries, gooseberries and apples in our backyard. Wild raspberries, strawberries and blueberries grew in the wooded section near our home. Blueberries were my favourite. The following recipe is almost exactly as my mother made it," says Mrs. Wanda Robson.

DOUGH

2 cups all-purpose flour
1 tablespoon baking powder
½ teaspoon salt
¼ cup butter
1 large egg
¾ cup cold milk

FILLING

2 to 3 cups fresh or frozen blueberries
1 cup granulated or packed brown sugar
1 teaspoon cinnamon
1 tablespoon lemon juice
½ cup water
Cream

DOUGH

Sift flour, baking powder and salt together into a large bowl. Cut in butter until mixture is crumbly. Add egg, then gradually add milk and mix until a soft dough forms. Turn the dough out on a lightly floured board and roll to a rectangle about 12 inches wide and ½-inch thick.

FILLING

Mix the berries with the sugar, cinnamon and juice. Spread over the dough, leaving about 2 inches as a border. Roll dough and berries up together, seal the edges well and turn the roll over so the seam is on the bottom. Place roll in a 9- by 13-inch baking pan. Add ½ cup of water. Baste frequently while baking at 350°F for 30 to 40 minutes, or until the juices have thickened and the crust is brown. Serve with cream.

Serves 6.

APPLE PAN DOWDY

. . . .

VIRJENE COLE, KENSINGTON, P.E.I.

A warm winter pudding whose origins are faded with time, but which remains a favourite, is made with apples from the trees in Virjene Cole's P.E.I. orchard.

1 cup water
1 cup packed brown sugar
¼ cup all-purpose flour
¼ teaspoon cinnamon
¼ teaspoon salt
1 teaspoon vanilla extract
1 teaspoon lemon juice
4 cups peeled, cored and chopped apples
Ice cream

BISCUIT DOUGH

1 tablespoon granulated sugar
¼ cup butter, softened
1 large egg
⅓ cup milk
1 cup all-purpose flour
2 teaspoons baking powder
¼ teaspoon salt

Cook first 5 ingredients in a saucepan over medium heat until thick, stirring often. Add vanilla and juice. Place apples on the bottom of a 1½-quart casserole or baking dish. Pour the cooked sauce mixture over the apples.

DOUGH

Beat sugar and butter. Add egg and milk, and mix. Stir in flour, baking powder and salt. Roll to fit the top of the baking dish and place over the apple mixture. Bake at 375°F for 40 to 45 minutes or until filling is bubbling and biscuit is no longer doughy underneath. Serve warm with ice cream.

Serves 6.

BLUEBERRY BUCKLE

. . . .

The word "buckle" identifies this cake as a Down East specialty. But the pleasure of blueberries, cake and a crumble topping is universal. Whipped cream, sour cream or ice cream on the make the treat perfect.

CAKE

½ cup butter, softened
½ cup packed brown sugar
1 large egg
1 teaspoon vanilla extract
2 cups all-purpose flour
1 tablespoon baking powder
½ teaspoon salt
¾ cup milk
3 cups blueberries

TOPPING

½ cup packed brown sugar
6 tablespoons all-purpose flour
½ teaspoon cinnamon
¼ cup cold butter, cubed

CAKE

Beat the butter, then beat in the sugar, egg and vanilla. In a separate bowl, sift together the flour, baking powder and salt. Mix into the butter mixture in 3 portions, alternately with the milk, in 2 portions. Spread evenly in a greased 8- by 12-inch cake pan.

Pour the blueberries over the batter in an even layer. Press down very lightly.

TOPPING

Combine the sugar, flour and cinnamon. Cut in the butter, working until the mixture is crumbly. Sprinkle evenly over the berries.

Bake in 350°F oven for 50 to 55 minutes, or until the crumble top is light golden, the berries juicy and a toothpick inserted into the cake comes out clean. Leave the buckle in the pan. Serve warm.

Serves 10 to 12.

STICKY APPLE PUDDING WITH TOFFEE SAUCE

EVANGELINE CAFÉ, GRAND PRÉ, N.S.

You will simply love this creation from the chef at Evangeline Café. A cross between old-fashioned gingerbread and sticky toffee pudding, the dessert won first place in the annual Annapolis Valley Apple Blossom Festival dessert competition in 2005.

2 cups apple cider
½ cup chopped dates
4 teaspoons baking soda
⅓ cup butter, softened
1¼ cups granulated sugar
3 large eggs
2 cups all-purpose flour
1 tablespoon baking powder
1 teaspoon cinnamon
½ teaspoon nutmeg
½ teaspoon cloves
2 Cortland apples, peeled, cored and cut in ¼-inch dice

TOFFEE SAUCE

¾ cup butter
1¼ cups packed brown sugar
¾ cup heavy cream (35% mf)
½ teaspoon vanilla extract

In a large saucepan, bring cider and dates to a boil. Boil until soft, about 5 minutes. Remove from heat and stir in baking soda (mixture will froth and increase in volume). Cool.

In a bowl, beat butter and sugar until light and fluffy. Add eggs, 1 at a time, beating after each addition.

In a bowl, combine flour, baking powder and spices. Stir flour mixture alternately with date mixture into the egg mixture, making 3 additions of dry ingredients and 2 of wet. Stir in diced apple.

Pour batter into greased 9- by 13-inch baking pan and bake in 350°F oven for 40 to 50 minutes, until a toothpick inserted in centre comes out clean. Serve warm.

TOFFEE SAUCE

Meanwhile, in a saucepan, melt butter over medium heat. Add sugar and stir until dissolved. Stir in cream and simmer until slightly thickened. Remove from heat and stir in vanilla. Serve warm with the pudding.

Serves 8.

BLUEBERRY BREAD PUDDING

· · · · · · · · · ·

CHIVES CANADIAN BISTRO, HALIFAX, N.S.

A warm country feel is what you get from bread pudding, and the little bursts of blueberry sauce are very homey and totally yummy.

3 large eggs
1½ cups blend cream (10% mf)
1 teaspoon allspice
1 tablespoon vanilla extract
½ cup packed brown sugar
1 cup fresh blueberries
4 cups cubed stale bread
Whipped Cream

BLUEBERRY SAUCE

2 cups fresh or frozen blueberries
½ cup granulated sugar
¼ cup brandy

In a large bowl, whisk eggs, cream, allspice, vanilla and sugar together. Mix in blueberries and bread. Soak 1 hour.

Pour into a greased 9- by 5-inch loaf pan or individual ramekins. Place the loaf pan in a larger pan containing 1 inch of hot water. Bake in a 300°F oven 30 minutes or until a knife inserted into the centre comes out clean.

SAUCE

In a large pot, simmer berries with sugar until they release their juice and become saucy. Remove from heat and add brandy. Serve with bread pudding and whipped cream.

Serves 4.

WILD BLUEBERRY POSSET

. . . .

ACTON'S GRILL AND CAFÉ, WOLFVILLE, N.S.

The chef at Acton's serves this luscious dessert in a glass dish garnished with a few sprigs of fresh mint, whole fresh blueberries and some cookies on the side.

2 cups wild blueberries, crushed
½ cup granulated sugar
2 cups heavy cream (35% mf), whipped
2 tablespoons lemon juice
4 large egg whites

Combine blueberries with sugar, cream and juice. Set aside. Beat egg whites until stiff but not dry. Carefully fold into blueberry mixture. Spoon into individual dessert dishes and serve immediately.

Serves 8.

STEAMED CRANBERRY PUDDING

. . . .

VIRJENE COLE, KENSINGTON, P.E.I.

Virjene Cole grew up on a farm where nothing was wasted. The family was lucky enough to have a patch of cranberries at the back of the property. They used everything they grew or picked for cooking and once they tried cranberries in a pudding instead of raisins. It proved a popular choice and the steamed cranberry pudding became a much-loved dessert.

1 tablespoon baking soda
¾ cup fancy molasses
¾ cup boiling water
2 cups all-purpose flour
1½ teaspoons baking powder
1½ cups cranberries

SAUCE
½ cup heavy cream (35% mf)
½ cup packed brown sugar
¼ cup butter

Combine baking soda, molasses and the boiling water. Sift the flour with the baking powder and mix into the molasses mixture with the cranberries. Place batter in a greased pudding bowl. Cover batter with round of waxed paper and bowl with foil. Tie the foil tightly to the bowl with string. Press foil up over the string. Steam on rack in large pot that has 1 inch of water until a toothpick inserted in the centre comes out clean, about 2 hours.

SAUCE

In the top of a double boiler, combine the cream, sugar and butter. Cook over boiling water until blended and thickened, about 15 minutes. Serve with pudding.

Serves 6 to 8.

BLUEBERRY AND RHUBARB CRUMBLE

· · · · · · · · · · · · ·

DALVAY BY THE SEA, DALVAY, P.E.I

At Dalvay by the Sea, this delicious fruit dessert is often served hot, with frozen berry yogurt.

FILLING

2 tablespoons butter
⅔ cup granulated sugar, or to taste
1½ tablespoons lemon juice
1 pound chopped rhubarb, about 3 cups
1 cup blueberries
½ teaspoon cinnamon
½ teaspoon vanilla extract
Frozen berry yogurt or whipped cream

CRUMBLE

⅓ cup butter, softened
½ cup granulated sugar
½ cup all-purpose flour
½ cup ground almonds
⅓ cup large-flake rolled oats

FILLING

In a saucepan combine butter, sugar and juice. Cook and stir over medium heat until light golden. Add rhubarb and increase heat to medium-high. Cook and stir until mixture starts to thicken, about 10 minutes. Add blueberries and cinnamon and cook for 4 minutes. Remove from heat, stir in vanilla and cool.

CRUMBLE

Beat butter and sugar until smooth. Combine flour, almonds and oats. Gradually rub into butter mixture until crumbly. Pour rhubarb-blueberry mixture into a greased 2-quart baking dish and sprinkle crumble mixture on top. Bake in a 425°F oven for 25 to 30 minutes, until top is browned. (May also be baked in 6 individual ramekins for 10 to 12 minutes.) Serve warm with frozen yogurt or whipped cream.

Serves 6.

BLUEBERRY GRUNT

. . . .

MOUNTAIN GAP INN AND RESORT, SMITHS COVE, N.S.

Blueberry Grunt is the homey kind of dessert we all shared around our grandmother's table. At Mountain Gap Inn, it is served warm with vanilla ice cream or whipped cream.

SAUCE

2 cups fresh or frozen blueberries
¼ to ½ cup granulated sugar
⅓ cup water

DUMPLINGS

1 cup all-purpose flour
2 teaspoons baking powder
1 teaspoon granulated sugar
¼ teaspoon salt
1 tablespoon butter
⅓ to ½ cup milk
Vanilla ice cream or whipped cream

SAUCE

Combine berries with sugar and water and bring to a boil in a large saucepan. Reduce heat and simmer until berries are soft and sauce begins to thicken, about 5 minutes.

DUMPLINGS

Whisk together flour, baking powder, sugar and salt. Cut in butter with a pastry blender. Stir in just enough of the milk to make a soft dough. Drop the batter by spoonfuls on top of the simmering berry sauce. Immediately cover saucepan and cook over medium heat without removing cover for 15 to 18 minutes. Serve warm with ice cream or whipped cream.

Serves 4 to 6.

EASY BLUEBERRY CRÈME BRÛLÉE

. . . .

QUACO INN, ST. MARTINS, N.B.

If you are looking for a quick and easy dessert recipe, look no further. This crème brûlée is beautiful in appearance and oh, so tasty!

1 pint blueberries
⅔ cup low-fat sour cream
½ cup plain yogurt
⅓ cup packed brown sugar
Mint leaves, for garnish

Divide blueberries among 6 heat-proof ramekins.

Combine sour cream and yogurt and spread over blueberries, being careful to cover completely. Sprinkle sugar over sour cream mixture and broil 3 inches from element until sugar caramelizes, approximately 3 to 5 minutes. Watch carefully, as topping can easily burn.

Serve immediately, garnished with mint leaves.

Serves 6.

CHOCOLATE STEAMED PUDDING

. . . .

VIVIEN FRASER, MONTAGUE, P.E.I.

The following recipe, created and handed down by Vivien Fraser's mother-in-law's sister, is now made for birthdays, Christmas and other special occasions.

PUDDING

2 large eggs
1 cup granulated sugar
1 teaspoon salt
1 teaspoon vanilla extract
2 cups all-purpose flour
7 tablespoons cocoa
1 tablespoon baking powder
1 cup milk

SAUCE

1 cup granulated sugar
½ cup butter
2 large eggs, separated

PUDDING

In a bowl, beat eggs until light in colour. Beat in sugar, salt and vanilla until well mixed. Sift flour, cocoa and baking powder together in a separate bowl. Add dry ingredients alternately with the milk to the egg mixture, making 3 additions of dry and 2 of milk. Put into a steamer dish and cover with round of waxed paper and then foil. Tie tightly with string. Set the bowl on a rack in a large pot that has 1 inch of water. Cover and bring the water to boil and steam for 1 hour.

SAUCE

Melt butter with sugar in a double boiler over low heat. Whisk in egg yolks and cook until slightly thickened. In a bowl beat the egg whites until stiff and fold into the butter mixture. Serve with the pudding.

Serves 6 to 8.

STICKY TOFFEE PUDDING

. . . .

For this recipe you need a scale. It makes small individual puddings. You can use ramekins, muffin moulds or timbales — they all make for an elegant presentation. Add a little whipped cream or vanilla ice cream to finish

1 pound pitted dates, chopped
1¾ cups water
½ teaspoon salt
2 tablespoons vanilla extract
¾ cups unsalted butter, softened
2 cups packed brown sugar
¼ cup fancy molasses or treacle
6 large eggs
½ cup milk
6 cups all-purpose flour
1 tablespoon baking powder
1 tablespoon butter
1 tablespoon granulated sugar

Bring dates and water to a boil and simmer for 10 minutes. Purée mixture until very smooth and add salt and vanilla. Set aside to cool.

Cream the butter, sugar and molasses in a mixer using the paddle attachment until light and fluffy. Add cooled date purée and beat well. Add eggs, 1 at a time, along with small amounts of milk. Combine flour and baking powder, gently fold in to date mixture. Grease 12 ramekins with butter and dust with sugar. Pour in batter and bake at 325°F for 30 minutes.

Serves 12.

GOOSEBERRY FOOL

. . . .

ALICE LEDUC, WATERVILLE, N.S.

A "fool" is a combination of stewed fruit and either cooked custard and cream together, or just cream. Ron and Diane Wiles, a retired English couple who ran a hobby U-pick at Berwick, N.S., grew gooseberries and followed this recipe from an old English cookbook.

1½ pounds gooseberries (6 cups)
2 tablespoons water
½ cup granulated sugar
1¼ cups heavy cream (35% mf), lightly whipped

Top, tail and wash gooseberries. Place in a pan with water over gentle heat, stirring frequently until gooseberries are soft. Reserve a few berries for garnish. Press remaining berries through sieve or food mill into a bowl. Stir in sugar. Allow to cool. Fold in whipped cream. Spoon into parfait glasses. Refrigerate until ready to serve. Decorate with reserved gooseberries.

Serves 8.

CARAMEL CHOCOLATE CRÈME WITH
WARM BLUEBERRY SAUCE

. . . .

DUFFERIN INN AND SAN MARTELLO DINING ROOM, SAINT JOHN, N.B.

This recipe was served by Margret and Axel Begner when they ran the Dufferin Inn in Saint John. This decadent crème caramel was topped with a warm blueberry sauce. The subtle addition of chocolate to the custard makes it a memorable dessert!

CUSTARDS

½ cup granulated sugar
1 tablespoon water
1 cup milk
1 cup heavy cream (35% mf)
2 squares white chocolate, chopped
3 large egg yolks
2 large eggs
Icing sugar, blueberries and white chocolate shavings

BLUEBERRY SAUCE

1½ cups blueberries
1 cup red wine
¼ cup granulated sugar
1 tablespoon cornstarch
1 teaspoon vanilla extract

Tip #1: Caramel reaches a very high temperature. It's a good idea to use oven mitts to protect yourself from splattering when the milk and cream are added.

Tip #2: While the sugar mixture is boiling, wash down the inside of the pan with a pastry brush dipped in water. This prevents the sugar from crystallizing.

CUSTARDS

Heat sugar and water in a heavy saucepan over low heat, shaking the pan occasionally until the sugar is dissolved. Turn heat to high and boil, without stirring, until caramel is golden brown. Watch carefully so that it does not burn.

Remove from heat and averting your face, cautiously stir in the milk and cream. Return to heat and bring almost to a boil then remove from heat. Add chocolate and stir until melted.

In a bowl, whisk yolks and whole eggs. Whisk a small amount of the hot mixture into the eggs, return egg mixture to hot mixture in saucepan and whisk to combine. Pour into 6 custard cups.

Place custard cups in a water bath (shallow roasting pan filled to 1 inch with hot water). Bake in a 350°F oven 30 to 35 minutes or until a knife inserted into the centre comes out clean. Cool, then refrigerate.

SAUCE

Meanwhile, cook blueberries, wine, sugar and cornstarch in a saucepan over medium heat until thick and bubbly. Remove from heat, stir in vanilla and keep warm.

To serve, unmould custards on individual serving plates dusted with icing sugar and top with warm blueberry sauce. Garnish with fresh berries and white chocolate shavings.

Serves 6.

COLD BLUEBERRY SOUFFLÉ

. . . .

LA PERLA, DARTMOUTH, N.S.

This is an impressive dessert that is easy to prepare in advance. At La Perla, it is presented in individual dishes decorated with a dollop of whipped cream, a few berries and fresh mint leaves or edible flowers.

5 cups fresh or frozen blueberries
⅓ cup water
2 tablespoons Grand Marnier liqueur
1½ envelopes unflavoured gelatin (1½ tablespoons)
3 large egg whites
½ cup granulated sugar
1½ cups heavy cream (35% mf), whipped

Fit a 1½-quart soufflé dish or individual ramekins with a foil collar.

In a deep saucepan, cook blueberries and 2 tablespoons of the water over medium heat until berries have broken down and mixture has become saucy. Remove from heat and stir in Grand Marnier. Keep warm.

In a small bowl, sprinkle gelatin over remaining cold water and stir. Set aside for 5 minutes to soften, then stir into warm blueberry sauce. Let cool.

Meanwhile, whisk egg whites and sugar until frothy and place in the top of a double boiler over hot (not boiling) water. Cook, whisking constantly, until thick and sugar is completely dissolved. Remove from heat and set double boiler insert in a bowl of ice and water to chill. Scrape into large bowl.

Carefully fold blueberry mixture into egg whites mixture. Fold in whipped cream and pour into the prepared soufflé dish. Refrigerate for 4 hours or until set.

To serve, remove foil collar and decorate as desired.

Serves 8.

BLUEBERRY BALLERINA

. . . .

INN ON THE COVE AND SPA, SAINT JOHN, N.B.

This spectacular dessert is easy to prepare and is a variation of the famous pavlova, a combination of strawberries and kiwi fruit over whipped cream and a soft meringue. The meringue is best made when the humidity is low.

MERINGUE

4 large egg whites, at room temperature
Pinch of cream of tartar
1 cup granulated sugar
1 tablespoon cornstarch
Pinch of salt
1 teaspoon vanilla extract
2 teaspoons cider vinegar
1 cup heavy cream (35% mf), whipped with
  1 tablespoon granulated sugar
1½ cups blueberries

BLUEBERRY COULIS

2 cups fresh or frozen blueberries
½ cup granulated sugar
¼ cup water
2 teaspoons cornstarch, dissolved in 1 tablespoon
  cold water
2 teaspoons lemon juice

MERINGUE

Beat egg whites and cream of tartar to soft peaks. Beat while gradually adding sugar until stiff peaks form. Fold in cornstarch and salt, then vanilla and vinegar.

Cut 2 pieces of waxed paper to fit a large baking sheet. Thoroughly wet waxed paper sheets with cold water and place on baking sheet. Pile meringue in a 10-inch circle with the sides slightly higher than the centre. Place in a 400°F oven and immediately turn off heat. Leave in oven 1½ hours. Remove, let stand 10 minutes then separate from waxed paper and cool.

COULIS

Meanwhile, in a heavy saucepan, bring blueberries, sugar and water to a boil, stirring occasionally, 5 minutes. Stir cornstarch mixture into pan. Add juice and simmer for 2 minutes, stirring constantly. Press sauce through sieve, then refrigerate until cold.

Place meringue on serving plate, fill with sweetened whipped cream and top with blueberries. Serve individual portions with Blueberry Coulis.

Serves 8 to 10.

CHRISTMAS PLUM PUDDING

. . . .

GAIL I. H. SMITH, CHESTER, N.S.

The tradition of plum pudding is one that many families observe, and there are many variations of the steamed dessert. For one family, it began with a great-great-grandmother who came to Nova Scotia from Prince Edward Island as a bride in 1860. She brought with her an English cookbook published in 1858. The same recipe is still followed, but the present-day daughter, Gail Smith, and her mother learned to adjust the quantity to suit fewer numbers and to reflect the package size of raisins and currants.

Of course plum pudding doesn't have any plums at all. The name dates back to a time when plum meant virtually any dried fruit. Cooked carrots are the main ingredient in this version and they make it rich and moist and also add a special sweetness.

½ pound ground suet

4 cups hot mashed cooked carrots

2 cups all-purpose flour

½ cup granulated sugar

1 teaspoon cinnamon

½ teaspoon cloves

¼ teaspoon nutmeg

¾ pound currants

¾ pound sultana raisins

8 ounces diced citron peel

RUM HARD SAUCE

½ cup butter

1 cup icing sugar

Rum

Mix suet into hot mashed carrots. Let stand so the suet will melt while the other ingredients are mixed.

In a large bowl, sift together flour, sugar, and spices. Add to the suet mixture, stirring until all the flour is absorbed. Stir in currants, raisins and peel. Pack in 2 greased stainless steel bowls or pudding bowls, 1½ quarts each. They should not be full because pudding rises as it steams. Cover with foil well down over the bowl. Tie foil tightly to the bowls. Place each bowl on a rack in a deep saucepan. Add boiling water to come halfway up the bowls. Cover and steam for 3½ hours replenishing the water as needed. The water should simmer, not boil vigorously. The pudding may be made early and reheated. Leftover pudding keeps well in the fridge.

SAUCE

In a mixer, beat butter and icing sugar at high speed. Add enough rum to make the mixture a soft icing consistency but not runny. Serve with wedges of hot plum pudding.

Serves 12.

MAPLE ICE CREAM

. . . .

Using maple syrup in ice cream is reminiscent of drizzling it over snow, as native Canadians did centuries ago. The coolness on the palate diminishes the overbearing sweet sensation and allows the flavours to emerge. It is simple to make if you have an ice-cream maker, and it works well with apple pie or angel food cake, or on its own.

4 cups heavy cream (35% mf)
2 cups whole milk
2 tablespoons maple extract
10 large egg yolks
2 cups Grade B or amber maple syrup
¼ cup glucose syrup, available in bulk and cake
   decorating stores

In a heavy-bottomed saucepan, heat cream, milk and maple extract until bubbles form around the edge of the pan. In a mixing bowl, thoroughly combine yolks, maple syrup and glucose. Temper this mixture with the hot cream mixture, one ladle at a time, stirring continuously. When all the cream mixture has been added, place this bowl over a pot of simmering water and cook while stirring with a rubber spatula. The eggs will cause the custard to thicken. When custard coats the back of a spoon, strain into bowl and refrigerate until it is very cold. Churn in an electric ice-cream maker, following the manufacturer's instructions. Store churned ice cream in a 4-pint plastic container in the freezer for a minimum of 2 hours before serving.

Makes 2 quarts.

LISCOMBE LODGE MAPLE SYRUP CREAM

. . . .

LISCOMBE LODGE, LISCOMB MILLS, N.S.

This simple, elegant dessert makes a beautiful presentation served in stemmed glasses, decorated with fresh seasonal berries and mint leaves.

1 tablespoon unflavoured powdered gelatin
   (1 envelope)
¼ cup cold water
½ cup milk, scalded
⅔ cup pure maple syrup
⅛ teaspoon salt
2 cups heavy cream (35% mf)
Fresh fruit and mint leaves, for garnish

Soak gelatin in cold water for 5 minutes. Stir into hot milk, stirring until dissolved. Add syrup and salt, and refrigerate until mixture begins to thicken, about 45 minutes. Whip the cream and gently fold into gelatin mixture. Pour into a large bowl or 6 individual serving dishes. Refrigerate several hours until firm. Garnish with fruit and mint leaves.

Serves 6.

MAPLE PARFAIT

. . . .

THE PALLISER RESTAURANT, TRURO, N.S.

Keltie Bruce of The Palliser told the story that as a child she refused to eat Christmas pudding. Her mother developed this recipe and served it only for the holidays, thus they affectionately call it "Maple Christmas."

½ cup pure maple syrup
2 large eggs, at room temperature
1 cup heavy cream (35% mf)
Crème de cacao, whipped cream and chocolate
   sprinkles

In a small saucepan, heat maple syrup almost to a boil. Pour into a bowl. Add eggs and beat with a mixer on medium-high speed until mixture is fully blended, approximately 5 minutes. Refrigerate until well chilled, several hours or overnight.

   Whip cream until stiff peaks form, then, using a mixer, beat into maple mixture. Pour into parfait glasses or brandy snifters, cover with plastic wrap and freeze. Remove from freezer 10 minutes before serving. Garnish with a teaspoon of crème de cacao, dollop of whipped cream and chocolate sprinkles.

Serves 6 to 8.

QUICK MAPLE PUDDING

. . . .

JOAN NEVERS, PLASTER ROCK, N.B.

The recipes of Joan Nevers's English grandmother were quite different from those found in New Brunswick when she arrived. But she used the ingredients that were available, and in the spring, maple syrup was one of them. When the woodcutters came in from the forests, she made this dessert. It was easy to prepare and they liked it.

1 tablespoon butter
3 tablespoons granulated sugar
1 cup all-purpose flour
2 teaspoons baking powder
¼ teaspoon salt
½ cup milk
1 cup maple syrup
Heavy cream (35% mf)

In a bowl, beat together the butter and sugar. In a separate bowl combine the flour, baking powder and salt. Stir half into the butter mixture, add the milk and then stir in the remaining dry ingredients "to make a nice batter."

   Heat maple syrup to boiling. Pour into a 2- or 3-quart casserole dish. Pour the batter over the syrup. Bake in 425°F oven until bubbling around the edges and the topping is firm to the touch, about 25 minutes.

Serves 6.

CREAM CROWDIE

. . . .

CAMPBELL HOUSE, CHESTER, N.S.

In Cream Crowdie, rolled oats and Drambuie reflect the strength of Scottish influence in Nova Scotian cooking.

3 tablespoons large-flake rolled oats
1 cup heavy cream (35% mf)
2 tablespoons Drambuie liqueur
1 tablespoon granulated sugar
6 scoops vanilla ice cream

Spread oats evenly on a baking sheet and bake at 350°F for 10 minutes, until golden brown. Remove from oven and cool. Place cream in a chilled bowl and whip until stiff. Add oatmeal, Drambuie and sugar. Place ice cream in a flat, shallow champagne glass (not a flute); top with cream mixture.

Serves 4 to 6.

PEACH SOUR-CREAM ICE CREAM

. . . .

RESTAURANT LE CAVEAU, GRAND PRÉ, N.S.

The fresh peaches of August inspired this delicately flavoured ice cream. For ultra-smooth results, use an electric ice-cream maker. Since homemade ice cream is very dense and firm, let it soften slightly in the refrigerator for 20 to 30 minutes before serving.

2 cups whole milk
¾ cup granulated sugar
7 large egg yolks
1½ cups sliced peaches
Zest of ½ orange
Zest of ½ lemon
1 cup sour cream
Whipped cream
1 peach, peeled and sliced

In a heavy saucepan, bring milk and sugar to a boil. In a small bowl, whisk yolks until pale. Remove milk mixture from the burner and whisk ½ cup into yolks. Reduce heat to low; whisk yolk mixture back into saucepan. Cook, stirring often, until thick enough to coat back of spoon (175°F). Remove, strain and let cool.

Using a blender, purée peaches and zests. Whisk into custard and stir in sour cream. Pour into an electric ice-cream machine and follow the manufacturer's instructions to freeze until fairly firm. Transfer to a 6-cup freezer container, allowing at least 1 inch of space at the top for expansion. Freeze until firm, about 4 hours or overnight. Scoop and garnish ice-cream balls with whipped cream and peach slices.

Serves 6 to 8.

MOLASSES AND MAPLE CRÈME BRÛLÉE

. . . .

OPERA BISTRO, SAINT JOHN, N.B.

You are guaranteed to leave the table with the senses fully satisfied after this exquisite dessert. It is the ultimate indulgence. Chef Margaret Begner enriches this crème brûlée with the "sweet sisters," molasses and maple syrup. No one can resist the crunchy caramelized topping followed by the delightfully creamy custard below. For convenience the custard can be made two to three days before serving. Caramelize the tops just before your guests arrive using a chef's blowtorch.

2 cups heavy cream (35% mf)
6 large egg yolks
2 tablespoons pure maple syrup
2 tablespoons fancy molasses
½ cup plus 1 tablespoon granulated sugar

Bring cream to a boil. In a bowl, combine yolks, syrup, molasses and 1 tablespoon of the sugar. Pour hot cream over egg mixture, whisking steadily until blended. Divide custard into 6 ramekins and place in large shallow pan. Add hot water to come up halfway up sides of ramekins. Bake for 45 minutes at 300°F. Let cool, cover and refrigerate. Sprinkle with remaining sugar and then caramelize the sugar with a blowtorch.

Serves 6.

POACHED PEARS IN RED WINE

SEASONS IN THYME, SUMMERSIDE, P.E.I.

This elegant dessert is simple to prepare and good for any occasion. Pears are available year round and Bosc and Bartlett varieties poach well. Chef Stefan Czapalay of the short-lived Seasons in Thyme restaurant used Zinfandel wine and recommended refrigerating the poached pears overnight before serving.

1½ cups fruity red wine
½ cup orange juice
5 peppercorns
5 whole cloves
1 cinnamon stick
½ teaspoon nutmeg
2 tablespoons honey
4 pears

Combine the wine, juice, spices and honey in a saucepan and bring to a simmer. Peel pears, leaving stems intact.

Place pears in liquid, cover and gently poach until just tender, about 20 minutes. Allow pears to cool in liquid, then refrigerate overnight in their poaching liquid.

Serves 4.

WHITE WINE AND PEAR SORBET

THE JUBILEE COTTAGE COUNTRY INN, WALLACE, N.S.

Daphne Dominy served this sorbet as a light dessert or as a refresher between courses when she operated the Jubilee Cottage as an inn. She found that Jost Riesling from a neighbouring winery is just perfect for the recipe.

8 large pears, peeled, cored and chopped
1 cup granulated sugar
1 cup filtered water
2 tablespoons lemon juice
1 cup medium-dry white wine

Combine pears, sugar, water and juice in a saucepan and bring to a boil over high heat. Reduce heat and simmer, covered, for 15 minutes or until pears are very soft. Remove from heat and strain, reserving poaching liquid.

Purée pears in a blender in batches until very smooth. Add to poaching liquid and cool. Stir in wine and refrigerate. Freeze the mixture in an ice-cream maker following the manufacturer's instructions. Transfer to an airtight container and freeze until firm, about 4 hours. Let sorbet soften in the refrigerator about 20 minutes before scooping and serving.

Serves 4 to 6.

RED WINE PLUM COMPOTE

. . . .

LITTLE SHEMOGUE COUNTRY INN,
PORT ELGIN, N.B.

Pungent fruit and wine flavours paired with hints of spice make this compote a favourite "adult" dessert.

6 large ripe red or blue plums
1½ cups dry red wine (preferably Merlot or Syrah)
1 cup granulated sugar
2 whole cloves
1 inch cinnamon stick
Whipped cream or vanilla ice cream (optional)

Cut plums in half, remove pits and place skin side up in a large saucepan. Combine wine, sugar and spices in a bowl. Stir to dissolve sugar. Pour into saucepan and bring to a boil over medium-high heat. Reduce heat and simmer plums, being careful not to boil, for 15 to 18 minutes, until fruit has softened. Remove plums and syrup to a serving dish. Discard cinnamon stick and cloves.

Plums may be served warm, cool or cold. Divide among dessert bowls and serve with whipped cream or ice cream, if desired.

Serves 6.

PUMPKIN CRÈME BRÛLÉE

. . . .

THE BLOMIDON INN, WOLFVILLE, N.S.

Rich, but oh so heavenly, chef Sean Laceby created a winning dessert with this variation on a traditional crème brûlée.

1½ cups heavy cream (35% mf)
4 large egg yolks
⅓ cup plus 1 tablespoon pumpkin purée
¼ teaspoon cinnamon
⅛ teaspoon each cloves, ginger and nutmeg
½ cup packed brown sugar
¾ teaspoon vanilla extract
Whipped cream, for garnish

Heat cream in a saucepan over medium heat until it simmers.

Meanwhile, in a bowl, whisk together yolks, pumpkin, spices and ¼ cup of the sugar. Gradually whisk in cream. Stir in vanilla and skim off foam. Divide among 4 6-ounce ramekins or custard cups. Place in a large shallow pan and pour in enough boiling water to come halfway up the sides of the ramekins.

Bake in 350°F oven until the edge is set but the centre jiggles and a knife inserted in the centre comes out creamy, about 30 to 35 minutes. Remove from water and let cool on racks. Cover and refrigerate until chilled and set.

To serve, place ramekins on a rimmed baking sheet. Sprinkle remaining brown sugar evenly over tops. Broil with a torch or under a broiler until sugar bubbles and darkens. Garnish with a dollop of whipped cream.

Serves 4.

CHRISTMAS PUDDING

· · · · · · · · · · ·

M. VILLETT, ISLINGTON, ONT.

A maternal grandmother's pudding was served with Christmas dinner at her farm home in North Wiltshire, P.E.I. As a little girl she travelled by horse and sleigh through the fields to reach the farm. It's still a tradition to serve this pudding at Christmas and the family is convinced it's the best they've ever tasted.

2 large eggs

½ cup fancy molasses

½ cup packed brown sugar

1 cup finely chopped suet

½ cup sour milk (add ½ teaspoon vinegar to sweet milk)

2 cups all-purpose flour

2 teaspoons baking soda

¾ teaspoon salt

½ teaspoon each cinnamon, nutmeg and cloves

1 cup sultana raisins

1 cup sticky seeded raisins, such as Lexia or Muscatels

½ cup chopped dates

½ cup chopped red and green cherries

¼ cup mixed peel

BUTTERSCOTCH SAUCE

½ cup packed brown sugar

3 to 4 tablespoons cornstarch

¼ teaspoon salt

2½ cups boiling water

1 tablespoon butter

½ teaspoon vanilla extract

In a large bowl, beat eggs and add molasses, sugar, suet and milk. In a separate bowl sift flour, baking soda, salt, and spices. Add flour mixture to molasses mixture and stir to combine. Then fold in raisins, dates, cherries and peel. Stir only until combined. Pour into a greased 2½-quart can or bowl. Cover the batter with a round of waxed paper. Make an additional cover with a piece of foil that extends down the side of the can. Tie firmly with string and trim the foil so there is a 2-inch overhang. Press foil up over string.

Place on a rack in a large pot. Pour in water to come two-thirds of the way up the can. Cover and steam for 3 hours, replenishing water as needed. Serve with butterscotch sauce.

BUTTERSCOTCH SAUCE

In a saucepan, mix the dry ingredients and slowly add boiling water. Cook over medium heat stirring often until thickened. Remove from the heat and add butter and vanilla.

Serves 12.

CREAMY RICE PUDDING WITH CINNAMON

· · · · · · · · · · · · · ·

Rice pudding, with its creamy texture, is a classic dessert in many European countries. This rich-tasting version is actually low in fat! The secret lies in evaporated milk and Arborio short-grain rice, which is high in starch. Flavoured with fresh lemon, cinnamon and maple syrup, this dessert will be a big hit. Add fresh berries if you like.

½ cup uncooked short-grain rice

1 cup water

2 strips lemon peel, each ½ by 2½ inches

1 3-inch cinnamon stick

¾ cup 2% evaporated milk

2¾ cups skimmed milk

2 tablespoons brown sugar

1 teaspoon cornstarch

2 tablespoons pure maple syrup

⅓ cup golden raisins

1 teaspoon vanilla extract

Cinnamon

Bring rice and water to a boil in a heavy saucepan. Cover and simmer on low heat for 10 minutes. Add lemon peel, cinnamon stick, evaporated milk and 1¾ cups of the skimmed milk.

In a bowl, combine sugar, cornstarch, remaining milk and syrup. Stir into rice mixture. Bring to a boil over medium-low heat and simmer, stirring often, over low heat for 25 minutes. Add raisins and continue cooking for 20 minutes longer, until slightly thickened, stirring often.

Remove from heat and discard lemon peel and cinnamon stick. Add vanilla. Serve warm or chilled, sprinkled with cinnamon. Pudding will thicken when chilled.

Serves 6 to 8.

RHUBARB COMPOTE

. . . .

Gently stewed and served in a crystal bowl, the compote is a fitting dish for a leisurely brunch.

8 cups chopped rhubarb, in 1-inch pieces
2 tablespoons finely chopped candied ginger
1½ cups granulated sugar, or to taste
¾ cup water

In a saucepan, combine all ingredients. Bring to a boil over medium heat. Reduce temperature and simmer gently, stirring often, until rhubarb is tender, approximately 15 minutes. Serve chilled.

Serves 8.

RHUBARB CRISP

. . . .

This rendition of an old-fashioned fruit crisp is easy to prepare and a wonderful winter dessert. It tastes best served with whipped cream.

4 cups chopped rhubarb
½ cup orange juice
¾ cup granulated sugar
½ teaspoon cinnamon
1 tablespoon butter

TOPPING
¾ cup all-purpose flour
¾ cup packed brown sugar
¾ cup large-flake rolled oats
¾ cup flaked coconut
½ cup butter

Combine rhubarb, juice, sugar and cinnamon in a greased 9-inch square baking dish. Dot with butter.

TOPPING
Combine flour, sugar, oats and coconut. Cut in butter with a pastry blender until crumbly. Sprinkle over rhubarb. Bake at 350°F until golden brown and bubbly, about 45 minutes.

Serves 6.

RASPBERRY UPSIDE-DOWN PUDDING

ALICE LEDUC, WATERVILLE, N.S.

There's no shortage of ideas on how to use summer's bounty of berries. You can use any type or combination for this pudding. Alice Leduc recommends raspberries as in recipe below or combines them with black currants.

½ cup butter, softened
½ cup packed brown sugar
2 cups raspberries
½ cup granulated sugar
1 large egg
½ teaspoon vanilla extract
1 cup sifted cake flour
½ teaspoon salt
¼ teaspoon baking powder
⅓ cup milk
Light cream (20% mf) or whipped cream

Melt half the butter in a 9-inch square pan. Sprinkle on the sugar and arrange berries over the top. Cream the remaining butter with sugar, then beat in the egg and vanilla. Sift the flour, salt and baking powder together and add alternately to the creamed mixture with the milk. Spread batter over the berries. Bake at 350°F until a toothpick inserted in the centre comes out clean, about 25 to 30 minutes. Invert on to a warm plate and serve with cream.

Serves 8.

OLD-FASHIONED SHORTCAKE

MARILYN VILLETT, ISLINGTON, ONT.

Summer visits to her grandmother's farm in North Milton, P.E.I., meant shortcake for dessert for Marilyn Villett. It could be strawberry, raspberry or blueberry, depending on the season.

2 cups all-purpose flour
4 teaspoons baking powder
⅔ cup granulated sugar
⅓ teaspoon salt
¼ cup butter, cubed
1 cup heavy cream (35% mf)
3 cups strawberries or raspberries (approximate)
Light cream (20% mf)

Combine flour, baking powder, salt and 2 tablespoons of sugar. Cut in butter with a pastry blender. Add heavy cream (with a little milk, if needed) and mix only until combined. Divide dough into 2 equal portions. Turn out on a floured surface and roll into 2 circles, each about 6 inches in diameter. Place in greased layer cake pans. Bake at 400°F for 10 to 15 minutes or until lightly browned. Meanwhile prepare the berries.

Crush the berries and add remaining sugar. Let stand until ready to serve the shortcake. Cover 1 layer of cake with crushed berries. Place the other layer on top and cover with berries as well. Serve with light cream. (For blueberry shortcake, bring 3 or more cups of blueberries to a boil and add ½ cup of sugar. Let simmer for 5 to 10 minutes. Serve as above.)

Serves 8.

RHUBARB FOOL

. . . .

An excellent dessert for late winter, when the first hothouse rhubarb appears on the market. This forced rhubarb has a mild flavour and a particularly pink colour that looks attractive swirled through the whipped cream. But don't neglect this dessert during garden rhubarb time. Just use the pinkest and most tender stalks.

4 cups finely chopped rhubarb, in ½-inch pieces
1 teaspoon orange zest
1 tablespoon orange juice
1 cup granulated sugar
1 cup heavy cream (35% mf)

Place the rhubarb, zest and juice in a heavy-bottomed saucepan over low heat. Cover and cook 20 to 25 minutes, or until the fruit is tender. Stir periodically and watch carefully, especially at the beginning, to prevent burning.

Add the sugar, stir and cook just long enough to dissolve the sugar. Purée in blender or pass through a food mill. Cool, cover and refrigerate. This step can be done 2 or 3 days before serving.

Just before serving, whip the cream. Transfer to a crystal or glass serving bowl. Fold in the chilled rhubarb purée, leaving swirled traces of cream and rhubarb.

Serves 6.

MAPLE SABAYON ON MARINATED BERRIES

. . . .

HARVEST DINING ROOM, FAIRMONT HOTEL MACDONALD, EDMONTON, ALTA.

This recipe was collected by Elaine Elliot working on her maple syrup cookbook. Naturally she thinks it works best with syrup from the Maritime provinces. The choice of berries in this recipe depends upon the season, but executive chef Patrick Turcot reports that he gets rave reviews all year from his patrons.

4 cups seasonal berries (strawberries, raspberries, blueberries)
½ cup Grand Marnier liqueur
3 large egg yolks
¼ cup granulated sugar
¼ cup pure maple syrup
¼ cup white wine
Mint leaves, for garnish

Place berries in a bowl and drizzle with Grand Marnier. Spoon into 4 heat-proof bowls and set aside.

Whisk yolks and sugar in a heat-proof bowl until foamy and pale. Set bowl over a pan of simmering water. Whisk constantly, adding syrup and wine, a little at a time, until the sabayon is fluffy and thickened.

Preheat broiler. Spoon sabayon sauce over berries and brown under a broiler until golden, 1 to 2 minutes. Serve immediately, garnished with mint leaves.

Serves 4.

FRESH STRAWBERRY FOOL

. . . .

ACTON'S GRILL AND CAFÉ, WOLFVILLE, N.S.

At Acton's, the ever popular "fool" is served using fresh seasonal fruit.

5 cups hulled strawberries
1 cup granulated sugar
1 teaspoon rum or brandy (optional)
1 cup heavy cream (35% mf)
Fresh mint, for garnish

Set aside a few whole berries for garnish. In a food processor or blender, purée remaining berries. Stir in sugar and liquor and set aside at room temperature for 1 hour, stirring occasionally. Cover and refrigerate several hours.

   Just before serving, whip cream and gently fold into strawberry purée. Turn into individual serving bowls, garnish with whole berries and mint.

Serves 6.

PEPPERED STRAWBERRIES WITH BALSAMIC VINEGAR AND MINT

. . . .

This is a great summer dessert when strawberries are in season. The unlikely combination of black pepper and balsamic vinegar complements the fruity sweetness of fresh strawberries.

3 cups strawberries, halved
Fresh mint sprigs
2 tablespoons packed brown sugar
2 teaspoons balsamic vinegar
pepper

Place strawberries in a bowl. Finely shred 4 mint leaves. Combine sugar and vinegar in a small bowl and stir in shredded mint. Pour over berries and gently toss to coat. Sprinkle with pepper.

   Serve in martini or wine glasses topped with a sprig of mint.

Serves 4.

STRAWBERRY RHUBARB CRUMBLE

. . . .

WEST POINT LIGHTHOUSE, WEST POINT, P.E.I.

Chef Liz Lecky serves this dessert warm from the oven, topped with vanilla ice cream.

2 cups hulled strawberries
3 cups chopped rhubarb
¾ cup granulated sugar
2 tablespoons minute tapioca

TOPPING
¾ cup packed brown sugar
½ cup all-purpose flour
½ cup large-flake rolled oats
1 teaspoon cinnamon
¼ teaspoon salt
⅓ cup butter, softened

Prepare strawberries and rhubarb, and spread in lightly buttered 8-inch square baking dish. Sprinkle with sugar and tapioca. Toss to mix.

TOPPING
In a medium bowl, mix together sugar, flour, oats, cinnamon and salt. Cut in butter using a pastry blender or fingertips. Sprinkle over filling and pat down lightly. Bake in 375°F oven for 30 to 35 minutes. Serve warm or cold.

Serves 6.

KIWIS AND STRAWBERRIES IN CHAMPAGNE

. . . .

LISCOMBE LODGE, LISCOMB MILLS, N.S.

Elegance and simplicity — this dessert presents beautifully in a stemmed glass! Serve when strawberries are bountiful.

2 kiwis, peeled and cut in ¼-inch slices
¼ cup granulated sugar
2 cups strawberries, halved
¾ cup Champagne or sparkling wine

Place kiwi in a large bowl and sprinkle with sugar. Let stand 30 minutes. Add strawberries. Divide between 6 dessert dishes or glasses. At serving time, drizzle Champagne over fruit.

Serves 6.

FIELD STRAWBERRIES WITH
ICE WINE SABAYON

• • • • • • • • • • • •

MARK GABRIEAU, GABRIEAU'S BISTRO, ANTIGONISH, N.S.

Mark Gabrieau has many great attributes as a chef and restaurateur, but he has always excelled in the pastry arts. His desserts are approachable and delicious — but he doesn't forget the flavour. When working with perfectly ripe, in-season strawberries, Mark knows not to mess around with them. Canadian ice wine and strawberries have become a bistro classic. When making this sabayon sauce, serve it without delay, as it will lose some foaminess and begin to separate if it is allowed to stand.

4 large egg yolks
6 tablespoons granulated sugar
3 ounces ice wine or late-harvest wine
½ teaspoon lemon juice
4 cups strawberries, hulled

In a stainless-steel bowl, beat yolks until foamy. Beat in half of the sugar, wine and juice. Place the bowl over a pot of simmering water and continue beating until sabayon is thick and hot.

Divide strawberries among 6 bowls. Cover with sabayon, sprinkle lightly with remaining sugar. Torch the top with a chef's torch until lightly caramelized.

Serves 6.

ETON MESS

ACTON'S GRILL AND CAFÉ, WOLFVILLE, N.S.

The meringue in this recipe must be made a day ahead, so plan accordingly. As a special strawberry treat, this dessert is delicious and well worth the extra calories.

4 large egg whites, at room temperature for 45 minutes
1 cup superfine sugar*
1 cup icing sugar
4 teaspoons cornstarch
3 cups strawberries, thickly sliced
3 tablespoons kirsch liqueur (optional)
1½ cups heavy cream (35% mf)
6 whole strawberries
6 mint sprigs

In a mixer, beat egg whites until almost stiff, about 2 minutes. With mixer running, add ⅔ cup of the superfine sugar, 1 tablespoon at a time, beating until sugar is completely dissolved and meringue is glossy and very stiff, about 3 minutes. Sift together icing sugar and cornstarch. Fold into meringue. Spoon meringue about 1-inch thick onto a parchment-lined baking sheet. Bake in 170°F oven for 3 hours. Turn oven off and let meringue cool in oven. Reserve in covered container.

In a bowl, combine strawberries, half of the remaining superfine sugar and kirsch. Stir to dissolve sugar and reserve at room temperature for 1 hour.

In a mixer, beat cream and remaining superfine sugar until stiff. In a large bowl, break up meringue into bite-size pieces. Add marinated strawberries and whipped cream, and toss to coat. Portion strawberry mixture into glass bowls and garnish with a whole strawberry and a sprig of fresh mint.

Serves 6.

* Superfine sugar is finely processed granulated sugar. You can buy it in any supermarket or make your own by whirling regular granulated sugar in a food processor until the granules are fine but not powdery.

RHUBARB STRAWBERRY ICE

JUDITH COMFORT, PORT MEDWAY, N.S.

Stewed rhubarb takes on new life when combined with its favourite partner, strawberries. But instead of a crumble or pie, a slush or ice is easily made in a metal pan in the freezer compartment of a fridge. If you prefer to make it in an ice-cream machine the texture will be smoother.

4 cups diced rhubarb
2 cups water
¾ cup granulated sugar
1 cup puréed fresh or frozen unsweeetened strawberries

Place the rhubarb and water in a large nonreactive (stainless steel or enamel-coated) saucepan. Bring to a boil, cover and simmer until the rhubarb is very soft, about 15 minutes. Strain the mixture through a cheesecloth-lined sieve, pressing the rhubarb gently to extract the juices without making the liquid cloudy. Discard or save the pulp for other purposes.

Pour the liquid back into the saucepan. Stir in sugar and bring to a rolling boil over high heat. Remove from the heat and cool to room temperature. Stir in strawberries. Pour into a 9-inch square metal pan. Place in the freezer. After an hour, ice will start to form on the edges. Stir the ice into the centre with a fork. Check every half hour or so for 2 to 3 hours, stirring until slushy consistency is achieved. Or freeze until almost solid. Whirl in batches in food processor until smooth. Refreeze in airtight container until firm enough to scoop.

Serves 8.

HARBOURVIEW CRÈME FRAÎCHE AND FRESH STRAWBERRIES

· · · · · · · · · · · ·

HARBOURVIEW INN, SMITHS COVE, N.S.

4 cups strawberries
½ cup crème fraîche or sour cream (30% mf)
3 to 4 tablespoons packed brown sugar

Rinse and dry strawberries, leaving the hulls intact. Place in a shallow bowl suitable for table presentation. Place crème fraîche in a small bowl and the sugar in a separate small bowl. To serve, invite guests to dip strawberries, first in crème fraîche and then in sugar.

Serves 4.

STRAWBERRY CRÈME BRÛLÉE

· · · · · · · · · · · ·

KAULBACK HOUSE HISTORIC INN, LUNENBURG, N.S.

You must watch carefully so as not to burn the sugar.

½ cup light sour cream
2 tablespoons packed brown sugar
2 cups sliced strawberries
4 whole strawberries, for garnish

Preheat broiler. Spread the sour cream in a broiler-safe pan. Sprinkle with brown sugar and broil only until sugar has caramelized, approximately 1½ minutes. Cool slightly, then add sliced strawberries, tossing to coat. Refrigerate 8 hours and serve, garnished with a whole strawberry.

Serves 4.

ELEGANT CHOCOLATE-DIPPED STRAWBERRIES

A. HIRAM WALKER ESTATE HERITAGE INN,
ST. ANDREWS BY-THE-SEA, N.B.

Elizabeth Cooney serves these delectable large strawberries for her afternoon high tea. If the strawberries are extra large, you might find them double dipped, one half in brown chocolate and the other in white.

15 to 20 large strawberries
½ cup chopped semisweet or white chocolate
⅓ cup pure maple syrup

Choose only the most perfect large strawberries and rinse and pat dry, leaving the green hulls intact.

In a small microwaveable bowl, combine chocolate and maple syrup. Microwave on medium, stirring at 30-second intervals until chocolate melts and maple syrup is incorporated, approximately 90 seconds. Gently dip strawberries in chocolate and place to harden on waxed paper. Arrange on a cake plate.

Serves 4 to 6.

FRESH FRUIT GRANDE

PANSY PATCH, ST. ANDREWS BY-THE-SEA, N.B.

Chocolate shells are available in large supermarkets and in specialty food stores.

3½ cups strawberries, quartered
¾ cup plus 2 tablespoons water
¼ cup granulated sugar
2 to 3 tablespoons cornstarch
3 tablespoons cold water
6 bittersweet chocolate shells
½ cup heavy cream (35% mf), whipped, for garnish
Chocolate curls, for garnish

Place 2 cups of the berries in a saucepan with ¾ cup water and sugar. Bring to a boil, reduce heat and simmer until strawberries are softened, approximately 3 minutes. Combine cornstarch with remaining water, add to saucepan and cook until clear and slightly thickened. Remove from heat, cool slightly and purée. Refrigerate sauce.

At serving time, divide remaining berries among chocolate shells. Spoon a small amount of sauce on individual serving plates, top with filled chocolate shells and garnish with whipped cream and chocolate curls.

Serves 6.

WINDS AND BRASS

. . . .

As pleasing as the resounding strains of a fine symphony, this dessert will fulfil the expectations of the most discriminating sweet lover.

4 ounces light cream cheese, softened
¾ cup light sour cream
2 tablespoons icing sugar
2 ounces semisweet chocolate, melted
1 tablespoon Grand Marnier liqueur
1½ tablespoons Cointreau liqueur
2 cups sliced strawberries
Orange zest, for garnish
Chocolate curls, for garnish

MERINGUE SHELLS

3 large egg whites
Pinch of cream of tartar
¾ cup superfine or fruit sugar
½ teaspoon vanilla extract

Whip the cream cheese until smooth. Stir in sour cream and whip until well blended. Stir in sugar, chocolate and liqueurs. Continue to whip until ingredients are well blended and mousse is fluffy. Refrigerate several hours in a well-sealed bowl.

At serving time, gently fold strawberries into mousse. Divide among meringue shells and garnish with zest and chocolate curls.

MERINGUE SHELLS

Beat egg whites and cream of tartar until soft peaks form. Gradually beat in the sugar, continuing to beat until all the sugar has dissolved and the whites are stiff and glossy. Fold in vanilla. For each shell, spoon about ⅓ cup meringue onto parchment paper-lined baking sheet and shape with the back of a spoon into a shell. Bake in 250°F oven for 1 hour, turn off heat and leave meringues in oven until cooled to room temperature or overnight.

Serves 6 to 8.

STEAMED BERRY PUDDING

SANDRA NOWLAN, HALIFAX, N.S.

This pudding recipe was used by Sandra Nowlan's mother and grandmother and probably had its origin in England. It is usually made with cranberries, probably because they are available in winter when one craves such substantial fare, but blackberries or blueberries will do very nicely.

1 cup all-purpose flour

1½ teaspoons baking powder

½ teaspoon salt

½ cup butter

½ cup fine dry breadcrumbs

½ cup granulated sugar

1½ cups cranberries, blueberries or blackberries

1 large egg, well beaten

⅔ cup milk

SAUCE

1 cup granulated sugar

2 tablespoons cornstarch

2 cups boiling water

3 tablespoons butter

Pinch each of nutmeg and salt

Sift together flour, baking powder and salt. Cut in butter with a pastry blender and add breadcrumbs and sugar. Gently mix in berries. (Cranberries should be cut in half.) Add egg and milk and stir only until dry ingredients are moistened. Pour into a greased 6-cup mould or heat-proof bowl.

Cover with a double layer of waxed paper and then a layer of foil. Tie tightly with string. Set the bowl on a wire rack in a large pot that has 1 inch of water.

Bring the water to a boil. Cover tightly and steam for 2 hours. Add more boiling water during cooking, if needed. Serve with sauce.

SAUCE

In a saucepan, mix sugar and cornstarch. Stir in boiling water and boil for 5 minutes. Stir in butter, nutmeg and salt. If the sauce is to be served with blueberry pudding, omit nutmeg and add 2 tablespoons fresh lemon juice.

Serves 4 to 6.

COOKIES AND SQUARES

FAT ARCHIES

. . . .

LORRAINE PYE, HALIFAX, N.S.

The true origins of many cookies are difficult to determine. This is especially so of Cape Breton cookies. Mary Gibbons, a lifelong resident of Sydney Mines, N.S., was known for her Fat Archies. One can only surmise they were named after someone called Archie who enjoyed the large soft molasses cookies.

2½ cups all-purpose flour
1 teaspoon salt
1 teaspoon ginger
½ teaspoon each cinnamon and nutmeg
½ cup butter, softened
½ cup packed brown sugar
½ cup granulated sugar
1 large egg
½ cup fancy molasses
2 teaspoons baking soda
½ cup boiling water

Sift together flour, salt, ginger, cinnamon and nutmeg. Cream butter with the sugars. Beat in egg, then molasses. Dissolve baking soda in boiling water and add to butter mixture. Add dry ingredients mixing quickly to a smooth dough. Refrigerate, roll out and cut with a cookie cutter. Place on a greased cookie sheets and bake at 375°F for 10 to 15 minutes or until slightly darkened on bottom.

Makes about 4 dozen cookies.

AUNT NELLIE'S SOFT MOLASSES COOKIES

. . . .

JUDITH BURDETT, BRIDGEWATER, N.S.

Growing up in the country in Prince Edward Island meant having molasses on the table along with the salt and pepper. Bread and molasses, pancakes and molasses, gingersnaps, gingerbread, molasses cookies — all were standard fare. Molasses was an essential ingredient in those days, and even the cows in the barn had their share.

A favourite treat at Grandmother's house was Aunt Nellie's soft molasses cookies, and a batch of these cookies with big sticky raisins in the centres didn't last long when young sisters went to visit. The recipe, in Grandmother's own handwriting, is a treasured possession.

1 large egg
1 cup packed brown sugar
1 cup fancy molasses
1 cup melted butter
4 teaspoons baking soda
¼ cup hot water
4½ cups all-purpose flour
1 teaspoon cream of tartar
¾ teaspoon salt
Seeded raisins or large sultana raisins

Beat egg in a large bowl. Beat in sugar, molasses and butter. Combine baking soda and hot water and stir into molasses mixture. Mix well. Sift flour, cream of tartar and salt. Stir into molasses mixture. Flour hands and shape the dough into large balls at least 1 tablespoon in size. Arrange 2 inches apart on greased cookie sheets. Flatten slightly into a circle and press a raisin into the centre. Bake in 350°F oven until just firm to the touch, 10 to 12 minutes.

Makes about 3 dozen large cookies.

MOLASSES OATMEAL RAISIN COOKIES

· · · · · · · · · · ·

KAMLOOPS CATERING,
ROCKY MOUNTAINEER RAILWAY, KAMLOOPS, B.C.

These soft and delicious cookies got rave reviews from guests on the Rocky Mountaineer Railway and were good enough that the recipe must have come from a transplanted Maritimer! You can make these cookies at home and enjoy receiving your own compliments.

1 cup granulated sugar

½ cup butter, softened

1 large egg

½ cup fancy molasses

1 teaspoon vanilla extract

2 cups all-purpose flour

1½ teaspoon baking soda

1 teaspoon salt

1 cup quick-cooking oats (not instant)

1 to 1½ cups raisins

1 cup chopped walnuts or pecans (optional)

Cream the sugar and butter together in a large mixing bowl. Add egg, molasses and vanilla. Beat well. Whisk together the flour, baking soda and salt. Stir into molasses mixture. Stir in oats, raisins and nuts (if using). Drop batter from a tablespoon onto greased baking sheets. Bake cookies at 375°F for 10 to 12 minutes, until lightly browned on the bottom.

Makes about 4 dozen cookies.

JUMBO RAISIN COOKIES

• • • • • • • • • • • •

LORRAINE PYE, HALIFAX, N.S.

Another special Cape Breton cookie is large and soft, loaded with raisins and nuts and scented with spices. Soft cookies are best stored in an airtight container and separated into layers by sheets of waxed paper. A piece of apple placed in the container will keep the cookies moist. These cookies spread, so they should be dropped two inches apart on the greased cookie sheets.

2 cups raisins
1 cup boiling water
1 cup butter, softened
2 cups granulated sugar
3 large eggs
1 teaspoon vanilla extract
4 cups all-purpose flour
2 teaspoons salt
1½ teaspoons cinnamon
1 teaspoon baking powder
1 teaspoon baking soda
½ teaspoon nutmeg
¼ teaspoon allspice
1 cup chopped almonds or walnuts

Combine raisins and boiling water in a saucepan. Bring to a boil and simmer for 5 minutes. Let cool. Cream butter and sugar. Add eggs 1 at a time and blend well. Add cooled raisin mixture and vanilla. In a separate bowl, blend all dry ingredients and add to raisin mixture. Add nuts. Combine thoroughly and drop from a tablespoon onto greased cookie sheets. Bake at 400°F for 10 to 12 minutes or until firm to touch.

Makes about 8 dozen cookies.

DOUBLE PEANUT BUTTER COOKIES

• • • • • • • • • •

LORRAINE PYE, HALIFAX, N.S.

Someone must have wanted an extra helping of cookies, or loved the extra taste of peanut butter sandwiched between the halves. Who knows, except the first Cape Breton cook to try them this way?

½ cup butter, softened
¾ cup peanut butter
⅓ cup granulated sugar
⅓ cup packed brown sugar
3 tablespoons orange juice
1½ cups all-purpose flour
½ teaspoon baking soda
¼ teaspoon salt

Cream butter and ½ cup of the peanut butter. Add sugars and juice and beat until fluffy. In a separate bowl combine flour, baking soda and salt. Add to peanut butter mixture and beat well. Shape into a 7-inch long roll. Wrap in waxed paper and refrigerate until firm. Cut into ¼-inch slices and place half the slices on ungreased cookie sheets, about 2 inches apart. Spread each cookie with about 1 teaspoon of the remaining peanut butter. Cover with remaining slices and press the edges to seal. Bake at 350°F for 12 to 15 minutes.

Makes about a dozen cookies.

OATCAKES

LAHAVE BAKERY, LAHAVE, N.S.

As wholesome and nutritious as Scottish oatcakes, but a good deal sweeter, these are delicious for breakfast, lunch or a late-night snack.

3 cups large-flake rolled oats
2 cups all-purpose flour
1 cup whole wheat flour
½ cup granulated sugar
½ cup packed brown sugar
1 teaspoon fine sea salt
1 teaspoon baking soda
1½ cups unsalted butter, cubed
⅓ cup water (approximate)
Extra rolled oats, for rolling

In a large bowl, combine all dry ingredients. Cut in butter with a pastry blender. Slowly add water, just enough to hold the dough together.

On a large work surface, generously cover dough with the extra rolled oats. Roll the dough to ¼ inch thickness. Cut into 2- by 4-inch cakes. Bake on parchment paper-lined baking sheets in 350°F oven until browned on bottom, about 15 to 20 minutes.

Makes about 8 dozen oatcakes.

SUGAR COOKIES

LORRAINE PYE, HALIFAX, N.S.

1 cup butter, softened
¾ cup granulated sugar
¼ cup packed brown sugar
1 large egg
1 teaspoon vanilla extract
2 cups all-purpose flour
2 teaspoons cream of tartar
1 teaspoon baking soda
¼ teaspoon salt
¼ teaspoon nutmeg
Granulated sugar, for sprinkling
Glazed cherries, quartered (optional)

Cream butter with sugars. Beat in the egg and vanilla. In a separate bowl, combine flour, cream of tartar, baking soda, salt and nutmeg. Stir into sugar mixture. Divide into 4 disks, wrap and refrigerate. Roll one disk at a time on a floured board and cut with cookie cutter. Sprinkle with sugar and garnish with glazed cherry quarters, if desired. Bake on parchment paper-lined or ungreased cookie sheets at 375°F for 8 to 10 minutes.

Makes about 3 dozen cookies.

CHOCOLATE CHIP COOKIES

. . . .

Chocolate chip is undoubtedly the most popular cookie in North America. The only problem with making them is that you never seem to make enough.

1 cup all-purpose flour
½ cup whole wheat flour
1 teaspoon baking powder
1 teaspoon baking soda
⅛ teaspoon salt
1 cup butter, softened
½ cup granulated sugar
1 cup packed brown sugar
1 large egg
1 teaspoon vanilla extract
1¼ cups large-flake rolled oats
¾ cup coconut
¾ cup chocolate chips

In a bowl, sift or whisk flours with baking powder, baking soda and salt.

In a large bowl, beat butter with sugars until light and fluffy, about 4 minutes. Add egg and vanilla. Beat for 1 minute. With mixer on low speed, add flour mixture and mix just until combined. With mixer on low speed, add rolled oats and coconut, and mix just until combined. Stir in chocolate chips.

Drop by rounded spoonfuls, about 2 inches apart, onto parchment paper-lined or greased baking sheets. Bake in a 350°F oven for 10 to 12 minutes until light brown. Cool slightly on baking sheets before removing cookies to rack.

Makes 3½ dozen cookies.

FALCOURT INN'S MAPLE MERINGUES WITH PEACHES

. . . .

FALCOURT INN, NICTAUX, N.S.

Meringues will keep for up to a week if stored in an airtight container. They are easy to prepare and are the basis of many stunning desserts.

4 large egg whites, at room temperature
¼ teaspoon cream of tartar
Pinch of salt
½ cup pure maple syrup
Drop of vanilla extract
16 fresh or canned peach slices
Mint leaves, for garnish

In a large bowl, beat egg whites, cream of tartar and salt until soft peaks form. Slowly add ¼ cup of the maple syrup and the vanilla and continue to beat until stiff glossy peaks form. Pipe or spoon onto a baking sheet lined with parchment paper, forming small rounds. Place in a 250°F oven and bake approximately 1 hour. Turn off heat and leave meringues in oven until cooled to room temperature. Remove and store in an airtight container up to 1 week. Makes 10 to 12 meringues.

Marinate peach slices in remaining maple syrup for at least 1 hour. To serve, place 2 or 3 meringues in centre of dessert plate with peach slices. Garnish with mint leaves.

Serves 4 to 6.

RUGELACH

BETTE TETRAULT, HALIFAX, N.S.

This recipe from Freida Perlin is the culmination of a Chanukah meal. The Jewish festival of Chanukah, or the festival of lights, comes at the beginning of winter. The dinner would include latkes, or potato pancakes and sufganiyot — jelly-filled, sugar doughnuts. After a main course of roast beef or turkey comes rugelach, delicious fruit- and nut-filled crescent-shaped cookies.

2 cups all-purpose flour

½ cup icing sugar

1 cup butter, cubed

6 ounces cream cheese, cubed

½ teaspoon salt

½ cup apricot or plum jam

1½ to 2 cups mixed sultanas, chopped toasted pecans
   or almonds and flaked coconut

1 large egg, beaten

¼ cinnamon sugar

In a bowl, mix together the flour and sugar. With a pastry blender, cut in the butter and cream cheese. Do not overhandle. Gather into a ball, flatten, wrap and refrigerate overnight.

Divide into 3 parts. On a floured work surface roll each into a 12-inch circle of ¼-inch thickness. Spread each with a third of the jam. Sprinkle a third of the sultana, nut and coconut mixture over the jam. Cut each circle into 12 wedges and roll each piece from the wide edge to the point (like a crescent roll).

Place rugelachs, points down, on greased cookie sheets. Brush with beaten egg and sprinkle with cinnamon sugar. Refrigerate for 15 minutes to firm the dough and then bake at 375°F for 15 to 20 minutes or until golden.

Makes 3 dozen.

Apricot
Jam

TURTLE SQUARES

. . . .

GLENEAGLE BAKERY, DARTMOUTH, N.S.

These caramel pecan delights will please even the most discerning sweet tooth.

BASE
4½ cups all-purpose flour
1½ cups packed brown sugar
1 cup butter, softened
1½ cups chopped pecans

TOPPING
1 cup butter
1⅓ cups packed brown sugar
½ cup light corn syrup
2 cups chocolate chips

Line a 9- by 13-inch square pan with parchment paper or foil extending 2 inches over the sides.

In a large bowl, combine the flour, sugar and butter until crumbly in texture. Spread evenly over prepared pan. Cover with pecans and press lightly.

In a heavy-bottomed saucepan, combine all ingredients for the topping, except the chocolate chips, and bring to a boil. Cook until thick. Pour over base and bake at 350°F until bubbly all over the top. Remove from oven and let cool slightly.

Sprinkle chocolate chips over top and spread with a palate knife. Refrigerate until set.

Lift the squares from the pan by gently pulling on the extended paper or foil. Cut into squares.

Makes 2 to 3 dozen squares.

AUNT HELEN'S CRANBERRY AND ORANGE OATMEAL SQUARES

. . . .

SANDRA NOWLAN, HALIFAX, N.S.

Says Sandra Nowlan, "My aunt Helen Smith from French Lake, N.B., baked up a big batch of these tasty squares for a family reunion. I have added orange zest and cranberries to give a nice tartness."

½ cup large-flake rolled oats
⅓ cup chopped dates
½ cup boiling water
¼ cup soft margarine
½ cup packed brown sugar
1 large egg, beaten
½ teaspoon vanilla extract
1 teaspoon orange zest
1 cup all-purpose flour
½ teaspoon baking powder
½ teaspoon baking soda
1 cup chopped cranberries
¼ cup flaked coconut
¼ cup chopped nuts
Icing sugar

Combine rolled oats, dates and water in a small bowl. Set aside to cool.

Cream margarine and sugar. Beat in egg, vanilla, zest and oat mixture. In a separate bowl, whisk flour, baking powder and baking soda. Stir into batter. (Batter will be stiff.) Add cranberries, coconut and nuts.

Spread evenly in a greased 9-inch square pan and bake at 350°F for about 25 minutes. Let cool, then dust with icing sugar.

Makes 3 dozen squares.

CRANBERRY SQUARES

. . . .

VIRJENE COLE, KENSINGTON, P.E.I.

There's usually some cranberry sauce in the freezer or the cupboard whether or not it's a holiday.

1⅓ cups all-purpose flour
1 tablespoon icing sugar
½ cup butter, softened
2 large eggs, beaten
1 cup granulated sugar
1 teaspoon almond extract
1 teaspoon baking powder
¼ teaspoon salt
½ cup flaked coconut
½ cup chopped walnuts or almonds
⅓ cup chopped raisins
⅔ cup cranberry sauce

BUTTER ICING

¼ cup butter, softened
1 cup icing sugar
½ tablespoon milk
¼ teaspoon vanilla extract
Pinch of salt

In a bowl, combine 1 cup of the flour and icing sugar. With a pastry blender, work in butter until crumbly. Press lightly over bottom of greased 8-inch square baking pan.

In a separate bowl, whisk eggs with granulated sugar and almond extract. Stir in remaining flour, baking powder and salt. Add coconut, walnuts and raisins. Stir in cranberry sauce. Spread over base. Bake in 350°F oven until base is golden and filling set. Let cool on rack. Spread with icing. Cut into squares.

BUTTER ICING

Beat butter, icing sugar, milk, vanilla and salt until smooth.

Makes 2 dozen squares.

MOM'S ALMOND SQUARES

. . . .

GRACE MCCLUNG, CHESTER BASIN, N.S.

A childhood Christmas treat is hard to duplicate when Mom's recipe doesn't exist. Experimenting over the years produced squares that are almost the same. One bite brings back memories of Christmases past.

½ cup butter, softened
1 cup granulated sugar
2 large eggs, separated
2 teaspoons almond extract
1½ cups all-purpose flour
1 teaspoon baking powder
1 cup packed brown sugar
1 cup slivered almonds

In a bowl, mix butter and granulated sugar. Stir in egg yolks and almond extract. In a separate bowl, combine flour and baking powder. Stir into butter mixture. Spread over bottom of a greased 9-inch square baking pan.

In a separate bowl, beat the egg whites to soft peaks. Beat in the brown sugar, ¼ cup at a time, beating to firm peaks. Stir in almonds and spread over base.

Bake in 350°F oven until almond topping is firm to touch and evenly golden brown, about 30 to 35 minutes. Let cool on a rack. Cut into squares.

Makes about 2 dozen squares.

RHUBARB COCONUT SQUARES

· · · · · · · · · · · · ·

THE MOUNTAIN GAP INN AND RESORT,
SMITHS COVE, N.S.

*Chef Hank Lewis at the Mountain Gap Inn suggested that for these squares
you leave the rhubarb filling rather tart because the topping is quite sweet.*

BASE

1⅓ cups all-purpose flour
½ cup granulated sugar
Zest of ½ an orange
½ cup unsalted butter, cubed

FILLING

2 cups diced rhubarb
¼ cup granulated sugar (approximate)
Juice of 1 orange
2 tablespoons butter
Pinch of nutmeg

TOPPING

2 large eggs
¾ cup granulated sugar
1½ teaspoons vanilla extract
Zest of ½ an orange
2½ cups shredded coconut
2 tablespoons all-purpose flour

BASE

Blend together the flour, sugar and zest. Cut in the butter until mixture is mealy. Spread evenly in a greased 9-inch square pan and press down firmly.

FILLING

Boil together rhubarb, sugar and juice until the mixture thickens. Taste, adding more sugar if desired. Remove from the heat and stir in butter and nutmeg. Allow to cool slightly then spread over base.

TOPPING

Blend together eggs, sugar, vanilla and zest. Stir in coconut and flour. Spread over filling and bake in a 350°F oven until lightly browned, about 25 to 30 minutes. Allow to cool before cutting.

Makes 2 dozen squares.

CANDY

NAN'S FUDGE

DONNA GOODWIN, LARRY'S RIVER, N.S.

Here's a Heritage Recipe Contest fudge that never fails.

3 cups packed brown sugar
1 cup butter
½ cup cocoa powder
¾ cup evaporated milk
1 teaspoon vanilla extract
3 cups icing sugar
½ cup chopped nuts or coconut

Place the first 5 ingredients in a large saucepan and boil for 5 minutes. Remove from heat. Add the icing sugar and nuts. Pour into a greased 9- by 13-inch pan. Refrigerate until firm. Cut into squares to enjoy.

Makes 36 squares.

PEANUT BRITTLE

LORRAINE PYE, HALIFAX, N.S.

2 cups granulated sugar
1 cup light corn syrup
¼ cup butter
½ cup water
2½ cups unsalted peanuts
1½ teaspoons baking soda

Lightly butter 2 large rimmed baking sheets. Mix sugar, syrup, butter and water in a 3-quart saucepan and cook over medium heat until the mixture boils, stirring constantly.

Cook over medium-low heat to the crack stage, 290°C on a candy thermometer. This should take about 40 minutes. Add peanuts. Remove from the heat. Sprinkle with baking soda and stir well. Quickly pour onto prepared cookie sheets. Cool completely and break into pieces.

Makes about 24 pieces.

SPONGE TOFFEE

LORRAINE PYE, HALIFAX, N.S.

1 cup granulated sugar
1 cup light corn syrup
4 teaspoons baking soda

Lightly butter a shallow pan, about 9 by 13 inches. Combine sugar and syrup in a 2-quart saucepan. Bring to a boil over medium heat, stirring until the sugar dissolves. Cook without stirring until the candy reaches the brittle stage, 305°C on a candy thermometer. Remove from the heat and quickly stir in the baking soda. Mix well. (It will double in volume.) Pour into prepared pan. Place the pan in the refrigerator to cool. It should not be moved again until the candy has set. Then break the candy into pieces.

Makes about 36 pieces.

WALNUTTY CHEWS

LORRAINE PYE, HALIFAX, N.S.

2 cups granulated sugar
1 cup light corn syrup
1 cup light cream (20% mf)
¼ cup butter
1 teaspoon vanilla extract
1½ cups chopped walnuts

Lightly butter an 8-inch pan. Mix the sugar, syrup, cream and butter in a 3-quart saucepan and cook over medium heat stirring constantly. Cook to the firm ball stage, 245°C on a candy thermometer. Remove from the heat and stir in vanilla and walnuts, and turn into the prepared pan. Let cool for 1 hour. Turn candy out of the pan. Cut into bite-size pieces and wrap with waxed paper or plastic wrap. The candy will keep for several weeks.

Makes about 24 pieces.

MOM'S BEST FUDGE

. . . .

LORRAINE PYE, HALIFAX, N.S.

2 tablespoons butter
2 cups granulated sugar
2 cups packed brown sugar
½ cup all-purpose flour
½ cup light corn syrup
1 cup milk
¼ teaspoon salt
1 teaspoon vanilla extract
½ cup coconut or chopped walnuts (optional)

Mix all ingredients, except walnuts and coconut, in a 3-quart saucepan. Cook over medium heat until mixture boils, stirring constantly. Continue to cook to the soft ball stage, 238°C on a candy thermometer. Remove from heat and let cool until it registers 110°C on a candy thermometer. Add nuts or coconut and beat until the mixture begins to thicken, becomes creamy and loses its glossy sheen. Spread quickly into buttered pan. Allow to cool and cut into squares.

Makes 24 pieces.

CHOCOLATE FUDGE
Add ¼ cup cocoa to the ingredients above.

Tip: Beating the candy mixture is easier with an electric mixer, but be careful, if you are using a hand mixer, not to tax the motor or it will burn out. A stand mixer is recommended. When the fudge begins to thicken, continue the beating by hand.

MOLASSES PULL TAFFY

. . . .

LORRAINE PYE, HALIFAX, N.S.

2 cups granulated sugar
1 cup fancy molasses
½ cup water
1 tablespoon white vinegar
¼ teaspoon cream of tartar
⅛ teaspoon baking soda
2 tablespoons butter

Mix the sugar, molasses, water and vinegar in a heavy 3-quart saucepan. Cook over medium heat, stirring constantly until the mixture comes to a boil. Add cream of tartar and cook to the hard ball stage, 260°C on a candy thermometer. Remove from the heat. Stir in baking soda and butter. Pour into a buttered 8-inch square pan. Cool quickly by placing the pan in cold water in the sink or, in winter, outdoors in the snow. When the mixture is cool enough to handle, pull and twist with buttered hands until it is light colored and difficult to pull. This should take about 20 minutes. Cut into 1-inch lengths with buttered scissors. Wrap with waxed paper or plastic wrap.

Makes a generous pound of taffy.

IRISH CREAM TRUFFLES

. . . .

GLENEAGLE BAKERY, DARTMOUTH, N.S.

For the best truffles you need to use the best-quality chocolate, such as Callebaut, Cacao Barry or Lindt.

1 cup heavy cream (35% mf)
20 ounces milk chocolate, finely chopped
¼ cup unsalted butter
⅓ cup Irish Cream liqueur
2 pounds white chocolate, roughly chopped, for
  enrobing

This can be used as a base recipe, and you may substitute your favourite liqueur in place of Irish Cream.

DAY ONE

In a small saucepan, bring the cream to a boil. Place the milk chocolate, butter and liqueur in a medium bowl. Slowly pour hot cream over the chocolate mixture. Gently stir with a heavy whisk until smooth. Cover with plastic wrap and refrigerate overnight.

DAY TWO

Remove the chocolate mixture from the refrigerator and, either by hand or using a small ice cream or portion scoop, place little balls onto on a rimmed baking sheet lined with parchment paper. Set aside.

To temper the enrobing white chocolate, place the white chocolate in a glass or stainless steel bowl and set over a saucepan of simmering water. Make sure the bottom does not touch the water and avoid any contact with steam, as this will make the chocolate seize. Stir the chocolate constantly until almost completely melted. Remove the bowl from the saucepan, and allow the residual heat to melt the remaining chocolate. When the chocolate begins to cool, stir every so often until it becomes thicker and loses its shine. At this point, place the bowl over the simmering water again and stir constantly until just fluid. Remove from heat.

Working with your fingers only, dip each centre in the white chocolate. Roll them around on your fingers to ensure they are totally covered. Place on a baking sheet lined with parchment paper. The appearance will be rustic, like little snowballs. However, if you prefer a smooth finish, re-dip truffles using a dipping fork.

When the truffles are dry, store in an airtight container in the refrigerator for up to 2 weeks.

Makes about 50 truffles.

RASPBERRY TRUFFLES

. . . .

GLENEAGLE BAKERY, DARTMOUTH, N.S.

Once you have mastered these raspberry truffles, you can begin experimenting with other flavours that lend themselves well to combining with chocolate.

1¾ cups heavy cream (35% mf)
1 pound semisweet chocolate, finely chopped
2 tablespoons raspberry liqueur
¼ cup seedless raspberry preserves
1½ lbs semisweet chocolate, for enrobing

DAY ONE

In a small saucepan, bring cream to a boil. Place the chocolate in a medium bowl. Slowly pour the hot cream over the chocolate. Gently stir with a heavy whisk until smooth. Add raspberry liqueur and preserves, stirring until combined. Cover with plastic wrap and refrigerate overnight.

DAY TWO

Remove the chocolate mixture from the refrigerator and, either by hand or using a small ice-cream or portion scoop, scoop little balls onto a baking sheet lined with parchment paper. Set aside.

To temper the enrobing chocolate for the centres, place the semisweet chocolate in a glass or stainless steel bowl and set over a pot of simmering water. Make sure the bottom does not touch the water and avoid any contact with steam, as this will make the chocolate seize. Stir the chocolate constantly until almost completely melted. Remove the bowl from the pot, and allow the residual heat to melt the remaining chocolate. When the chocolate begins to cool, stir every so often until it becomes thicker and loses its shine. At this point, place the bowl over the simmering water again and stir constantly until just fluid. Remove from heat.

Working with your fingers only, dip each centre in the chocolate. Roll them around on your fingers to ensure they are totally covered. Place the covered truffles on a clean baking sheet lined with parchment paper. The appearance will be rustic. If you prefer a smooth finish, redip truffles using a dipping fork.

When the truffles are dry, store in an airtight container for up to 2 weeks.

Makes about 50 truffles.

CARAMEL CORN

. . . .

LORRAINE PYE, HALIFAX, N.S.

Remember the most popular house on the block when you were growing up? From its kitchen came candy that was better because someone else's mom made it. She was often a friend's mother or grandmother and as the neighbourhood kids ran home from school, they slowed down as they passed her door. They always hoped this was the day she had made some of her sweet concoctions and would notice them and call them in.

Not a figment of childish imagination, there is just such a woman in Sydney Mines, N.S. — Ruby Pye, mother of nine and grandmother of six children. She is renowned in the area for her love of cooking, but especially for her sweet treats and homemade candy.

These are projects in which everyone can become involved, and Ruby Pye has some of the best recipes and memories of candy-making. "I remember as a child," she says, "it was such a treat when Mom made pull taffy. We would gather round [she was one of 12 children] and wait for the candy to cook. Then we would put the pot in the snow to cool it quickly since we didn't have a refrigerator back then."

Young and old alike will enjoy trying Ruby Pye's classic candy recipes from the days when the best thing to do on a cold winter night was to gather in the warm kitchen and make a variety of delicious treats.

8 cups popped corn, about ⅓ to ½ cup unpopped
¾ cup packed brown sugar
⅓ cup butter
3 tablespoons light corn syrup
¼ teaspoon baking soda
½ teaspoon vanilla extract
2 to 4 cups unsalted peanuts (optional)

Place popcorn in a large greased baking dish. Keep popcorn warm in a 300°F oven while making the caramel. In a 2-quart saucepan combine sugar, butter and corn syrup. Cook over medium heat until it boils, about 8 to 10 minutes, stirring constantly. Continue cooking until candy reaches the hard ball stage, 255°C on a candy thermometer. Remove from heat. Add baking soda and vanilla and stir until well blended. Pour caramel and peanuts over popcorn and toss until the popcorn is coated. Bake at 300°F for 12 minutes. Stir and bake for 8 more minutes. Cool and break into small pieces.

Makes enough for a family with 9 children.

PRESERVES:
JAMS, JELLIES, CHUTNEYS, RELISHES, PICKLES AND SAVOURY SAUCES

BLUEBERRY JAM

. . . .

*A bottle of homemade jam makes a wonderful hostess
gift, so be sure to make extra to share with friends.*

6 cups wild blueberries
3 cups granulated sugar
¼ cup lemon juice

Rinse and pick over blueberries, discarding small
stems or leaves. Crush berries and place them in a
large heavy pot. Stir in sugar and juice. Over low heat,
stir until sugar is dissolved, then bring mixture to a
full rolling boil. Cook uncovered for 10 to 12 minutes,
stirring frequently. Remove pot from heat and let
it stand for 5 minutes, skimming off any foam with
a large metal spoon. Pour jam into hot preserving
jars. Seal and process for 10 minutes according to
instructions on page 311.

Makes about 4 cups.

SUMMER SEASON
FRUIT JAM

. . . .

ALICE LEDUC, WATERVILLE. N.S.

*After the first rush of fresh strawberries, it's time for
a different kind of jam. Only then it seems that all
the fruits and berries come into season at the same
time. The answer to capturing the season's best
— whether it's bought at a local farmers' market,
roadside stand or a U-pick — is to make a multi-fruit
jam to enjoy all winter.*

3 cups chopped sweet pitted cherries
3 cups crushed topped and tailed gooseberries
3 cups red currants
2½ cups crushed raspberries
7 cups granulated sugar

In a large heavy pot combine fruits and boil for 15
minutes, stirring often. Add sugar, stir to dissolve.
Bring mixture to a full rolling boil. Boil rapidly until
set, about 12 to 15 minutes. Remove from the heat.

Stir and skim for 5 minutes. Pour into hot
preserving jars, leaving ¼-inch headspace. Seal and
process for 10 minutes according to instructions on
page 311.

Makes about 10 cups.

SPIRITED CRANBERRY-ORANGE SAUCE

. . . .

Choose either fresh or frozen cranberries for this refrigerator preserve.

Juice and zest of 2 oranges
1 teaspoon lemon juice
¾ cup granulated sugar
½ cup finely diced peeled apple
3 cups cranberries, thawed if frozen
1 tablespoon brandy or cognac

In a large pot over medium heat, combine juices, zest, sugar and apple. Bring to a boil, stirring constantly, until sugar is dissolved. Cook 4 minutes. Add cranberries and return to a boil, stirring. Reduce heat and simmer, stirring frequently, until cranberries pop, about 7 minutes. Remove from heat and stir in brandy. Refrigerate in covered jars, for up to 1 week.

Makes about 2 cups.

SOUR CHERRY JAM

. . . .

SANDRA NOWLAN, HALIFAX, N.S.

Sandra Nowlan recounts her memories of family cherry picking: "In mid-July my children begin to coax us to take them to the Annapolis Valley to pick sour cherries, so that they can have their favourite cherry jam. It is a pleasurable experience to see the bright red cherries dotting the trees, to taste the tart, succulent fruit and to have the juice run down our arms and drip off our elbows. Once the cherries are brought home, it is a family activity to stem and pit them. Many bags of them are put in the freezer, but some are reserved for a batch of jam, to pay off the work of the little pickers."

2 quarts sour cherries, stemmed and pitted
4½ cups granulated sugar
1 2-ounce package fruit pectin crystals
½ teaspoon butter
¼ teaspoon almond extract

Mash the cherries. For a less-coarse jam put about a cup or so of the fruit in the food processor and chop. Measure out 4½ to 5 cups of the prepared fruit and put into a large, heavy pot. Measure out the sugar and set aside.

Mix pectin crystals with the fruit. Bring to a rolling boil over high heat, stirring constantly. Add butter to prevent foaming. Stir in the sugar all at once. Bring to a hard rolling boil and boil for 1 minute. Remove from the heat and let cool for 5 minutes, stirring occasionally to prevent floating fruit. Skim foam off the top with a metal spoon. Add almond extract. Ladle into hot preserving jars leaving ¼-inch headspace. Seal and process for 10 minutes according to the instructions on page 311. Or freeze the airtight containers, leaving ¼-inch headspace.

Makes about 6 cups.

THE BEST-EVER STRAWBERRY JAM

BLUENOSE LODGE, LUNENBURG, N.S.

Former innkeeper Grace Swan said that this homemade freezer strawberry jam was one of the most popular items on the inn's breakfast buffet. Guests frequently requested her recipe, which requires less sugar than many other jams.

2½ pounds strawberries (2 very full quart boxes), hulled
2 cups granulated sugar
1 package freezer jam gelling powder

Mash strawberries in a large bowl. Add sugar to berry mixture, stirring to dissolve completely. Let stand at room temperature for 20 minutes, stirring occasionally. Sprinkle gelling powder over berry mixture, a little at a time, stirring until it is completely dissolved. Let stand overnight, then pour into airtight containers, leaving ¼-inch headspace. Refrigerate for up to 3 weeks or store in freezer for up to 1 year.

Makes 6 cups.

RASPBERRY JAM WITH COINTREAU

Cointreau, or any orange liqueur, adds a subtle flavour to this sweet preserve.

4 cups raspberries
¼ cup lemon juice
6½ cups granulated sugar
1 3-ounce package liquid fruit pectin
2 tablespoons Cointreau liqueur

Thoroughly crush berries, a layer at a time, and press half the purée through a sieve to remove seeds, if desired. Place in a large heavy pot, add lemon juice and sugar, stirring until sugar is dissolved. Place over high heat and bring to a full rolling boil, stirring constantly. Boil hard for 1 minute. Remove from heat and immediately stir in the liquid fruit pectin. Stir and skim for 5 minutes. Stir in liqueur.

Pour into hot preserving jars, leaving ¼-inch headspace. Seal and process for 10 minutes according to instructions of page 311.

Makes 8 cups.

APPLE BUTTER

THE INN AT SPRY POINT, SPRY POINT, P.E.I.

Those who love the flavour of spicy apples will appreciate this recipe for this old-fashioned apple preserve. Serve warm or cold on toast, muffins and breads. Choose apple varieties that appeal to your personal taste, as the end flavour depends upon the type of apple you use.

9 cooking apples, peeled, cored and quartered
1 cup apple cider
1½ cups granulated sugar
½ cup packed brown sugar
1½ teaspoons cinnamon
¼ teaspoon allspice
Pinch nutmeg
2 tablespoons cider vinegar

In a large heavy pot over medium heat, bring apples and apple cider to a boil. Cover, reduce heat to simmer and cook, stirring occasionally, until apples are very soft, about 25 to 30 minutes.

In a food processor or with an immersion blender, purée the apples until smooth. Return to the pan and add remaining ingredients. Cook over low heat, stirring frequently until mixture becomes thick, about 30 minutes. Spoon into freezer containers, cover and freeze, or pour into hot preserving jars, leaving ¼-inch. Seal and process for 10 minutes according to instructions of page 311.

Makes 5 cups.

1,2,3 MARMALADE

JOAN NEVERS, PLASTER ROCK, N.B.

Joan Nevers was given this easy and tasty recipe from her grandmother, who brought it with her from England. The flavours mingle so delightfully.

2 lemons
5 oranges
1 grapefruit
2 cups chopped rhubarb
½ cup chopped pitted cherries
Granulated sugar

Cut lemons, oranges and grapefruit into large chunks, removing the seeds. Chop, in batches, in a food processor or to a pulp with distinct pieces of peel.

Measure pulp into a large bowl. To every cup of pulp add 3 cups of water. Let stand overnight.

Transfer with rhubarb and cherries to a large heavy pot. Bring to a boil over medium-high heat, stirring regularly. Boil gently until the peel is very tender. Cover and let stand overnight.

Measure pulp. Combine with 1 cup sugar per 1 cup pulp. Bring to boil, stirring, over high heat. Boil until marmalade sets, stirring constantly. Pour into hot preserving jars, leaving a ¼-inch headspace. Seal and process for 10 minutes according to instructions on page 311.

Makes about 8 cups.

PLUMS MACERATED IN BRANDY

. . . .

WICKWIRE HOUSE, KENTVILLE, N.S.

"This is not an instant dessert," cautioned innkeeper Darlene Peerless, who bottled her plums in early October for use over the Christmas holidays. The plums are delicious over vanilla ice cream. Choose only uniformly shaped, unblemished plums. The fruit must be left whole, otherwise the flesh will cloud the brandy.

3 cups brandy
1 cup granulated sugar
1 quart whole purple plums, washed

Combine brandy and sugar, stirring until sugar is dissolved. Pack plums into sterilized quart jars. Pour brandy mixture over fruit, covering completely. Seal and let stand in a cool dark place for at least 2 months.

Makes 2 quarts.

RHUBARB JELLY

. . . .

TREVA MCNALLY, SHERWOOD, P.E.I.

In the early summer when rhubarb starts to grow fast, it can sometimes get ahead of you and you can end up with 5 or 10 pounds of it. This recipe will use up 4 pounds of rhubarb at a time and makes a beautiful rosy jelly.

4 pounds pink rhubarb
7 cups granulated sugar
2 3-ounce packages liquid fruit pectin
2 to 3 drops red food colouring, optional

Remove the leaves and trim the ends of the rhubarb. Cut into short lengths and finely chop in a food processor or grinder. Place rhubarb in a fine-mesh sieve and press out as much juice as possible. Measure 3½ cups of juice. If you are short of juice, make up the difference with apple juice or rosé wine. Pour juice into a Dutch oven or large heavy pot. Stir in sugar and bring to a rolling boil, stirring constantly. Add pectin and return to a rolling boil for 1 minute. Add colouring, if using, and remove from heat. Skim the top. Pour quickly into hot preserving jars, leaving ¼-inch headspace. Seal and process for 10 minutes according to instructions on page 311.

Makes about 6 cups.

GREEN TOMATO CHOW CHOW

. . . .

Oh, what to do with that abundant supply of green tomatoes? You know, the ones that refuse to ripen after the first frost. Green Tomato Chow Chow makes a tasty accompaniment to fall and winter fare.

5 quarts green tomatoes
6 large onions
⅓ cup coarse pickling salt
4 cups white or cider vinegar
6 cups granulated sugar
¼ cup pickling spice

Wash, trim and thinly slice unpeeled tomatoes, place in a large glass bowl. Thinly slice onions and add to tomatoes. Sprinkle with salt, stirring to coat vegetables evenly. Cover and let stand overnight. Thoroughly rinse vegetables with cold running water and press out excess moisture.

In a large heavy pot, bring vinegar and sugar to a boil. Tie pickling spice in a cheesecloth bag and add to pot. Add vegetables and simmer, stirring often, until liquid thickens and vegetables are soft, about 1½ hours. Ladle into hot preserving jars leaving ½-inch headspace. Seal and process for 10 minutes according to instructions on page 311.

Makes 12 cups.

CHRISTMAS CRANBERRY CHUTNEY

. . . .

CATHERINE J. BLENKHORN, ATHOL, N.S.

Catherine Blenkhorn makes this salt-free Christmas Cranberry Chutney not only as an alternative to traditional cranberry sauce, but also to hear her husband say, "Boy, this smells good."

7 cups fresh cranberries
1 cup white or golden raisins
3 cups water
1 tablespoon cinnamon
1½ teaspoons ginger
¼ teaspoon cloves
2 cups granulated sugar
3 medium cooking apples, pared, cored and diced neatly
2 medium onions, chopped
1½ cups diced celery
½ teaspoon nutmeg

In a large heavy pot, cook cranberries and raisins in water for 15 to 20 minutes. In a bowl, mix the cinnamon, ginger and cloves with the sugar then add to the cranberry mixture. Add the apples, onions and celery. Stirring often, cook for 25 to 30 minutes on medium heat.

Watch carefully, you might need to lower the heat for the last 10 minutes. Break the cranberries with a wooden spoon as the chutney cooks. Add the nutmeg. Ladle into hot preserving jars leaving ½-inch headspace. Seal and process for 15 minutes according to instructions on page 311. Store chutney for a week to allow the flavours to develop.

Makes about 8 cups.

PICKLED BEETS

• • • • • • • • • • • • •

Choose firm baby beets of uniform size. Store jars in a cool, dark cupboard so beets keep their colour.

5 pounds baby beets, washed
6 cups white vinegar
1½ cups water
3 cups granulated sugar
1½ teaspoons pickling salt
⅓ cup pickling spices
2 teaspoons mustard seeds

In a covered saucepan, simmer beets until tender when pierced with a skewer, about 45 minutes. Drain and slip the skin, root and stems from the beets with your fingers.

Meanwhile, combine vinegar, water, sugar and salt in a large heavy pot, and bring to a boil. Tie pickling spices and mustard seeds in a cheesecloth bag. Add to pot, simmer 10 minutes and remove bag. Pack beets in hot preserving jars to within ¾ inch of the rim. Cover with vinegar mixture leaving ½-inch headspace. Seal and process for 30 minutes according to instructions on page 311.

Makes 16 cups.

BEET AND HORSERADISH RELISH

• • • • • • • • • • • • • •

GRACE MCCLUNG, CHESTER BASIN, N.S.

Autumn activity produced this staple dish served in Grace McClung's home at almost every meal when she was growing up.

Grace remembers that the relish was kept in a stone crock in the cold room and she was sent down with a bowl and a spoon to get some before mealtime. After leaving home, she asked family members for the recipe to try for her own children. No one had it. The relish was a way of using all the available vegetables and then storing them for the winter so they would last until spring. The present recipe is drawn from memories of what was in that stone crock.

6 cups finely chopped cabbage
6 cups cooked, peeled and chopped beets
½ to 1 cup grated horseradish, or to taste
4 cups granulated sugar
2 tablespoons salt
3 cups white vinegar

Combine ingredients in a large heavy pot and bring to a boil. Reduce heat and simmer for 10 to 15 minutes. Transfer to airtight containers and refrigerate.

Makes about 10 cups.

PICKLED EGGS

. . . .

JOAN NEVERS, PLASTER ROCK, N.B.

1 teaspoon peppercorns
1 teaspoon dried basil
½ teaspoon mustard seed
½ teaspoon celery seed
3 cups white vinegar
1½ cups water
1½ teaspoons pickling salt
12 large eggs

Put the spices in a cheesecloth bag. In a large saucepan bring the vinegar, water, salt and spice bag to a boil. Simmer for 10 minutes. Cool. Hard cook eggs, shell and let cool. Place in a large, sterilized screw-top jar. Pour pickling liquid over eggs. Refrigerate for up to 2 to 3 weeks.

Makes 12 pickled eggs.

APPLE TOMATO CHUTNEY

. . . .

LISCOMBE LODGE, LISCOMB MILLS, N.S.

This recipe came from a chef who worked at Liscombe Lodge on Nova Scotia's Eastern Shore when it was a fine dining destination. The chutney's pungent flavour and wonderful colour make it a fitting addition to meat and seafood entrées.

3 pounds tomatoes
4 cups peeled, cored and diced apples
1 cup seedless raisins
½ cup finely chopped onion
1 cup packed brown sugar
½ cup pure maple syrup
⅔ cup cider vinegar
1½ teaspoons mixed pickling spices
½ teaspoon whole cloves

Bring a saucepan of water to a boil, immerse tomatoes until skin begins to split. Remove with a slotted spoon and immediately slide off the skin. Cut away stem section and dice.

Place tomatoes in a bowl, cover and put a heavy weight on top. Press overnight and in the morning pour off the juice.

Transfer tomatoes to a large saucepan and add apples, raisins, onion, sugar, syrup and vinegar. Tie up spices in a cheesecloth bag and add to the saucepan. Bring to a boil, stirring constantly. Reduce heat and simmer until thick, about 1½ hours, stirring regularly. Remove spice bag. Pour chutney into hot preserving jars leaving ½-inch headspace. Seal and process for 15 minutes according to instructions on page 311.

Makes 6 cups.

FALL HARVEST
PEAR CHUTNEY

. . . .

TATTINGSTONE INN, WOLFVILLE, N.S.

Several fruit trees grace the beautiful grounds of the Tattingstone Inn. Former innkeeper Betsey Harwood used her pears to make this spicy chutney. She advises that this recipe may be adjusted to make peach, apple or even cranberry chutney.

8 cups peeled, cored and cubed pears
4 or 5 cloves garlic, minced
1 small onion, diced
1 cup raisins or currants
3 cups packed brown sugar
1½ teaspoons ginger
1 teaspoon dry mustard
1½ teaspoons cinnamon
1 teaspoon crushed chili peppers
⅓ teaspoon salt
1 cup cider vinegar

Combine all ingredients in a large stainless steel kettle, bring slowly to a boil, stirring often. Simmer, uncovered and stirring occasionally, reducing heat as chutney begins to thicken, approximately 1¼ hours.

Ladle into hot preserving jars leaving ½-inch headspace. Seal and process for 15 minutes according to instructions on page 311.

Makes 6 cups.

PLUM TOMATO CHUTNEY

. . . .

INN AT SPRY POINT, SPRY POINT, P.E.I.

When Shirleen Peardon was chef at Inn at Spry Point, she served this tomato chutney with pork, fish, poultry and beef entrées. She even spread it on crostini as an appetizer.

½ cup red wine vinegar
¾ cup apple cider vinegar
⅔ cup granulated sugar
¾ teaspoon salt
½ teaspoon pepper
½ teaspoon chili powder
1 pound plum tomatoes, diced
1 sweet red pepper, diced
5 green onions, sliced

In a medium saucepan over medium-high heat, bring vinegars, sugar, salt, pepper and chili powder to a boil. Add tomatoes, red pepper and green onions, and bring back to boil. Reduce heat and simmer, uncovered, stirring occasionally until thickened and reduced to 1½ cups, about 1 hour. Cool and store, in an airtight container, in the refrigerator for up to 2 weeks.

Makes 1½ cups.

BLUE PLUM CHUTNEY

• • • • • • • • • • • •

MURRAY MANOR BED & BREAKFAST,
YARMOUTH, N.S.

Innkeeper Joan Semple prepares this delightful chutney when plums are at the peak of their season. It is a wonderful accompaniment to chicken and pork dishes.

3 pounds blue plums, pitted and finely chopped
1 pound apples, cored, peeled and chopped
1 pound onions, finely chopped
½ pound pitted dates, chopped
½ pound sultana raisins
4 cups granulated sugar
2½ cups malt vinegar
3 tablespoons pickling spice
2 tablespoons finely chopped fresh ginger

Combine plums, apples, onions, dates and raisins in a large heavy pot. Add sugar and vinegar, stirring until sugar is dissolved.

Place pickling spice and ginger in a spice bag and add to plum mixture. Bring to a boil, reduce heat and simmer, stirring regularly, 1½ to 2 hours.

Remove spice bag. Pour into hot preserving jars leaving ½-inch headspace. Seal and process for 15 minutes according to instructions on page 311.

Makes 6 to 8 cups.

SWEET ZUCCHINI RELISH

• • • • • • • • • • • •

To allow the flavours to blend, store the relish two to three weeks before serving.

5 pounds zucchini, seeded and chopped
3 cups chopped onion
1 cup chopped sweet red pepper
½ cup chopped sweet green pepper
⅓ cup pickling salt
3 cups white vinegar
4½ cups granulated sugar
2 teaspoons dry mustard
1½ teaspoons celery seed
¾ teaspoon pepper
¾ teaspoon turmeric
1 tablespoon cornstarch dissolved in 1 tablespoon cold
    water

In a large bowl, combine zucchini, onion, and peppers. Stir in pickling salt and let stand, covered, for 2 hours. Drain vegetables in a colander and rinse with cold running water. Squeeze out excess moisture.

In a large saucepan, combine vinegar, sugar, dry mustard, celery seed, pepper and turmeric. Bring to a boil. Add vegetables and simmer 30 minutes, stirring frequently. Stir cornstarch mixture into vegetables and continue to simmer 5 minutes until mixture is slightly thickened. Ladle relish into hot preserving jars. Seal and process for 10 minutes according to instructions on page 311.

Makes 10 to 12 cups.

RHUBARB RELISH

VIRJENE COLE, KENSINGTON, P.E.I.

The tartness of rhubarb lends itself well to a condiment that's aromatic with spices.

8 cups chopped rhubarb
8 cups chopped onions
3 cups vinegar
3 pounds brown sugar
1 teaspoon cinnamon
1 teaspoon allspice
1 teaspoon cloves
½ teaspoon salt

In a large heavy pot, cook the rhubarb, onions and vinegar for 10 minutes. Add sugar and spices. Bring to a boil, stirring. Reduce heat to simmer for 1 hour, stirring regularly or until thickened.

Pour into hot preserving jars leaving ½-inch headspace. Seal and process for 10 minutes according to instructions on page 311.

Makes about 10 cups.

LADY ASHBURNHAM'S PICKLES

COLLEEN THOMPSON, FREDERICTON, N.B.

Maria Anderson, known as "Rye," was a telephone operator in Fredericton, N.B., in the late 1800s. Her voice and charm captivated the distinguished Englishman Capt. Thomas Ashburnham, and their wedding was the social event of the era. The captain became heir to his father's title and family fortune and "Rye" became the Countess of Ashburnham, along with other titles. The lord and his lady shared their wealth with every good cause in Fredericton and their home was the social centrepiece of the city.

6 large cucumbers
¼ cup pickling salt
Water
4 cups finely chopped onions
2 sweet red peppers, diced
1 sweet green pepper, diced
2 cups granulated sugar
3 tablespoons all-purpose flour
1 tablespoon dry mustard
½ teaspoon turmeric
1 teaspoon mustard seed
1 teaspoon celery seed
2 cups white vinegar

Peel and seed cucumbers, and cut into pieces the size of sugar cubes. In a large bowl, mix with salt and enough water to cover. Let stand overnight. Drain. Add onions, red and green peppers. Thoroughly mix sugar, flour and spices and add a little of the vinegar to make a smooth paste. In a large, heavy pot blend the paste with the remaining vinegar, stirring until it's smooth. Add the cucumber mixture. Cook until the sauce becomes clear, about 1 hour on low to medium heat, stirring regularly. Ladle into hot preserving jars leaving ½-inch headspace. Seal and process for 10 minutes according to instructions on page 311.

Makes about 8 to 10 cups.

MUSTARD BEAN PICKLES

. . . .

COLLEEN THOMPSON, FREDERICTON, N.B.

Wanda Jonah of Hillsborough, N.B., has been preparing batches of these pickles for over 30 years. Her aunt Dot, who provided the recipe, has been at it for more than 45 years. The origins can be traced back to Wanda's grandmother Smith of Bouctouche, near Moncton. Prior to that, details are dimmed by time and memory. The pickles are especially tasty with sweet baked beans, as a sandwich garnish or a piquant accompaniment to a breakfast of poached eggs. Recipients of a gift bottle of mustard bean pickles have been known to hoard it, permitting its appearance on the table for special occasions only.

8 quarts yellow string beans
Water
¾ cup pickling salt
1 cup dry mustard
1 cup all-purpose flour
1 teaspoon turmeric
2 teaspoons celery salt
6 cups cider vinegar

Cut beans in 1 to 1½-inch lengths, place in a large pot and just cover with boiling water. Add pickling salt and bring back to a boil. Boil just until crisp tender, no longer. Drain in a colander while the sauce is being prepared.

Mix together all the dry ingredients. Combine with vinegar in the pot. Bring to a boil. Return the beans to the pot. Bring to a boil and boil for 5 minutes. Pour into hot preserving jars leaving ½-inch headspace. Seal and process for 10 minutes according to instructions on page 311.

Makes 8 cups.

CELERY RELISH

. . . .

VIRJENE COLE, KENSINGTON, P.E.I.

Almost everyone in Prince Edward Island has a vegetable garden and there are only so many soups and salads that require celery. Add some cucumbers, cabbage or cauliflower for a crunchy mustard relish.

2 quarts cucumbers
2 quarts onions
1 large cabbage or cauliflower
½ cup pickling salt
Boiling water
5 cups vinegar
2 cups all-purpose flour
½ cup dry mustard
8 cups packed brown sugar
1 tablespoon mustard seed
1 tablespoon turmeric
2 large bunches of celery, trimmed and finely chopped
2 sweet red peppers, finely chopped

Peel the cucumbers and onions and chop finely. Shred the cabbage or cut the cauliflower in small pieces. Put in a large crock or bowl and cover with salt and enough boiling water to cover vegetables. Let stand 4 to 5 hours or overnight. Drain well.

In a large, heavy pot, make a syrup of 2 cups of the vinegar, the flour and dry mustard. Add the remaining vinegar, brown sugar, mustard seed, turmeric, celery, peppers and drained vegetables. Bring to a simmer, cook slowly until thickened and clear, about 2½ to 3 hours. Pour into hot preserving jars leaving ½-inch headspace. Seal and process for 10 minutes according to instructions on page 311.

Makes 10 to 12 cups.

QUICK PICKLED RED ONIONS

. . . .

These pickled red onions find their way into numerous vinaigrettes, condiments, salads and even sandwiches. Their colour is lovely and the taste is tangy and sweet, without any "oniony" aftertaste. They're good to have on hand at all times as they are really simple to prepare and can be made year round.

2 pounds red onions
1 cup red wine vinegar
1 cup granulated sugar
1 bay leaf
1 teaspoon cracked black peppercorns
2 tablespoons grenadine
1 teaspoon salt

Peel and thinly slice onions into rings about ⅛-inch thick. In a pot, bring all remaining ingredients to a boil. Pack onions tightly into preserving jars and pour hot liquid over the top. Seal when still hot and refrigerate for up to 1 month.

Makes 4 cups.

SOLOMON GUNDY

. . . .

DEBORAH METHERALL, HALIFAX, N.S.

In Nova Scotia, pickled herring means more than a jar at the back of the fridge. In the south shore community of Blue Rocks, Lunenburg County, where German immigrants settled and brought their "salmagundi" recipes. Here's the recipe that many in the community use for this delicacy.

6 salt herring
2 medium onions, sliced
2 cups vinegar
2 tablespoons pickling spice
½ cup granulated sugar

Remove the heads and tails from the herring. Clean the insides and remove the skins. Cut in pieces about 1 inch thick and fillet the pieces. Soak in cold water for about 24 hours. Squeeze the water from the herring. Place in preserving jar with a wide mouth in alternate layers with the slices of onion. In a saucepan heat the vinegar, pickling spice and sugar just to boiling. Let cool, then pour over the herring in the jar. Refrigerate 4 to 6 days for the pickling liquid to penetrate.

Makes 1 jar.

BREAKFASTS

CREAMY TOFU FRUIT SHAKE

- - - - - - - - - -

This delicious, nutrition-packed, high-potassium shake will convince non-tofu lovers that tofu is edible in a pleasant form. It is important to use the soft silken tofu for a smooth creamy shake. When I have a fresh pineapple, I always dice and freeze some to make this drink. Other fresh or frozen fruits such as blueberries, raspberries or mango can be used. This shake also makes a refreshing dessert, garnished with a sliced strawberry or a sprig of fresh mint.

½ cup silken tofu
1 cup skim milk
¼ cup fat-free plain yogurt
1 cup fresh or frozen strawberries
½ cup frozen pineapple cubes
1 ripe banana
2 tablespoons frozen orange juice concentrate

Combine all ingredients in a blender and purée until smooth. If too thick, add more milk. Pour into tall glasses.

Makes 3 1-cup servings.

A PAIR OF SMOOTHIES

- - - - - - - - - -

Smoothies are not only easy to prepare, they are also delicious and nutritious. Whip one up for breakfast when you are in a rush or blend one in the middle of the day when you need a quick pick-me-up.

BANANA YOGURT SMOOTHIE

1 ripe banana
½ cup fresh orange juice
½ cup plain or fruit yogurt
1 tablespoon liquid honey

FRESH STRAWBERRY SMOOTHIE

2 cups fresh strawberries, washed and hulled
½ cup milk
1 cup strawberry yogurt

In a blender, add all ingredients and purée until smooth. Pour into glasses and enjoy.

Makes 2 large or 4 small servings.

CRANBERRY, ORANGE AND BANANA FRUIT FLIP

· · · · · · · · · · · · · ·

THE DELTA PRINCE EDWARD,
CHARLOTTETOWN, P.E.I.

Chef Paul Paboudjian first developed this flip as a refreshing low-fat drink to serve for cocktail parties as an alternative to alcoholic beverages. He noted that it is equally delicious served as a "breakfast on the run."

½ cup fresh cranberries
½ cup orange juice
½ cup sliced banana
½ cup skim or low-fat milk
½ cup plain yogurt
½ cup low-fat vanilla ice cream
Granulated sugar, to taste

GARNISH

2 orange segments, 6 fresh cranberries and
  2 thick banana slices

Incorporate cranberries, juice, sliced banana, milk, yogurt and ice cream in a large blender and purée on high until smooth. Add sugar, as desired, and pour into parfait glasses. Serve with a skewer of an orange segment, 3 cranberries and a slice of banana.

Serves 2.

MAPLE BUTTER

· · · · · · · · · · · · · ·

Beautiful on biscuits, a piece of roasted trout or pancakes, maple butter is worth a little extra work for special occasions. Use salted butter as it gives a nice balance to the sweet syrup.

½ pound salted butter
¼ cup pure amber maple syrup (approximate)

Bring butter to room temperature. Whip butter and the maple syrup together until light and fluffy, about 5 minutes, using a stand or hand mixer for best results.

  To serve, fill a butter dish with maple butter and smooth over the top with a knife. Drizzle a few drops of maple syrup on the top to garnish.

Makes 2 cups.

CANTALOUPE AND BLUEBERRY WAKE-UP

. . . .

HATFIELD HERITAGE INN, HARTLAND, N.B.

Chef Richard Boulier of Hatfield Heritage Inn, which operated in Harland, N.B., combined vine-ripened cantaloupes with fresh wild blueberries and yogurt to make a fine breakfast dish that was not only attractive but also nutritious. Cantaloupes and blueberries contain antioxidants known to provide certain health benefits to the cardiovascular and immune systems. To ensure that the cantaloupe is fully ripened, choose one with a sweet, fruity fragrance that is heavy for its size.

1 large cantaloupe
2 cups fat-free yogurt
1 teaspoon vanilla extract
1 tablespoon liquid honey
2 cups wild blueberries

Slice the cantaloupe into 8 wedges, discarding the seeds. In a bowl, whisk yogurt, vanilla and honey. Spoon about ¼ cup of yogurt over the cantaloupe and sprinkle with blueberries. Or, with very small melons, cut each in half, scrape out seeds and fill with yogurt mixture and blueberries.

Serves 8.

MUM'S BUCKWHEAT PANCAKES

. . . .

DAWN BREMNER, JEMSEG, N.B.

Since the 19th century, buckwheat has been an important dietary staple in a countryman's diet. Census records tell that in 1860, 50 bushels of buckwheat were grown on the Bremner family's seven acres. The buckwheat would have been threshed, taken to the grist mill and ground into flour. A lot of the flour found its way into buckwheat pancakes.

2 cups buckwheat flour
1 cup all-purpose flour
4 cups buttermilk
Pinch of salt
¾ teaspoon baking soda
Warm water

Mix the first 4 ingredients together at least 1 hour before frying. Let mixture sit in a batter pitcher at room temperature until needed. When ready to begin cooking, add the baking soda dissolved in a little warm water and stir well. Put a properly seasoned and cured griddle over medium heat. Rub with the flat surface of a raw peeled potato to prevent smoking. When hot, pour some batter on the griddle and cook until the edges curl a little and the surface seems dry

Turn over and cook for 1 or 2 minutes on the other side. Continue to rub the griddle with a fresh surface of the potato as needed. Keep pancakes warm in the oven until several are ready to serve.

(Note: If the potato method doesn't work, the pancakes can be fried on a griddle greased with pork or bacon fat, or in this "modern age of scandalous waste," one can use cooking oil or butter).

Makes 20 to 24 pancakes.

WICKWIRE HOUSE MAPLE PECAN BANANA PANCAKES

· · · · · · · · ·

WICKWIRE HOUSE BED AND BREAKFAST, KENT-VILLE, N.S.

"Maple caresse" fresh cheese is available in the yogurt section of many supermarkets. Toast the pecans by sprinkling them on a cookie sheet and baking in a moderate oven for 2 to 3 minutes.

2 extra-large eggs
2 cups buttermilk
2 cups mashed bananas
¼ cup pure maple syrup (approximate)
¼ cup vegetable oil
2¼ cups all-purpose flour
1 tablespoon baking powder
1 teaspoon baking soda
¼ teaspoon salt
1 cup chopped pecans, toasted
3 medium bananas, sliced
3 cups strawberry halves
Maple caresse fresh cheese

Beat eggs in a large bowl until fluffy, approximately 2 minutes. Whisk in buttermilk, bananas, maple syrup and oil, and set aside. In a separate large bowl, combine flour, baking powder, baking soda, salt and pecans. Add liquid ingredients, stirring only until just blended.

Heat a nonstick griddle or skillet over medium-high heat to 375°F, greasing lightly as necessary. Pour approximately ¼ cup batter per pancake onto griddle and cook until puffed and dry around the edges, then turn over and cook until golden brown. Serve with bananas, strawberries and a dollop of maple caresse cheese. Drizzle with additional maple syrup.

Makes 24 4-inch pancakes.

GOLDEN PANCAKES WITH ORANGE MAPLE SYRUP

· · · · · · · · · ·

Just like a sun-filled morning, these pancakes will leave you smiling and begging for them another day. They are easy to prepare and simply delicious.

1½ cups all-purpose flour
2 tablespoons granulated sugar
1½ teaspoons baking powder
½ teaspoon baking soda
½ teaspoon salt
½ teaspoon cinnamon
Pinch each of nutmeg and cloves
1¾ cups buttermilk
½ cup pumpkin purée
1 large egg
1 large egg white
2 tablespoons vegetable oil, plus extra for cooking
Butter

ORANGE MAPLE SYRUP
1 cup pure maple syrup
Zest of 1 orange

In a large bowl, sift together dry ingredients.

In another bowl, beat buttermilk, pumpkin, egg, egg white and oil until smooth. Add liquid to dry ingredients, stirring until just blended.

Heat griddle to medium-high and coat with vegetable oil. Dollop the batter, ¼ cup at a time, on hot griddle. Cook pancakes until surface begins to bubble. Turn and bake until golden. Remove pancakes and keep warm.

ORANGE MAPLE SYRUP
Meanwhile, in a small saucepan, combine syrup and orange zest. Over low heat, gently heat and steep, being careful not to boil.

To serve, arrange pancakes on warmed plates. Top with butter and warm Orange Maple Syrup.

Makes about 14 pancakes.

BLUEBERRY WAFFLES WITH MAPLE SYRUP

. . . .

Luscious, golden waffles are a nice variation for Sunday brunch. Treat yourself to a warm waffle covered with butter and maple syrup.

1½ cups all-purpose flour
2 tablespoons granulated sugar
1 teaspoon baking powder
½ teaspoon salt
½ teaspoon baking soda
1½ cups buttermilk
2 large eggs, beaten
¼ cup vegetable oil or melted butter
½ cup fresh blueberries

Combine flour, sugar, baking powder, salt and baking soda in a large bowl. In another bowl, whisk together buttermilk, eggs and oil. Add liquid to dry ingredients, stirring only until smooth.

    Heat waffle iron according to manufacturer's directions. Pour batter onto hot waffle iron and sprinkle with 1 tablespoon blueberries. Bake until steaming stops and waffle is golden.

Makes 12 waffles.

BUTTERMILK BLUEBERRY PANCAKES

. . . .

Elaine Elliot and Virginia Lee have been making these pancakes for so long that the recipe is firmly imprinted in their memories. Once you try them they will become the pancake of choice for your family as well!

1½ cups all-purpose flour
1 teaspoon baking powder
½ teaspoon salt
½ teaspoon baking soda
2 tablespoons granulated sugar
1¾ cups buttermilk
2 tablespoons vegetable oil
1 large egg
½ cup fresh or frozen blueberries
Syrup of choice

Sift flour, baking powder, salt, baking soda and sugar into a large bowl. In another bowl, beat together buttermilk, oil and egg. Add liquid to flour mixture, stirring only until combined. Drop by large spoonfuls onto a greased hot griddle and sprinkle with blueberries. Cook until pancake bubbles. Turn and cook on other side until golden brown. Serve hot with syrup of choice.

Makes 10 to 12 medium pancakes.

CRANBERRY ALMOND PANCAKES

WHITMAN INN, KEMPT, N.S.

Situated near "nature's treasure," Kejimkujik National Park, guests at the Whitman Inn are offered substantial breakfasts, often featuring local berries and pure maple syrup.

2 cups all-purpose flour
¼ cup large-flake rolled oats
1 tablespoon baking powder
½ teaspoon salt
2 large eggs, beaten
1¾ cups milk
1 cup fresh or frozen cranberries
1½ cups granulated sugar
½ cup slivered almonds
1 teaspoon vanilla extract
Butter and pure maple syrup

In a large mixing bowl, combine flour, oats, baking powder and salt. Stir in eggs and milk. In a food processor, combine cranberries, sugar, almonds and vanilla, processing until finely chopped. Stir cranberry mixture into pancake batter.

Pour ⅓ cup of batter onto a hot greased griddle. Cook until surface bubbles. Flip and cook the other side until browned. Serve warm with butter and pure maple syrup.

Makes 15 to 20 pancakes.

OVEN-PUFFED MAPLE PANCAKES

JUDITH COMFOR, PORT MEDWAY, N.S.

Maple syrup is graded on a spectrum of colour, clarity and density according to federal regulations. It ranges from top-grade extra light, to light, then to medium. The syrup gets darker and cloudier as the season progresses and last-run syrup rarely makes it to the marketplace. But the late syrup is used commercially to give flavour to everything from bacon to cigars.

Whether spooned up plain or dripping down the sides of hot, butter-topped pancakes, the indescribable flavour of maple syrup is a real spring tonic. Try a different approach to pancakes by baking them in the oven with the maple syrup already included. For maximum effect, make sure all eyes are upon you as you open the oven door, for soon after . . . it becomes flat as a pancake.

6 large eggs
1 cup milk
1 cup all-purpose flour
1 teaspoon vanilla extract
½ cup melted butter
1⅓ cups maple syrup

Whisk together eggs, milk, flour and vanilla in a large bowl. Pour melted butter into the bottom of 2 large high-sided baking pans, glass or metal, each about 13 by 9 by 2 inches. Pour half of the batter into each pan. Drizzle ⅔ cup of maple syrup over the batter in each pan leaving a 2-inch border around the edges. Bake in a 450°F oven for 15 to 20 minutes until puffed with golden-brown edges. Don't peek until almost done.

Serves 4.

OATMEAL PORRIDGE WITH RASPBERRY JAM AND ALMONDS

. . . .

SANDRA NOWLAN, HALIFAX, N.S.

Oatmeal is one of the best ways to start the day, but it never appealed to Sandra Nowlan until her daughter, Claire, served this delicious version dressed up with raspberry jam and toasted almonds. Oatmeal is recognized by the U.S. Department of Agriculture with the ability to help lower cholesterol and reduce the risk of heart disease. Cooking time varies from 3 to 10 minutes depending on whether you use quick or old-fashioned large-flake rolled oats.

2 cups water
1 cup oatmeal or rolled oats
3 tablespoons raspberry jam (approximate)
½ cup slivered almonds, toasted*

Bring water to a boil in a saucepan over high heat. Gradually stir in oats and when porridge is boiling, reduce heat to low and cover. Simmer porridge until thick and tender, up to 10 minutes, stirring occasionally. Stir in raspberry jam.

Spoon into 4 bowls and add a dab of jam on top, if desired. Sprinkle toasted almonds over the top and serve with milk.

Makes 4 servings, ½ cup per serving.

* *To toast almonds, spread them in a pan and bake at 350°F for about 8 to 10 minutes. Watch carefully to ensure that they don't burn.*

CARLTON COUNTY FIDDLEHEAD FRITTATA

. . . .

HATFIELD HERITAGE INN, HARTLAND, N.B.

A New Brunswick delicacy, fiddleheads are harvested during the spring, just before they unfurl into ferns. Fiddleheads should be firm and have a deep rich green colour.

1 cup shredded Swiss cheese
½ cup shredded Cheddar cheese
1 cup fresh fiddleheads, cleaned, dried and chopped
¼ cup chopped leeks, white part only
½ cup sliced mushrooms
4 strips crisp bacon, crumbled
8 large eggs
4 large egg whites
1 cup milk
1 cup heavy cream (35% mf)
Generous pinch of nutmeg
Pepper to taste

Spray a 12-inch square baking dish with cooking spray. Spread cheeses over the bottom of dish. Top with vegetables, mushrooms and bacon.

In a bowl, whisk together eggs, whites, milk, cream, nutmeg and pepper. Pour over cheese, vegetables and bacon, and bake at 375°F for 45 minutes or until a knife inserted into the centre comes out clean. Let stand for 5 minutes. Cut into squares and serve warm.

Serves 8.

HEALTHY GRANOLA FRUIT PARFAIT

· · · · · · · · · · · · ·

The quantities in this recipe will serve one, but it's easy to increase the amounts to allow for more servings. Choose a mixture of fruits, mixing colours for the ultimate presentation. This granola recipe is less sweet than most packaged granola cereals, and can be stored in an airtight container for up to 1 month.

½ cup granola cereal (recipe follows) or store-bought granola
½ cup low-fat plain yogurt
½ cup fresh fruit, such as kiwi, banana, strawberries and melon

GRANOLA

4 cups large-flake rolled oats
1¼ cups wheat bran
1¼ cups chopped pecans
1¼ cups slivered almonds
1 cup sunflower seeds
½ cup sesame seeds
⅓ cup canola oil
2¼ cups raisins
1½ cups chopped dates
¾ cup flaked coconut
⅓ cup liquid honey
1 tablespoon vanilla extract
1 tablespoon orange zest

To serve, sprinkle granola over the bottom of a serving dish, saving some to use as a garnish. Top with yogurt, fruit slices and a sprinkling of granola.

Serves 1.

GRANOLA

In a large bowl, combine rolled oats, wheat bran, pecans, almonds, sunflower seeds and sesame seeds. Pour in oil and stir to coat. Spread on 2 rimmed baking sheets. Bake in a 325°F oven, stirring every 10 minutes, for 30 minutes or until golden. Transfer to a large bowl. Stir in raisins, dates and coconut.

In a separate bowl, combine honey, vanilla and zest. Stir mixture into granola until well combined. Let cool completely before storing in airtight container.

Makes 15 cups.

EGGS LOYALIST

. . . .

HOMEPORT HISTORIC BED AND BREAKFAST INN, SAINT JOHN, N.B.

Chef Ralph Holyoke admits that the name of this dish is a historical play on words, considering that Saint John, N.B., is known as the Loyalist City — and one of its famous Loyalist settlers was Benedict Arnold.

3 English muffins, split
Butter, to spread
Water
1 teaspoon vinegar
6 large eggs
6 ounces smoked salmon, thinly sliced
Pinch of cloves
6 watermelon wedges

QUICK HOLLANDAISE SAUCE

1 cup milk
1 package hollandaise-sauce mix
¼ cup butter, cut in pieces
3 dashes Worcestershire sauce
3 ounces smoked Gruyère cheese, finely diced

Lightly toast muffins. Spread with butter and keep warm in oven.

In a saucepan large enough to poach all the eggs, pour enough water to depth of 2 inches, add vinegar and bring to a simmer. One at a time, crack eggs into a saucer and gently slip them into water. Poach to desired doneness, about 5 minutes. Remove eggs with slotted spoon, draining excess water. Place eggs on muffins. Top with smoked salmon, add a large dollop of Quick Hollandaise Sauce and a very light sprinkle of cloves. Serve on warmed plates with watermelon wedges.

Serves 6.

QUICK HOLLANDAISE SAUCE

In a small saucepan, whisk milk and packaged sauce mix until smooth. Add butter and bring to a boil over medium heat, stirring constantly. Reduce heat to medium-low. Stir in Worcestershire sauce and Gruyère cheese. Continue stirring and cooking until sauce is smooth and creamy, about 1 minute. Serve immediately.

CHEESE AND BACON STRATA

. . . .

You can prepare this popular brunch dish a night ahead then simply cover with plastic wrap and refrigerate until an hour before, uncovering, baking and serving.

12 slices of day-old white bread, crusts removed and cut into cubes

½ pound bacon

½ cup sliced mushrooms

½ cup sweet red pepper, diced

1½ cups mixed shredded cheeses (Edam, creamy fontina, white Cheddar and Parmesan cheeses)

6 large eggs

2 large egg whites

2 teaspoons dry mustard

¾ teaspoon salt

Generous grating of pepper

3 cups whole milk

Grease a 9- by 13-inch baking dish and sprinkle bread cubes over the bottom. Fry bacon until crisp, drain on paper towel and crumble. Sprinkle bacon over bread. Remove all but 1 teaspoon of bacon drippings from pan and sauté mushrooms and pepper until barely tender, about 2 minutes. Sprinkle vegetables and shredded cheese over bacon. In a large bowl, whisk together eggs, egg whites, mustard, salt, pepper, and milk. Pour over bread mixture. Cover and refrigerate overnight.

Bake strata in a 325°F oven for 1 hour or until puffy and golden brown. Cut into squares and serve warm.

Serves 8.

FRESH ASPARAGUS AND HAM GRATIN

· · · · · · · · · · ·

ACTON'S GRILL AND CAFÉ, WOLFVILLE, N.S.

Acton's has long been known for using seasonal produce at its peak of freshness and flavour. Here's a way to offer delicious local asparagus.

36 slender asparagus spears, peeled and trimmed
12 thin slices of ham
3 cups Mornay Sauce (recipe follows)
3 tablespoons freshly grated Parmesan cheese

MORNAY SAUCE

¼ cup butter
¼ cup all-purpose flour
2 cups milk, scalded*
4 ounces shredded aged Cheddar cheese
2 ounces freshly grated Parmesan or Reggiano cheese
¼ teaspoon nutmeg
⅛ teaspoon cayenne pepper
Salt and white pepper to taste

In a large saucepan of boiling water, blanch asparagus for 3 minutes. Drain and immerse in cold water to stop cooking. When asparagus is cooled, drain and reserve.

Lightly butter a 3-quart shallow casserole dish or individual au gratin dishes. Roll 3 asparagus spears in each slice of ham. If using a casserole dish, place all rolls in a single layer; if using individual au gratin dishes, place 2 rolls in each dish. Cover ham rolls with Mornay Sauce and sprinkle with Parmesan cheese. Bake in a 375°F oven for 15 to 20 minutes until bubbly and lightly browned.

Serves 6.

MORNAY SAUCE

In a saucepan over low heat, melt butter. Raise heat to medium-low, add flour and whisk constantly for 1 to 2 minutes. Raise heat to medium, whisk in scalded milk and cook, stirring constantly, until sauce thickens. Reduce heat to low and simmer, stirring frequently for 5 minutes. Stir in cheeses and season with nutmeg, cayenne pepper and salt and white pepper to taste.

* To scald milk, heat it to just below the boiling point until bubbles form around the edge.

DRINKS

HOT MULLED CIDER

. . . .

Here are two versions of hot mulled cider. One "with" and one "without." Pick your potion!

MULLED CIDER (WITH)

1 quart sweet apple cider
¼ cup dark rum
3 tablespoons brown sugar
2 tablespoons lemon juice
2-inch piece cinnamon stick
¼ teaspoon whole allspice

Combine all ingredients in a large saucepan and heat until nearly bubbling. Do not boil.

Strain into 6 serving cups.

MULLED CIDER (WITHOUT)

1 quart sweet apple cider
1 teaspoon whole cloves
1 teaspoon whole allspice
2-inch piece cinnamon stick

Combine ingredients in a large saucepan or coffee urn and heat slowly for half an hour. Do not boil. Discard spices and if desired, strain. Serve piping hot.

Serves 6.

FRUITED ICED TEA

. . . .

Here's a solution for those who crave a daily cup of tea even when the weather is hot and sticky. Satisfy your thirst with this New World variation on brewed tea.

6 cups water
4 tea bags
2 cups cold juice of choice (cranberry or raspberry)
Ice cubes
1 lemon, thinly sliced
Mint sprigs
Granulated sugar or artificial sweetener (optional)

Bring fresh cold water just to a boil. Pour small amount boiling water into a 6-cup teapot. Swirl water and discard. Add tea to pot, pour hot water over tea and brew 5 minutes. Remove tea bags, pour tea into pitcher and refrigerate. Add juice to pitcher, stirring to blend.

To serve, add ice cubes, lemon slices and mint to tall glasses, pour tea mixture over ice and serve immediately. If a sweeter tea is desired, stir sugar into individual servings.

Serves 6.

LEMON GRASS GINGER LEMONADE

. . . .

DUNES RESORT, BRACKLEY BEACH, P.E.I.

A new twist on the old favourite — the lemon grass's subtle, exotic flavour and ginger's heat should make this one of your new favourites. The amounts of sugar and ginger can be adjusted for personal taste.

1 cup granulated sugar
2 to 4 stalks lemon grass,* sliced
1 2-inch piece fresh ginger, peeled and sliced
4 cups water
Juice of 3 lemons
Juice of 2 limes
Pinch of sea salt
2 cups ice cubes

In medium saucepan, combine sugar, lemon grass, ginger and water and bring to a boil. Simmer for 20 minutes. Remove from heat and let sit for 1 hour to steep and develop flavour. Strain into a pitcher. Add juices, salt and ice.

Makes 4 tall glasses.

* When choosing lemon grass, look for plump, moist lower stalks. This is the only part you'll use for this drink.

OLD-FASHIONED LEMONADE

. . . .

The signature drink of summer, this lemonade is just tart enough to quench your thirst without too much pucker.

4 cups water
1 cup granulated sugar
1 cup lemon juice (6 lemons)
Zest of 2 oranges
Juice of 2 oranges

In medium saucepan, combine water and sugar. Bring to boil and stir until sugar dissolves. Let cool. Add lemon juice, orange zest and orange juice. Cover and let stand 1 hour, then strain and refrigerate. Serve chilled.

For pink lemonade, add a tablespoon of raspberry or strawberry syrup.

Makes 4 tall glasses.

AWESOME ORANGEADE

. . . .

Nothing beats the taste of fresh-squeezed orange juice. For a different-looking orangeade, try blood oranges. These red-fleshed oranges are every bit as juicy and vitamin-C packed as their more conventional cousins.

1 cup water
1 cup granulated sugar
Zest of 1 orange
Zest of 1 lemon
2 cups orange juice
¼ cup lemon juice
3 cups ice water

In medium saucepan, combine water and sugar. Bring to boil and stir until sugar dissolves. Add orange and lemon zest. Boil gently until syrupy and thinly coats the back of a spoon, about 10 minutes. Strain and cool. In container, combine syrup, orange juice, lemon juice and ice water. Stir. Refrigerate and serve chilled.

Makes 6 tall glasses.

PLOUGHMAN'S COOLER

. . . .

OPA!, HALIFAX, N.S.

This recipe was handed down from the chef's father and grandfather. "In those days," notes Chef Joseph, "there was no Coca-Cola." It's an unusual drink, but well-suited for hot summer days, especially when doing outside work like gardening. Opa! became Ela!, but the downtown Halifax restaurant remains itself.

1 cup seedless raisins
4 cups cold water
Rind of ½ orange, chopped
Rind of ½ lemon, chopped
Pine nuts, for garnish

In large glass container, mix raisins, water, and rinds. Refrigerate overnight. Strain and serve chilled. Garnish with pine nuts.

Makes 4 water glasses.

RHUBARB NECTAR

. . . .

Positively one of the best-liked, old-time summer drinks coast to coast — maybe because the nectar is so delicious and rhubarb is so easy to grow. Combined with spices and orange, it certainly makes a very refreshing drink. Try to use the pinkest rhubarb.

12 cups chopped rhubarb, in 1-inch pieces
4 cups water
1 lemon
1 orange
4-inch piece cinnamon stick
3 cups granulated sugar

Place the rhubarb and water in a large pot. Pare the zest off the lemon and orange. Crush the cinnamon lightly and add it with the zests to the pot.

Bring to the boil over high heat, then reduce the heat, stir, cover and simmer 10 minutes. The rhubarb should be well broken up. Wet a jelly bag and wring it out. Strain the rhubarb mixture through the bag. Squeeze out as much juice as possible. There should be 6 cups. Pour into a large saucepan and add ½ cup sugar for each cup juice. Squeeze the lemon and orange and strain their juice into the saucepan. Stir well. Bring to a boil and boil 3 minutes. For use within 2 weeks, pour into hot sterile jars, seal, cool and store in the refrigerator for up to 3 weeks. For longer storage, pour the boiling syrup into hot preserving jars, leaving ¼-inch headspace. Seal and process for 15 minutes according to instructions on page 311.

To serve, combine with equal amounts of cold soda water. Add ice, a slice of orange and a sprig of mint.

Makes 8 cups nectar.

RASPBERRY VINEGAR

. . . .

There's nothing quite like a shot or two of raspberry vinegar, made with fresh berries, to liven up a glass of water.

4 cups red wine vinegar
24 cups raspberries
Granulated sugar

In a bowl, pour vinegar over half the berries, and let stand 6 to 8 hours or overnight. Strain through cheesecloth onto a bowl containing the remaining berries. Let stand 6 to 8 hours. Strain again. For each cup of liquid, add ¼ cup sugar and boil for 20 minutes. Pour into sterilized preserving jars and refrigerate.

Use the vinegar to flavour water or soda water, 2 tablespoons per 8-ounce glass.

Serve in tall, frosted glasses over ice cubes. For a special touch, freeze a raspberry in each cube, or add raspberries to the pitcher.

Makes 8 to 10 cups.

CHAI TEA

· · · · · · · · · · · · · · ·

Hot or cold, chai tea is delicious, but hot tea is popular in India, even in summer time, for cooling down the body!

4 cups water
4 tea bags
½ teaspoon crushed fresh ginger
1 medium cinnamon stick
¼ teaspoon fennel seeds (optional)
¼ teaspoon cardamom seeds (optional)
2 to 3 teaspoons sugar or honey, or to taste
1½ cups whole milk

In large saucepan, bring water to a boil. Add tea bags, ginger, cinnamon, fennel and cardamom, if using. Simmer 3 to 4 minutes, covered. Add milk and return to a boil. Stir in honey or sugar. Strain and enjoy.

Serves 4.

GINGER BEER

· · · · · · · · · · · · · · ·

Ginger beer is an excellent thirst quencher but definitely an acquired taste. A staple in warm climates, such as Jamaica, it's the forerunner of more commercial, sweeter ginger ale.

2 ounces fresh ginger, minced
2 lemons, sliced
1 lime, sliced
1 teaspoon cream of tartar
1 pound granulated sugar
1 gallon boiling water
1 teaspoon active dry yeast

In large container, such as a 2-gallon jug, combine ginger, lemons, lime, cream of tartar and sugar. Pour in boiling water and stir. Let sit until mixture is just warm, then stir in yeast. Tightly cover jug and let sit for 24 hours. Strain, chill and serve.

Serves 10 beer mugs.

PREBAKING A PIE SHELL

Some recipes call for a prebaked shell. To make one, line the pastry with foil and fill it with pie weights (available at cookware shops) or with dried beans, lentils or peas. (You can reuse the beans for years — just be sure to note on the container that these beans are for prebaking pie shells, not to eat.)

Bake the pie shell in the bottom rack of a 400°F oven until the edge of the pastry is light golden, about 20 minutes. Remove the weights and foil and return the shell to the oven to bake to an even golden colour, about 5 to 10 minutes. When prebaking with pie weights, you may need less time than with beans.

Some recipes call for a partially baked shell. To make one, prepare the shell, lining and pie weights as above, but bake for 20 minutes, or the time called for in the recipe. The length of time a pie is baked after the pie shell is filled will determine how long the shell needs to be prebaked.

SEAL-AND-PROCESS PROCEDURE

These are the steps to take when preserving jams, jellies, marmalades, fruit, relishes and pickles for storage for up to a year.

Always use preserving jars available in grocery and hardware stores. These jars are reusable as long as they are not chipped or cracked. Wash, rinse and air dry before using.

Each time a jar is used, you need a new disc (lid). Before filling and sealing the jars, warm the lids in luke warm water.

Jar rings or bands are reusable as long as they are not rusted or bent out of shape.

Heat the preserving jars before filling. The best way to do this is in the boiling water canner. Fill the canner two-thirds full with hot water. Arrange the jars upside down on the rack and lower the rack into the hot water. Cover and bring to a simmer, timing this process so the jars are hot when the preserve has finished cooking. You can hold the jars in hot water until needed if the preserve needs a few more minutes.

Remove preserving jars from the canner with canning tongs and set upright on a tray. Canning tongs that grip the shoulder of the jars are essential for the safe handling of hot jars and preserves.

Use a funnel and small metal cup or ladle to fill the jars to the headspace noted in each recipe. For chunky preserves run a plastic knife down the inside of the jar to press out any air bubbles. Adjust the headspace level if necessary. Wipe the jar rim with moistened paper towel if any of the preserve has slopped onto it.

Centre a disc on top of the jar and screw on a jar ring until resistance is met, then, with fingertips, tighten without forcing.

Place the jars upright on the rack in the canner. Lower the rack, add more boiling water if needed to come 1 inch above the top of the jars. Cover the canner, bring to a brisk boil, timing the processing time from this point.

Turn off the heat under the canner, remove the lid from the canner and let the boiling subside, about 5 minutes.

Using canning tongs, lift the jars onto a rack or folded towel to cool, about 1 day. Check that the discs have snapped down, i.e., that they are well sealed. If any of the lids are still curved up, refrigerate the jar and use within 3 weeks.

Wipe and label the jars. Remove the jar rings if desired. Store preserves in a cool, dark and dry spot.

RECIPE SOURCES

Apples by Elaine Elliot and Virginia Lee
Apple and Rutabaga Casserole, Apple Nut Pound Cake, Apple Tomato Chutney, Classic Apple Crisp, Hot Mulled Cider, Organic Greens with Orange Shallot Vinaigrette, Sticky Apple Pudding with Toffee Sauce, Torta di Mele Alla Panna (Apple Cream Pie)

Blueberries by Elaine Elliot and Virginia Lee
Amherst Shore Chicken with Blueberry Sauce, Blueberry and Rhubarb Crumble, Blueberry Ballerina, Blueberry Cinnamon Coffee Cake, Blueberry Flan, Blueberry Grunt, Blueberry Jam, Blueberry Lemon Muffins, Blueberry Scones, Buttermilk Blueberry Pancakes, Caramel Chocolate Crème with Warm Blueberry Sauce, Classic English Trifle, Cold Blueberry Soufflé, Easy Blueberry Crème Brûlée, Wild Blueberry Posset

Chowders, Bisques and Soups by Elaine Elliot and Virginia Lee
Chilled Blueberry Soup; Chilled Sweet Pea, Mint and Yogurt Soup; Cream of Cauliflower Soup; Fish Stock; Gingered Carrot Soup; Minestrone Soup; Quick Romano Bean and Pasta Soup; Roasted Vegetable Stock; Skillet Croutons

Cranberries by Elaine Elliot
Brant's Pie; Brie Baked en Croute with Cranberry Sauce; Cranberry, Orange and Banana Fruit Flip; Cranberry Almond Pancakes; Cranberry Orange Muffins; Crown Roast of Spring Lamb with Cranberry Wine Jus; Peerless Cranberry Carrot Cake; Red Ribbon Cranberry Coffee Cake; Seasons' Cranberry-Glazed Chicken

Delicious DASH Flavours by Sandra Nowlan
Banana Flax Muffins, Cantaloupe and Blueberry Wake-Up, Creamy Tofu Fruit Shake, Fresh Steamed Fiddleheads, Hodge Podge, Oatmeal Porridge with Raspberry Jam and Almonds, Poached Pears in Red Wine, Stoneground Whole Wheat Bread

Delicious Small Dishes by James MacDougall
Blueberry Bread Pudding, Corn and Crab Fritters, Nova Scotia Duck Breast with Flageolets

Fall Flavours by Elaine Elliot and Virginia Lee
Apple Butter; Autumn Squash Casserole; Braised Red Cabbage with Apples and Onion; Buttermilk Biscuits; Cream of Chanterelle Soup; Eggplant and Chèvre Gratin; Green Tomato Chow Chow; Harvest Vegetable Polenta Torte; Herb-Rubbed Turkey with Sherry Gravy; Maple-Baked Apples; New Brunswick Potato Cake; Old-Fashioned Molasses Brown Bread; Peppered Beef Tenderloin; Pickled Beets; Plum Tomato Chutney; Pumpkin Bread; Raspberry Jam with Cointreau; Red Wine Plum Compote; Roasted Garlic, Stilton and Potato Pavé; Salmon Terrine; Seasoned Bread and Potato Stuffing; Smoked Salmon Crostini; Spirited Cranberry-Orange Sauce; Spirited Pumpkin Mousse Cake; Steamed Carrots with Dill Sauce; Sweet Zucchini Relish

Fresh & Frugal by Craig Flinn
Fried Green Tomato Parmesan; Fried Sweet Potatoes with Maple Syrup and Grilled Sausages; Gardener's Pie; Glazed Beef Short Ribs with Roast Corn Polenta; Grilled Lamb Kebabs with Tangy Couscous Salad; Jiggs' Dinner with Pease Pudding; Marinated Flank Steak with Fried Potato Gnocchi, Fiddleheads, Balsamic and Pecorino Romano; Pan-fried Haddock with Soft-Poached Egg and Green Beans; Pork Schnitzel with Fried Free-Range Egg, Swiss Chard and Brown Butter; Rappie Pie; Roasted Beet, Walnut and Goat Cheese Salad; Salmon à

la King with Sweet Peas, Leeks and Chopped Egg; Smoked Mackerel, Apple and Celery Root Salad; Venison Goulash; Whole Roast Loin of Pork with Caramelized Apples, Spaghetti Squash and Brussels Sprout Petals

Fresh & Local by Craig Flinn
Acadian Sugar Pie; Chicken Stock; Darren's Coq au Vin; Fiddlehead Soup with Smoked Gouda Soufflés; Fish 'n' Chips; Free-Range Chicken Pot Pie; Fresh-Ginger Gingerbread, Butterscotch Apples and Cinnamon Crème Anglaise; Fruits de Mer Salad with Sauce Marie Rose; Grilled Asparagus with Tomato Vinaigrette; Heirloom Tomato Salad with Bocconcini, Basil, Aged Balsamic Vinegar and Olive Oil; King Crab and Mascarpone Risotto; Maple Butter; Maple Ice Cream; Quick Pickled Red Onions; Roast Chicken with Root Vegetables (Poulet Roti); Root Vegetable Tart; Smoked Bacon, Oka Cheese and Sweet Potato Gratin; Smoked Line-Caught Haddock Cakes with Sweet Corn and Tartar Sauce; Sticky Toffee Pudding; Swiss Pan Potato Gratin; Tourtière Pie

Fresh Canadian Bistro by Craig Flinn
Butter-Roasted Halibut with Asparagus "Noodles" and Beurre Blanc; Cheesecake with Rhubarb in Rosé Wine Syrup; Chicken Fricot with Sweet Potato Dumplings; Corn Cob and Aged Cheddar Soufflé; Elegant Split Pea Soup with Smoked Turkey; Field Strawberries with Ice Wine Sabayon; Fricot au Lapin des Bois (Braised Wild Rabbit Hot Pot); Glazed Lamb Shanks with Simply Perfect Risotto; Lobster Chowder; Oyster and Snow Crab Gratin; Penne with Smoked Salmon and Cream Cheese Sauce; Poutines à Trou (Dumplings with a Hole) with Rum Butter Sauce and Vanilla Bean Crème Anglaise; Smoked Haddock Fish Cakes with Celery Root, Apple and Golden Beet Salad; The Tastiest Shepherd's Pie

Heritage Recipes from the Maritimes and Newfoundland by the readers of *Atlantic Insight*
1,2,3 Marmalade, Applesauce, Applesauce Cake, Atlantic Maple Syrup Cake, Blueberry Roly-Poly, Bread and Apple Custard Pudding, Carrot Cake Surprise, Chiard, Chocolate Steamed Pudding, Christmas Cranberry Chutney, Coriander Fruit Crumble, Corn Bread, Country Ham Loaf, Cranberry Lemon Loaf, Cullin Skink, Fricot Soup, Glazed Cinnamon Butter Rolls, Grandma's Gumdrop Cake, Island Seafood Chowder, Mum's Buckwheat Pancakes, Old-Fashioned Chicken Dumplings, Onion Soup, Pickled Eggs, Potato and Cheese Soup, Potato Bran Bread, Rhubarb Jelly, Rolled Moose Steak, Scallop Chowder, Scotch Eggs, Sour Cherry Jam, Split Pea Soup, Steamed Berry Pudding

Lobster by Elaine Elliot and Virginia Lee
Atlantic Blue Mussel Chowder, Cream Cheese Crab Cakes, Fresh Atlantic Lobster Soufflé, Fresh Steamed Lobster, Hot Atlantic Crab Dip, Lobster Club Sandwich, Lobster Rolls, Simply Steamed Clams

Low-Salt DASH Dinners by Sandra Nowlan
Aunt Helen's Cranberry and Orange Oatmeal Squares, Creamy Rice Pudding with Cinnamon, Peppered Strawberries with Balsamic Vinegar and Mint

Maple Syrup by Elaine Elliot
Acadian Apple Pie, Algonquin Maple and Mustard Barbecued Lamb Chops, Blueberry Waffles with Maple Syrup, Dundee Maple Butter Tarts with Maritime Maple Sauce, Falcourt Inn's Maple Meringues

with Peaches, Liscombe Lodge Maple Syrup Cream, Maple Apple Coffee Cake, Maple Parfait, Maple Sabayon on Marinated Berries, Maple Syrup Gingerbread, Maple Syrup Pie, Maple-Glazed Ham, Nova Scotia Maple Syrup Baked Beans, Peerless Cranberry Maple Sugar Scones, Wickwire House Maple Pecan Banana Pancakes, Wild Rice and Mushroom Soup

Maritime Flavours by Elaine Elliot and Virginia Lee

Apple Pie, Asparagus Soup with Cream and Parmesan, Berry Layer Muffins, Bumble Berry Pie, Butterscotch Pie, Captain Burgess Rum Cake, Chicken and Peaches, Chicken Supreme, Cream Crowdie, Cream of Fiddlehead Soup, Dutch Appel Taart, Grilled Breast of Chicken with Apple Brandy Sauce, Grilled Salmon with Sage Butter, Grilled Vegetable Medley, Heavenly Chicken, Honey Mustard Dressing, Hot Apple Cake with Caramel Pecan Sauce, Lemon Almond Tart, Lobster Shannon, Lobster Thermidor, Lobster-Stuffed Mushroom Caps, Baked Mi'kmaq Haddock Fillets, Nut and Seed Bread, Pork Tenderloin with Peppercorn-Mustard Crust and Cider Gravy, Potato and Mussel Salad, Prize Butter Tarts, Raspberry Pie, Rhubarb Coconut Squares, Rhubarb Crisp, Scallop Bubbly Bake, Seafood Cocktail, Sicilian Chicken, Spring Lamb Chops, Tatties and Neeps (Potatoes and Turnips)

Molasses Inspirations by Joy Crosby

Blomidon Inn Bread, Molasses and Maple Crème Brûlée, Molasses Oatmeal Raisin Cookies, Pulled Pork Sandwich with Molasses Barbecue Sauce

Pasta by Elaine Elliot

Dilled Shrimp and Pasta Salad, Gabrieau's Fettuccini with Scallops and Shrimp, Seafood Lasagna

Patisseries by James MacDougall

Irish Cream Truffles, Lemon Roulade, Oatcakes, Raspberry Truffles, Scandinavian Apple Cake, Turtle Squares

Peaches, Pears & Plums by Elaine Elliot

Blue Plum Chutney, Fall Harvest Pear Chutney, Plums Macerated in Brandy, White Wine and Pear Sorbet, Wickwire House Peach Cardamom Cake

Pumpkin & Squash by Elaine Elliot and Virginia Lee

Curried Butternut Squash and Cauliflower Soup, Golden Pancakes with Orange Maple Syrup, Harvest Pumpkin Cheesecake, Pumpkin Cream Cheese Muffins, Pumpkin Crème Brûlée, Pumpkin Pie

Salads by Elaine Elliot

Green Salad with "Tide's Table" Dressing, Maritime Caesar, Spinach and Orange Salad with Poppy Seed Dressing, Warm Potato Salad

Salmon by Elaine Elliot and Virginia Lee

Cedar-Planked Salmon, Fillet of Salmon with Cream Leek Sauce, Highland Salmon, Honey Mustard Glazed Salmon, Poached Salmon, Salmon and Spinach Lasagna, Salmon Loaf with Parsley Egg Sauce, Salmon Roll, Smoked Salmon Quiches

Scrumptious and Sustainable Fishcakes edited by Formac Cookbook Team

Crab Cakes de Bouctouche, Fish Cakes, Salmon Cakes, Traditional Breaded Fish Cakes

Strawberries by Elaine Elliot

Best Ever Strawberry Jam, Chilled Strawberry Soup, Elegant Chocolate-Dipped Strawberries, Fresh Fruit Grande, Fresh Strawberry Butter, Fresh Strawberry Fool, Harbourview Crème Fraîche and Fresh Strawberries, Kiwis and Strawberries in Champagne, Liscombe Lodge Fresh Strawberry Pie, Strawberry Crème Brûlée, Strawberry Pecan Muffins, Strawberry Rhubarb Crumble, Strawberry Rhubarb Pie, Strawberry Rhubarb Soup, Winds and Brass

Summer Berries by Elizabeth Baird

Blueberry Buckle, Blueberry Orange Cake, Rhubarb Fool, Rhubarb Nectar

Summer Drinks by Elizabeth Feltham

Awesome Orangeade, Chai Tea, Ginger Beer, Lemon-Grass Ginger Lemonade, Old-Fashioned Lemonade, Ploughman's Cooler, Raspberry Vinegar

Summer Flavours by Elaine Elliot and Virginia Lee

A Pair of Smoothies, Apple Crisp, Asparagus with Almonds, Atlantic Smoked Salmon with Creamed Horseradish Sauce, Baked Leeks, Baked Sweet Onions, Carlton County Fiddlehead Frittata, Cheese and Bacon Strata, Chocolate Chip Cookies, Down East Apple Cake, Eggs Loyalist, Eton Mess, Fresh Asparagus and Ham Gratin, Fresh Minted Peas, Fruited Iced Tea, Grilled Corn on the Cob, Grilled Halibut, Grilled Vegetable Paquets, Grilled Vegetable Pita Pockets, Healthy Granola Fruit Parfait, Lemon Poppy Seed Muffins, Peach Sour-Cream Ice Cream, Portobello Veggie Burgers, Raisin Ginger Bran Muffins, Rhubarb Compote, Rice Pilaf, Roasted Rosemary Potatoes, Rumrunner's Salmon, Rustic Plum Tart, Steamed Mussels Acadian Style, Stuffed Chicken Breasts with Blueberry-Maple Sauce, Summer Vegetable Pasta Salad, The Dunes' Curried Mussels, Tomato and Basil Salad with Balsamic Vinaigrette, Vegetable Crudités with Dip, Zippy Beef Burgers

Summer Vegetables by Elaine Elliot

Baked Broccoli Casserole, Beets Dijonnaise, Broccoli Salad, Creamy Carrots and Parsnips, Five-Onion Risotto with Charred Pepper Coulis, Grilled Portobello Mushrooms with Mixed Peppers and Cassis, Harvest Gold Soup, Murray Manor Polish Onions, Mushroom Spread, Ratatouille, The Last Word in Latkes

The Atlantic Cookbook by the readers of Atlantic Insight, edited by Patricia A. Holland

Acadian Wild Blueberry Pâté, Apple Pan Dowdy, Aunt Nellie's Soft Molasses Cookies, Baked Stuffed Whole Haddock, Barbecued Lamb Chops, Bay of Fundy Clam Chowder, Beet and Horseradish Relish, Berry Layer Cake, Blackapple Pie, Blueberry Cake, Caramel Corn, Carrot Pineapple Muffins, Celery Relish, Challah, Chocolate Beet Cake, Chocolate Chip Loaf, Christmas Plum Pudding, Christmas Pudding, Cranberry Blueberry Streusel Cake, Cranberry Jelly Mould, Cranberry Squares, Deer Island Fish Chowder, Double Peanut Butter Cookies, East Coast Lobster Salad, Fat Archies, Fresh Asparagus Omelet, Gooseberry Fool, Graham Bread, Grandmother's Cranberry Loaf, Ham and Potatoes au Gratin, Hazel Haskell's Blueberry Pie, Honeyed Paprika Chicken, Jumbo Raisin Cookies, Lady Ashburnham's Pickles, Lebanese Bread (Hobus Lubany), Lobster Potato Salad Supreme, Lobster Supreme, Maple Syrup Pie, Maple Syrup Tarte, Maritime Cheddar Vegetable Chowder, Mary Rush's Pork and Sauerkraut, Molasses Pull Taffy, Mom's Almond Squares, Mom's Best Fudge, Mustard Bean Pickles, My Mother's Baked Beans, Nan's Fudge, Old-Fashioned Cabbage Salad, Old-Fashioned Shortcake, Oven-Puffed Maple Pancakes, Pâté (Acadian Meat Pie), Peanut Brittle, Prize-winning Blueberry Pie, Quiches au Crabe, Quick Maple Pudding, Rabbit in Garlic, Raspberry Upside-Down Pudding, Rhubarb Relish, Rhubarb Strawberry Ice, Rugelach, Solomon Gundy, Sponge Toffee, Steamed Cranberry Pudding, Sugar Cookies, Summer Season Fruit Jam, Tilly's Coleslaw, Turnip Surprise, Walnutty Chews

Tomatoes by Elaine Elliot and Virginia Lee

Grape Tomato Clafouti, Green Tomato and Apple Chutney, Heirloom Tomato Salsa, Italian Seafood Stew, Mediterranean Braised Lamb Shanks, Medusa Mussels, Oven-Roasted Plum Tomatoes

INDEX

METRIC CONVERSION CHART

Imperial	Metric
1 ounce	28 g
1 pound	454 g
1 teaspoon	5 mL
1 tablespoon	15 mL
1 fluid ounce	30 mL
1 cup	240 mL (usually 250 mL)
2 cups (1 pint)	470 mL (usually 500 mL)
1 quart	1 L
4 quarts (1 gallon)	3.8 L (usually 4 L)